Theory in a Time of Excess

Theory in a Time of Excess

Beyond Reflection and Explanation in
Religious Studies Scholarship

Edited by
Aaron W. Hughes

SHEFFIELD UK   BRISTOL CT

Published by Equinox Publishing Ltd.

UK: Office 415, The Workstation, 15 Paternoster Row, Sheffield,
South Yorkshire S1 2BX
USA: ISD, 70 Enterprise Drive, Bristol, CT 06010
www.equinoxpub.com

First published 2017

British Library Cataloguing-in-Publication Data

A catalogue record for this book is available from the British Library.

ISBN   978 1 78179 423 4 (hardback)
         978 1 78179 424 1 (paperback)

Library of Congress Cataloging-in-Publication Data

Names: Hughes, Aaron W., 1968– editor.
Title: Theory in a time of excess : the case of the academic study of
   religion / edited by Aaron W. Hughes.
Description: Sheffield, UK ; Bristol, CT : Equinox Publishing, Ltd., [2017]
| Includes bibliographical references and index.
Identifiers: LCCN 2016020802 (print) | LCCN 2016037575 (ebook) | ISBN
   9781781794234 (hb) | ISBN 9781781794241 (pb) | ISBN 9781781795118 (e-PDF)
   | ISBN 9781781795125 (e-epub)
Subjects: LCSH: Religion—Methodology. | Religion—Study and teaching.
Classification: LCC BL41 .T487 2017 (print) | LCC BL41 (ebook) | DDC
   200.71—dc23
LC record available at https://lccn.loc.gov/2016020802

Typeset by JS Typesetting Ltd, Porthcawl, Mid Glamorgan.
Printed and bound in Great Britain by Lightning Source UK Ltd., Milton Keynes
and Lightning Source Inc., La Vergne, TN

Contents

Part IV

Part V

Part VI

Introduction

Theory in a Time of Excess

Aaron W. Hughes

Not every scholar of English literature regards herself as a literary critic. Nor does every historian style himself as an expert in historiography. Yet, for some reason, the majority of scholars of religion now seem to claim to be specialists in something called "theory and method." A quick perusal of most departmental websites often reveals something like the following after most scholars' names: "Area of expertise: [insert given religious tradition here], [insert related geographical area here], and theory and method."

The simultaneous vagueness and ubiquity of the latter phrase's deployment, however, ought to alert us to the fact that surely everyone cannot be a specialist in said subject. Either the field of religious studies is the most theoretically sophisticated in the humanities or the term "theory and method" has become so transparent and amphibolous as to render it useless. If everyone engaged in theory and method as claimed, we should have no need for the North American Association for the Study of Religion (NAASR) or its journal *Method and Theory in the Study of Religion* (MTSR)—two institutions committed solely to such topics. For if everyone was as theoretically sophisticated as they claimed, we would encounter a healthy field (evidenced at its conferences, its published papers, its departments' curricula and hiring decisions) that was critical, self-reflexive, interested in the genealogy of terms, and engaged in the analysis of social actors and social facts.

That alternative universe, sadly, does not exist. What does exists, however, is a field whose members regularly make appeals to the "sacred," seeking to show how religion intersects with diverse topics that often includes social justice, environmental stewardship, and interfaith dialogue. Rather than have an entire field engaged in theory what we really have is the conflation of various ecumenical concerns and a now largely innocuous concept of theory.

In its newly perceived ubiquity, theory is surprisingly absent. At least if we define theory as a system of thought based on a set of historically based, reflective assessments of society and a critique of culture based on the systematic and ostensibly objective application of questions supplied by the humanities. Despite its traditional emphasis on critical reflection, critique, and dismantling inherited discourses, theory—now stripped of precisely this critique, dismantling, and reconstruction—risks becoming one of those terms that can mean all things to all people. This, it seems to me, explains why so many can now claim to engage in theory, yet all the while we witness a field of study that has changed very little over the past twenty years in its basic concerns and core values. Rather than be used in its technical and secular form of critique, theory now regularly includes, but is certainly not limited to, an investment in truth claims or the desire to work such claims out for a religious community (e.g., Armour 2016).

We therefore might now be wise to distinguish between "theory" and "critical theory" (though understood a little more broadly than the Frankfurt School). Everything is a theory in the sense that there is no theory-less based knowledge. But not all theory is *critical* and by this I mean that it is not engaged in the systematic rethinking (i.e., theorization) of an object of study—in our case "religion"—as opposed to its further reification.

A quick perusal of some of the works of David P. Gushee—elected by the general membership of the American Academy of Religion as its 2016 Vice-President (and thus its President-Elect in 2017)—takes us to the heart of this ambiguity. His works have titles such as *Getting Marriage Right: Realistic Counsel for Saving and Strengthening Relationships* (2004), *The Sacredness of Human Life: Why an Ancient Biblical Vision Is Key to the World's Future* (2013), and *A Letter to My Anxious Christian Friends: From Fear to Faith in Unsettled Times* (2016). All of these works, written by a scholar of religion no less, necessarily use theories, though I am not sure that he would use this term, since Gushee presumably has a systematically arranged set of assumptions, that he applies empirically, about what religion, or at least his religion, does or ought to do in the world. But it is not apparent that he, like so many in the field, recognizes this, for it seems that his descriptions are reflections of the world rather than the result of his stance and situation. The latter acknowledgement has something to do with what those of us who have devoted our academic lives to working with theory mean by the term.

This ambiguity in how the term is used is precisely the problem. It would also seem to be the major reason behind why so many can now claim to be theoretical experts. Theory seems to have morphed in the minds of many from a mistrust of our inherited intellectual worlds and the desire to interrogate the constructed nature of our terms and categories into something that is safe and that can be displayed on CVs and webpages to accentuate credentials. For is it really the case that the majority of scholars in our field are actively engaging in the topics of theory and/or method? I would venture to argue that they are not. Rather, saying one does "theory" has come to function as a type of code to signal to others that one is somehow better versed or qualified in the field than one may well be.

We must therefore realize that what is theory to one person may not be what it is to another. We thus return to the amphibolous or equivocal nature of the term. Someone engaged in the study of Sanskrit texts, for example, uses philological *method* and a *theoretical* model that involves, among other things, painstaking manuscript work that is a large part of the process of what it means to create a critical edition. I am not sure, however, that such an individual would describe his or her task as engaging in "theory and method," at least in the manner that other religionists use this term. Nor am I certain that such a scholar would list "theory and method" as one of his or her areas of expertise.

So what then does it mean to "do theory" or "be theoretical" in the study of religion today? Is imagining a permanent subfield for it that is somehow distinct from specific religions or geographic regions yet another way of marginalizing the term and the concept? After all, the claim that one works on Islam *and* theory does not necessarily means that one applies theory *to* Islam. Usually it means that one works on Islam and has read Eliade & Co. a little (but not too much), J. Z. Smith a little (but again, not too much), Asad, perhaps, along with a selective smattering of now-trendy postcolonial writers. A little theory is a good thing, it is assumed, but a lot of theory can become a problem. Here we hear the customary refrains: "theorists don't read sources in their original languages" or "theorists don't get their hands dirty." Even the most casual of saunters through the hallowed halls of the AAR's annual meeting, however, does not reveal scores of dirty-handed philologists. On the contrary, it often showcases (implicitly or sometimes quite explicitly) a form of ecumenicism and interfaith dialogue that characterizes the feel-good approach of the "big tent." This is on full display, for example, in the presidential "themes" that will define the 2016 ("Revolutionary Love") and 2017 ("Religion and the Most Vulnerable") Annual Meetings.

Where's the There?

Of course one can be a scholar of Islam, a scholar of Judaism, a scholar of Buddhism, and so on. But our field does not really permit one to be a theorist of religion or religions or, perhaps better, a social theorist ("Why aren't you working in a sociology department?" such a person might be asked by a colleague). A quick perusal of the classifications in the AAR's online job database, *Openings*, should reveal this in full Technicolor. The field of religious studies is a domain based on specific traditions, but rarely, if ever, on the discourses (both emic and etic) that have created such traditions in the first place. One is supposed to study "stuff," but not how we ask why this "stuff" and not that "stuff."

An example might be illustrative. In late 2014 Reza Aslan (who, though now a media personality, still prominently lists his credentials as a scholar of religion) published a post on the International Qur'anic Studies Association (IQSA) website entitled "Qur'anic Clues to the Identity of Muhammad's Community in Medina" (Aslan 2014). Therein he argued that "According to the Qur'an, Jews and Christians are 'People of the Book' (*ahl al-kitab*), spiritual cousins who, as opposed to the pagans and polytheists of Arabia, worship the same God, read the same scriptures, and share the same moral values as the Muslim community." He continued:

> Even Muhammad's claim to be the Prophet and Apostle of God, on the model of the great Jewish patriarchs, would not necessarily have been unacceptable to Medina's Jews. Not only did his words and actions correspond perfectly to the widely accepted pattern of Arabian Jewish mysticism, but Muhammad was not even the only person in Medina making these kinds of prophetic claims. Medina

was also the home of a Jewish mystic and Kohen named Ibn Sayyad, who, like Muhammad, wrapped himself in a prophetic mantle, recited divinely inspired messages from heaven, and called himself "the Apostle of God." Remarkably, not only did most of Medina's Jewish clans accept Ibn Sayyad's prophetic claims, but the sources depict Ibn Sayyad as openly acknowledging Muhammad as a fellow apostle and prophet.

I wrote a response on the same blog entitled "A Literary Portrait of Qur'anic Origins," wherein I argued that, while Aslan's piece was a nice ecumenical one, we do not have a shred of evidence when it comes to the Jews of the sixth-century Arab Peninsula (A. W. Hughes 2015). I reminded him that we know next to nothing about the Jews that Muhammad ostensibly encountered. We have no material or other archeological remains that tell us how they lived, no contemporaneous textual evidence of what they believed, and thus little to no idea who they were let alone how they conceived of Judaism. This, however, has not stopped many from projecting a later ethnic and religious normativity backward in time, onto these "Jews." I also pointed out that anachronism has never prevented scholars of religion—I'll leave it for readers to assess whether Aslan, a professor of creative writing, is a scholar of religion—from telling a good story for the purposes of their present.

My concern here, though, is less with Aslan's original piece than it is with a response to my reply written by Devin Stewart and titled "Growing Pains of Qur'anic Studies" (Stewart 2015). In it, he writes that "one could trump up a case and characterize Aaron Hughes as an expert in Jewish philosophy who is less than ideally qualified to issue judgments about the Qur'an or early Islamic history." This brings me to my main point: for Stewart, as for so many in the academic study of religion, one is pigeonholed into a religious tradition. One is a scholar of Judaism, or Hinduism, or Christianity. It never dawned on him to write that "Hughes is a theorist of identity formation who regularly works on data supplied by Jewish and Muslim sources in the premodern period" because such a characterization makes no sense in his intellectual world. It is therefore probably unfathomable to Stewart, as indeed it is to many, that one can be an expert on social theory and identity formation. I have a Ph.D. in religious studies, not Islamic studies and not Jewish studies, after all. Yet, if the academic study of religion is to mean anything, it has to have some sort of *raison d'être*.

This attention to category formation and genealogies, I submit, is where theory—properly calibrated and deployed—ought to fit within the academic study of religion. It appears that Stewart does not want me to be a part of the conversation (i.e., legitimized as an interlocutor) because I do not have the same philological and historical training that he does. Instead, he tells us that the problem is that "many writers on the Qur'an have only limited knowledge of Arabic and maybe one or two other languages and so do not take adequate account of what has been done in medieval and modern scholarship in many different languages" (Stewart 2015). In Stewart's world, again indicative of so many in the field, one cannot specialize in "theory" (and if one does, then one's work has little if any relevance for "serious scholars") because theory is not helpful in finding solutions to their problems. One finds answers to historical questions in the primary sources (which is, of course, nothing more than a *theoretical* claim itself).

The question then becomes, if scholars of a particular dataset (to stick with the above example, Qur'anic origins) are not interested in what social theorists have to say about identity formation and other such topics, why should we not regard such scholars as part of the very dataset that they purport to study? For now their works, inasmuch as they unreflectively take their data for granted, become primary sources for the theorist of religion, *not secondary ones.* But this distinction, I fear, is lost on most scholars of religion, including the very ones who are claiming theory as an area of specialization. That this has to be listed as somehow distinct from the specific religion and area that they happen to work on shows that the point is lost on them.

Excesses

As already noted, the terms "method and theory" are now regularly found in course titles, degree requirements, and as the subjects of comprehensive exams, regardless of subfield. Recent years have also witnessed the formation of both a variety of groups at the annual meeting of the AAR and many other scholarly conferences that now regularly itemize theorizing among the topics that they examine and carry out.[1] The Critical Theory and Discourses on Religion Group (CTDR) at the AAR, for example, defines its task as follows,

> The Critical Theory and Discourses on Religion (CTDR) group offers an interdisciplinary and international forum for analytical scholars of religion to engage the intersection of critical theory and methodology with a focus on concrete ethnographic and historical case studies. Critical theory draws on methods employed in the fields of sociology, anthropology, history, literary criticism, and political theory in order to bring into scrutiny all kinds of discourses on religion, spanning from academic to nonacademic and from religious to nonreligious.[2]

Or, consider the description of a related group, the so-called Study of Religion as an Analytic Discipline (SORAAAD), which runs its own annual workshop at the AAR meeting:

> The workshop is optimal for social science and critical humanities scholars of any rank who are looking to sustain or reenergize their work, or who are new to an approach. The workshop and presentations should appeal to established scholars producing relevant work, whether they are on the panel or in the audience. The workshop is also designed for graduate students developing dissertation proposals or chapters; and it should appeal to entry-level graduate students who want engagement with theoretically sophisticated and well-crafted research. The workshop is not a substitute for coursework in method and theory, much less "Method and Theory in Religion 101." Attendees and participants have professional commitments to this type of scholarly work, and they have already set down this path. The program and both the "suggested" and "further readings" are designed to

attract our constituency: people who will see the readings as smart, useful, timely, or otherwise "on plan" with their research. The readings, nominated by our speakers, are selected for reasons of topical relevance and/or theoretical and methodological challenge.[3]

While such groups are certainly a welcome addition to the otherwise ecumenical and interfaith work that currently passes for scholarship at the North American field's largest annual conference, it would seem that neither of these groups nor the various workshops devoted to "theory" are particularly interested in either meta-reflection on the practical conditions of the field or rigorously explanatory studies of religion's cause (or causes) or function (or functions). So, despite the appearance of tremendous advances in the field since NAASR's founding 30 years ago as what was then the only place in the US or Canada for carrying out theory in the study of religion, it can be argued that little has changed. Indeed, the term theory is today so widely understood as to make it coterminous with virtually all forms of scholarship on religion. The same works goes on as before. The only difference now is that people have convinced themselves that they are being theoretically responsible or sophisticated.

It is in this excess of theory that we currently find ourselves. The question we must now ask ourselves is, how do we find a way out of the abyss? How do we maintain standards of historicity and philology in our own specific subfields while simultaneously being responsible to the intellectual standards that define *critical* theory? There are at least two ways out. The first is what I like to call the "post-theory" posture, which assumes everything has been worked out, and the other is to systematically rethink all that we hold dear and to try to hold our colleagues up to a higher set of standards. While I subscribe to the far more ambitious latter position, let me briefly outline the alternative as I see it.

Post-Theory

"Post-theory" assumes that all is well, or has now been made well, in the field. All the debates have been resolved and rather than worry about earlier ideological battles, we should simply proceed to the interpretation of data, albeit with an imagined awareness of "theory." The data now, however, in many cases is less texts produced in different times and cultures than it is largely American and often derived from the domain of popular culture. The theoretical insight seems to be that the study of religion is so broad that it can be used to examine that which has traditionally been ignored. Not infrequently in this literature we hear the invocation of terms like "lived religion" (e.g., Hall 1997; Tweed 1997; McGuire 2008) or "material religion" (e.g., J. S. Hughes 2010; Promey 2014; Plate 2015). Such terms would seem to signal for their authors a new, more grounded emphasis, as if previous generations had somehow missed out on the actual "lived" or "material" aspect of religion. But note that the term "religion" is never queried. It remains untouched and the emphasis is now on the adjective to describe it in more nuance than had previous generations of scholars.

Overlooked in this post-theoretical turn is critical theory and how, in order to get to where we are today, many intellectual and institutional battles were waged. Here I am reminded of the recent review essay on J. Z. Smith's work and career that was written by Lofton (2014) that accused Smith of not practicing in the classroom what he preached in his pedagogical essays. Therein, she writes,

> Yet, there is an imperceptible center to all this talk of difference and its manage-
> ment, a coldness that often leads readers of Smith to feel he is explaining well
> the abstract meaning behind a ritual, myth or community decision, but that he is
> not capturing anything like their anthropological or psychological reality. (Lofton
> 2014: 537)

For Lofton, Smith misses out on the human—dare I say, "lived," perhaps even authentic—component of religion. Her students, she writes, frequently "experience a kind of alienation from [Smith's] subjects, unable to see what is relatable and human amid all his relating of religion" (ibid.). Since Lofton was an undergraduate student of Smith, as she informs us throughout her essay, she seems to invite readers to accept her on her own authority. That Smith's work abhors such insider knowledge and information privy to only a select few never seems to bother her. A theoretical stance based on untestable hypotheses (i.e., her reminiscences and thus undocumented personal anecdotes) violates both the spirit and letter of Smith's written corpus, suggesting that her approach is not so much post-theory as it is pre-theory.

Lofton's essay, and here I use it as exemplary of a post-theoretical approach, is therefore problematic because it reads as if it ignores the history of our field, the battles that have defined us, and the hazards that await us if we insist on reinventing the wheel every ten to fifteen years. Lofton seems interested in rhetoric and in telling us a good story—and there is no doubt that, in that capacity, she is among our field's most gifted. And so when everyone ostensibly does theory and it can now be defined by its sheer ubiquity, one must now look to transcend theory in order to appear *au courant*—the next big thing. But the result of this approach is that everything that has been done can now be undone only to be done again, all in the name of "theory" (with an ironic nod to Eliade's "eternal return"). If theory, as I propose defining it, ought to historicize and contextualize, thereby exposing various wills to power that define what gets to count as data, and how that data is manipulated, post-theory returns us to the data as if none of these other issues is significant.

A good example of what I have in mind of "post-theory" is the relatively new book series (co-edited by Lofton and John Lardas Modern) at the University of Chicago Press, titled "Class 200: New Studies in Religion." The series, in its own words, while resting "on a generation of critical scholarship that reevaluated the central categories of the field ... aims to surpass that good work by rebuilding the vocabulary of, and establishing new questions for, religious studies."[4] Critical scholarship is here intimated to be passé, something that can now be safely "surpassed" by the task of "rebuilding." But rebuilding what? Rebuilding the very vocabulary that critical theory has attuned us to be critical of? Does this mean that this vocabulary, now interrogated, is safe to use again? The series' description continues in the following vein:

> The series will publish authors who understand descriptions of religion to be always bound up in explanations for it. It will nurture authorial reflexivity, documentary intensity, and genealogical responsibility. The series presumes no inaugurating definition of religion other than what it is not: it is not reducible to demographics, doctrines, or cognitive mechanics. It is more than a discursive concept or cultural idiom. It is something that can be named only with a precise and poetic wrestling with the nature of its naming.

In not naming religion, however, the series paradoxically identifies religion as the unnamed (i.e., that which goes without saying) or that which cannot be named. This unnamed naming sounds remarkably similar to a previous generation's use of vague and imprecise terms that posit the sacred's irreducibility and that invoke phrases like Otto's *"mysterium tremendum et fascinans."* What is more is that for the editors of this new series, religion is "more than" culture or a cultural idiom. Religion, it would seem, can only be "wrestled with" poetically. All the ideological battles waged—only those of a previous generation are mentioned, yet no mention of those of us involved in such work today—now amount to very little. Work in religion carries on the way it always has only now such work can be labeled as somehow theoretically sophisticated. It seems to me that this is the reason that so many can now say they do theory and can list it as an area of expertise. Despite the superficial changes we see to theory here I dare say that absolutely nothing has changed.

   This book series is, to my way of thinking, all that is wrong with the field at the current moment. Under the guise of theoretical sophistication we instead find a return to the status quo. This status quo names religion (even if by unnaming it), puts pride of place on data (now derived from popular culture as opposed to classical texts written in other languages), and emphasizes rhetorical flourish over analytical skill. Note, for example, the use of "authorial reflexivity" as opposed to scholarly reflexivity in the previously quoted passage. In an excess of theory one can now distinguish oneself as engaging in "post-theory."

The 2015 NAASR Program

It was with these questions and issues lurking in the background that NAASR's Annual Meeting took place in 2015. Our meeting was devoted to the topic of this volume, namely, "Theory in a Time of Excess." All of the panels worked on the assumption that all was not well in the academic study of religion, despite (or indeed because of) this renewed interest in theory. The Association asked four relatively early and mid-career scholars—Jason N. Blum, K. Merinda Simmons, Claire White, and Matthew C. Bagger—to provide bold visions of what they thought the term "theory" ought to signify and to work with theories they thought best exemplified where the field should be heading. Rather than comment on their papers here, I will leave it to readers to assess what they have offered. Needless to say each of these scholars comes out of a "subfield" in the study of religion: history of religions (Blum), literary theory (Simmons), cognitive science (White), and philosophy (Bagger). Just as significantly, we then asked a series of early career scholars, primarily senior graduate students, to offer critical responses to these papers. Criteria for selection of these respondents were that they *not* work in the same area as the main paper so that they would not simply assent to the paper's first principles, but examine them. As NAASR Vice President and the one in charge of the annual program, I chaired all the sessions, the lively discussions, and the informative and extended Q&A sessions that followed each panel. In editing this volume, however, I have invited the presenters of the main papers to respond briefly to their respondents, writing pieces not previously heard at the 2015 meeting. My hope is that when each topic is taken as a whole—the following four sets of papers, responses, and replies to the responses—something significant, a multi-hued theoretical vision, will emerge therefrom.

In addition to this set of papers, NAASR asked Leslie Dorrough Smith, who was part of the NAASR Presidential Panel, to contribute an essay to this volume. Her chapter, the final chapter in the volume, thinks with and updates the important essay by two of the founding members of the organization, Donald Wiebe and Luther Martin, titled "Establishing a Beachhead: NAASR, Twenty Years Later," also published here as our opening chapter. The volume closes with an afterword by Russell McCutcheon, the current President of NAASR, which seeks to move the discussion into the future.

Aaron W. Hughes holds the Philip S. Bernstein Chair of Jewish Studies in the Department of Religion and Classics at the University of Rochester.

Notes

1. See, for example, the recent conference at the University of Vermont entitled "Shifting Boundaries: The Study of Islam in the Humanities" (details online at http://blog.uvm. edu/imorgens-shiftingboundaries). Panels included "Islam in/and the Humanities," "New Methods, New Frontiers," and "Critical Pedagogies and Pedagogy as Criticism."
2. See https://papers.aarweb.org/content/critical-theory-and-discourses-religion-group.
3. See https://sites.google.com/site/religiondisciplineworkshop/about-soraaad.
4. The full description may be found online at http://press.uchicago.edu/ucp/books/series/CLA200.html.

References

Armour, Ellen T. 2016. *Signs and Wonders: Theology After Modernity*. New York: Columbia University Press.

Aslan, Reza. 2014. "Qur'anic Clues to the Identity of Muhammad's Community in Medina." *International Qur'anic Studies Association Blog*. Online at: https://iqsaweb.wordpress.com/2014/11/17/muhammads-community-in-medina.

Hall, David D. (ed.). 1997. *Lived Religion in America: Toward a History of Practice*. Princeton, NJ: Princeton University Press.

Hughes, Aaron W. 2015. "A Literary Portrait of Qur'anic Origins." *International Qur'anic Studies Association Blog*. Online at: https://iqsaweb.wordpress.com/2015/01/05/hughes_literary-portrait

Hughes, Jennifer Schepper. 2010. *Biography of a Mexican Crucifix: Lived Religion and Local Faith from the Conquest to the Present*. New York: Oxford University Press.

Lofton, Kathryn. 2014. "Review Essay." *Journal of the American Academy of Religion* 82.2: 531–542.

McGuire, Meredith B. 2008. *Lived Religion: Faith and Practice in Everyday Life*. New York: Oxford University Press.

Plate, S. Brent (ed.). 2015. *Key Term in Material Religion*. London: Bloomsbury.

Promey, Sally M. (ed.). 2014. *Sensational Religion*. New Haven, CT: Yale University Press.

Stewart, Devin. 2015. "Growing Pains of Qur'anic Studies." *International Qur'anic Studies Association Blog*. Online at: https://iqsaweb.wordpress.com/2015/01/19/stewart_growing-pains.

Tweed, Thomas A. (ed.). 1997. *Retelling U.S. Religious History*. Berkeley, CA: University of California Press.

Part I

1

Establishing a Beachhead: NAASR Twenty Years Later

Luther H. Martin and Donald Wiebe

Next year, 2005, NAASR will be celebrating the twentieth anniversary of its founding.[1] Given the current discussions about the future of NAASR, we thought it might be of some interest to revisit the reasons we founded NAASR in the first place and to rehearse and assess what we take to be some of its more significant achievements.

Acting as an ad hoc organizing committee, E. Thomas Lawson, Luther H. Martin, and Donald Wiebe founded the North American Association for the Study of Religion in 1985, in the words of its mission statement,

> to encourage the historical, comparative and structural study of religion in the North American community of scholars, to promote publication of such scholarly research, and to represent North American scholars in the study of religion to, and connect them with, the international community of scholars engaged in the study of religion.[2]

As we stated in the initial letter of invitation to prospective members (2 October 1985), it had increasingly

> become apparent to a number of scholars, especially those engaged in the history or religions, comparative religions, or the scientific study of religions, or simply those who [felt] the need for theoretical work in the field, that the American Academy of Religion [had] become such a complex and competing repository of interests that the academic study of religion was in danger of being lost in the process.

The American Academy of Religion (AAR) came into existence in 1964 as successor to the National Association of Biblical Instructors (NABI), which had been founded in 1909 and dedicated to assisting in the practical development of the religious life of students and increasing the spirit of fellowship, as they put it, among religion instructors in American colleges and universities. By the mid-1950s and early 1960s these religious objectives came under review because of the increasing diversity of religious views among the Association's membership and because of changes in the academic study of religion. Although Claude Welch announced in his presidential address (1970) that the new AAR had self-consciously committed itself to a scholarly-scientific agenda, the Academy had not, in his view, moved very much beyond the hegemonic liberal Protestant framework that had dominated the NABI. As Welch had feared, and William Clebsch confirmed in his presidential address a decade later, the Academy fell back into the arms of religiously oriented interests where it has largely remained to this day. There were some in the AAR who by this time had become frustrated with the Academy's inability to transform itself into an institution that was able to encourage the development of a genuine scientific/scholarly approach to the study of religion, free from religious influence. The original membership of NAASR, consequently, sought to establish an alternative venue in which to work toward the establishment of a sound, academic study of religion, not in opposition to the AAR but complementary to it.

At its first organizational meeting in Anaheim (1985), program proposals were also discussed. Rather than continuing the conventional academic tradition of presenting successive days of individual papers on unrelated topics, initial program proposals included invited speakers, panel presentations on specific topics or themes (e.g., extended critiques of recently published studies of theory and/ or method, and structured occasions for both formal and informal discussion).

In addition, we founded NAASR to extend the collegial and institutional relationships of North American scholars. NAASR was actually founded in the context of the XIVth Congress of the International Association for the History of Religions (IAHR) in Sydney, Australia (August, 1985). At the time, the only U.S. association affiliated with the IAHR was the American Association for the Study of Religion (AASR), an association whose membership is limited and is by invitation only. We felt strongly that United States scholars should be represented in international organizations by democratic associations. At the conclusion of the Sydney congress, we submitted an application to the Executive Committee of the IAHR for affiliation of NAASR. According to the by-laws of the IAHR, this application could only be acted upon by the meeting of its General Assembly at its next quinquennial Congress in 1990, when it was, indeed, accepted.

It was also our proposal to offer the AAR a means whereby its interested members might also become officially associated with the IAHR through NAASR. We envisioned NAASR becoming an AAR "related scholarly organization" and that AAR members interested in affiliation with the IAHR could do so through membership in NAASR. In this way, AAR could avoid paying dues to the IAHR on behalf of its total membership, many—perhaps most—of whom had no special interest in a relationship with the IAHR, while at the same time allowing for a cooperative and mutually supportive relationship between the AAR and the international community of scholars of religion. The AAR was uninterested in this relationship.

A brief institutional history of NAASR includes:

- **August 1985** – founded, Sydney, Australia and application for affiliation with the IAHR submitted and officially received.

- **November 1985** – U.S. organizational meeting, Anaheim, CA.; application submitted to AAR for affiliation as a "related scholarly organization"

- **November 1986** – constitution and by-laws adopted (amended 1987).

- **February 1987** – incorporation in the State of Vermont as a non-profit, tax-exempt corporation (thus establishing the academic association under the legal protection of NAASR, Inc.)

- **November 1987** – application to the AAR for affiliation as a "related scholarly organization" rejected by the Executive Committee of the AAR.[3]

- **January 1988** – affiliation with the Council of Societies for the Study of Religion (CSSR).

- **August 1990** – official approval of affiliation with the IAHR by its General Assembly, Rome. (Affiliation of AASR with IAHR dropped in 1995.)

- **August 1991** – first NAASR sponsored international conference/IAHR regional Conference.

- **January 1993** – *Method & Theory in the Study of Religion* adopted as the official journal of NAASR (initially published by Mouton de Gruyter, subsequently by E. J. Brill).

- **October 1994** – informal relationship established with the Society for the Scientific Study of Religion (SSSR) as a venue for regional meetings of NAASR.

- **March 1998** – second application for affiliation as a "related scholarly organization" resubmitted to AAR; accepted May 1998.

Our relationship with other professional societies has been strong. Given that one of the reasons for the founding of NAASR was to affiliate with the IAHR, it is not surprising that our relationship with this association has been most productive. In addition to organizing and sponsoring two IAHR regional conferences,[4] NAASR has offered logistical and financial support to the IAHR. As well as regular payment of our annual dues, NAASR has contributed $1000.00 to the IAHR endowment fund. NAASR members have been active in the IAHR as elected officers on the Executive Committee, as members of the International Committee, and as organizers of panels and as presenters at every IAHR quinquennial congress and at many regional conferences since 1990. NAASR has also supported the collegial and scholarly aims of the Council of Societies for the Study of Religion (CSSR). Members of NAASR have served on the General Counsel of the CSSR, have served as editors for the *Bulletin of the CSSR*. In addition to the *Bulletin*, all NAASR members receive the *Religious Studies Review,* to which members of NAASR contribute and which is also published by the CSSR.

NAASR has an informal relationship with SSSR in which NAASR members may attend, present, and organize panels without being SSSR members. A number of panels so organized have been published.[5]

NAASR's annual meetings have been held, since our first meeting, coincident with the annual meetings of the AAR. In 2001, NAASR was recognized as an AAR "related scholarly organization."

MTSR, founded as a scholarly journal by graduate students at the University of Toronto, has flourished since being adopted as the official journal of NAASR. Under the leadership of its first NAASR editor, Russell McCutcheon, MTSR became a widely read and highly respected international journal devoted to theory and method in the academic study of religion.

Organizing interesting and relevant annual programs has, in many ways, been the most challenging problem NAASR has had to address. As stated above, we had hoped, from the beginning, to establish an innovative format alternative to the traditional academic modality of individual presentations on unrelated topics as an introduction to four more days of the same in the context of the AAR. This intent has proved to be difficult to sustain. While numerous fascinating and significant papers have been presented at NAASR over the years (a number of which have subsequently been published), some of our most successful programs in the past have included, in our opinion, panels organized to critically address specific methodological and/or theoretical initiatives in the field. For example, the cognitive science of religion and rational choice theory have emerged over the past years as two important theoretical approaches to the study of religion and NAASR has played an important supportive role to scholars involved in these projects.

Program proposals that have not been acted upon include a standing offer for members to organize conferences with NAASR sponsorship and a standing offer to members to organize ongoing seminars, research projects, discussion groups, and so on, in the context of the annual meeting program.

In addition to formal programs, panels, etc., one of the more appreciated contributions NAASR has made to our members—or so we have often been told—has been the sometime receptions organized in connection with annual meetings and international conferences. These receptions have offered NAASR members and their guests a collegial occasion—otherwise lacking in the context of large meetings—to meet old friends, make new friends, and even to initiate plans for collaborative work in the field.

In our judgement, the challenges still facing NAASR still include the creation of genuinely alternative and creative annual program formats. In addition, NAASR needs to develop a more inclusive and efficient organizational structure; work towards increasing active membership; and continue to facilitate our international connections. We conclude that the membership of NAASR can be justifiably proud of its accomplishments over the past twenty years. For a small scholarly organization, it has made significant contributions to a theoretically based study of religion both nationally and internationally.

Luther H. Martin is Professor Emeritus of Religion at the University of Vermont. He is the author/editor of numerous books and articles on theory and method in the study of religion.

Donald Wiebe is Professor of Philosophy of Religion at Trinity College, University of Toronto. He is the author/editor of a number of books and articles on the study of religion in the modern university.

Acknowledgements

This chapter originally appeared as "Establishing a Beachhead: NAASR, Twenty Years Later" in *Conversations and Controversies in the Scientific Study of Religion: Collaborative and Co-authored Essays*, edited by Luther H. Martin and Donald Wiebe (Leiden: Brill, 2016), 36–41. It is reprinted here by permission.

Notes

1. This paper was originally written in 2004 to commemorate the twenty-year anniversary of NAASR. It appeared online at https://naasrreligion.files.wordpress.com/2014/01/establishingabeachhead.pdf.
2. NAASR Statement of Purpose, 1985. E. Thomas Lawson, one of the three founders of NAASR with the present authors, is currently in residence in Belfast as Co-director of the new Institute for Cognition and Culture, Queen's University of Belfast.
3. James B. Wiggins, Executive Director of the AAR, wrote the following letter to NAASR to inform it of the decision of the Board of Directors:

   > Although I know that you were informally told by others, I write officially to communicate that the Board of Directors of the American Academy of Religion did not approve the petition from the North American Association for the Study of Religion to become a Related Scholarly Organization. The reasons were, as I heard them, essentially these: (1) Nothing about such a relationship is required for the NAASR to achieve its affiliation with the IAHR. (2) Nothing in such a relationship is required for any AAR members so inclined independently to have a relationship with the NAASR. (3) Since the NAASR was not seeking an Affiliated Society relationship with the AAR, the AAR would gain nothing from it. (4) All three of the AAR initials appear in the NAASR letters.

   The Board was overwhelmingly opposed, in terms of numbers.

   It seemed to us that, on the face of it, these reasons are spurious and that the Board of Directors simply did not wish an association with our stated goals to be a part of its "umbrella" organization—a conclusion confirmed to us confidentially by "friendly members" of the Board present when the decision was taken and present subsequent years at continuing discussions by the Board concerning "what to do about NAASR."

4. August 1991: NAASR-sponsored international conference/IAHR regional Conference (with additional support from the University of California, Santa Cruz and the University of Toronto), the University of Vermont, "Religious Transformations and Socio-Political Change" (proceedings published 1993 by Mouton de Gruyter); August 1998: NAASR-sponsored international conference/IAHR regional conference, in cooperation with the Czech Society for the Study of Religion, Masaryk University,

Brno (with additional support from the East-East Foundation of the Czech Republic and the Spencer Foundation), "The Academic Study of Religion during the Cold War" (proceedings published 2000 by Peter Lang Press).

5. E.g., two panels at the November 1997 meeting of SSSR: a panel on "The Definition of Religion in the Context of Social Scientific Study," published as a special issue of *Historical Reflections/Réflexions Historiques* 25(3) (1999), and a symposium on "Rodney Stark's *The Rise of Christianity: A Review Symposium*," published as "Review Symposium on Rodney Stark's *The Rise of Christianity*," *Religious Studies Review* 25(2) (1999).

Part II

2

On the Restraint of Theory

Jason N. Blum

What did the indigenous informant say to the postmodern anthropologist?
"Enough about you, let's talk about me now."

—David Schneider

Caricatures are funny because they exaggerate the prominent features of their subjects: at the core of their humor is a nugget of truth. Such is the nature of this joke. In the wake of postmodern critique, scholarship sometimes evinces such a degree of suspicion regarding explanation and such an acute emphasis on methodological self-reflectivity as to reach a nearly neurotic pitch. And—much as it has often taken its theoretical lead from anthropology in the past—the discipline of religious studies is once again tempted to follow in that field's footsteps, this time down the rabbit hole of incessant self-critique and obsessive self-doubt of its theoretical integrity.

Theory and theoretical self-consciousness are good things, but one can have too much of a good thing. While both theory and theoretical self-critique (what Russell McCutcheon calls "theory-as-critique") are necessary in the study of religion (as they are in any academic discipline), both have their proper place, and overemphasis of either has the potential to stymie scholarship and to dissolve the object/s of the study of religion. While critical awareness of the heuristic, constructed nature of our categories and reflection on the potentialities and limits of theory are indeed necessary, these intellectual practices must themselves be carried out with discipline. Without an anchor in empirics and philosophically sophisticated methods of analysis, theorizing in the study of religion risks degenerating into fictionalizing and omphaloskepsis. Theory, in other words, must be restrained in order to maintain its intellectual integrity. This may be effected by acknowledging two basic features of theory: the inherent limitations of its explanatory power, and its dependency on methods of analysis, including interpretation.

The Limitations of Theory

The first step in formulating an approach to research on religion that is theoretically self-reflective without paralyzing itself through incessant self-critique is to acknowledge that theory is imperfect. Religion—like politics, society, culture, and a host of other academic disciplines—is a constructed category. This is true not only because religion is not a natural type, but because it is constituted by a disparate array of types of phenomena. As such, the expectation that religious studies could coalesce around a single, monolithic theory or even an uncontested set of theories for the explanation of its object is not only unrealistic, but undesirable. First, because the phenomena out of which religion is constructed are so variegated—ranging from behaviors, institutions, experiences, traditions, psychological comportments, discourses, texts, etc.—it is obvious that a range of theories operating at different levels will be necessary to address these different, though typically interrelated, objects of interest. McCutcheon aptly summarizes the point and its disciplinary implications, endorsing an interdisciplinary model that includes multiple theories and which eschews the search for "one metaphysically reductive metatheory" (McCutcheon 2003: 210). Religious studies has always been an interdisciplinary field, and in its early stages the need to pilfer theories from adjacent fields derived largely from the fact that it lacked its own theoretical history. Although religious studies scholars clearly should develop their own theories, to ignore the inherently multidimensional—and therefore interdisciplinary—nature of our object of study is to needlessly hamstring our ability to carry out scholarship.[1] Religious studies should, and will, continue to cross-pollinate theory with related disciplines, just as they should, and will, cross-pollinate with ours.

Second, because the phenomena we study under the umbrella term "religion" are not immutable Platonic forms but socially embedded practices that operate through historically situated consciousnesses, it is equally obvious that our theories will need to change over time. The notion that religion consists of some kind of unchanging, ahistorical essence has been thoroughly and repeatedly thrashed by a host of contemporary scholars. If the "religion as essence" party has ended, the expectation of a final and comprehensive "theory of religion" is a hang-over from it. Because the collection of phenomena we study change through history, the tools we use to study that collection must also change. "Religion," after all, is not merely an academic term of art, but is now an element of many popular lexicons. The boundaries that define what qualifies as religion (over which we continue to debate anyway) are therefore fluid and shifting. It is when a discipline reaches consensus about its theories and methods that intellectual stagnation sets in and disciplinary irrelevance becomes a real possibility.[2] Therefore, what some see as theoretical instability, I see as adaptability; what some see as theoretical disarray I see as intellectual vitality. If theories must be disciplined through continual self-interrogation and empirical testing, dynamism and debate concerning theory are not signs of intellectual confusion and disorder, but evidence of the healthy continuance of that disciplining process (Hughes 2013: 1).

It is also the case that our theoretically informed endeavors to study, understand, and explain—no matter how rigorously refined—are always imperfect representations of reality. In the act of observing, selecting, and analyzing phenomena, those phenomena themselves are altered:

> The impact of post-Kantian social constructionism and a wave of critical theories
> that have moved through the Arts and Humanities (namely third wave feminism,
> postmodernism, poststructuralism, postcolonialism, queer theory etc.), has been
> to highlight the ways in which the object of study is itself constructed in the act
> of examination itself ... the kind of object one considers "religion" to be and the
> kinds of claims one makes about that object is significantly determined by the
> disciplinary lens and formative assumptions that ground that analysis in the first
> place. (King 2013: 142)

The comfortable Enlightenment assumption that, if disciplined and applied properly, the human mind could attain "truth" *simpliciter* has been thoroughly undermined by a range of philosophical and theoretical insights: that subjectivity is
always historically constructed; that theory is always contextually situated and
influenced; that the interests and assumptions that guide inquiry operate in per-
vasive and often unacknowledged ways. These realizations are valuable, and suggest that a certain degree of humility with regard to the power of theory is not
only advisable, but necessary. It is only in recognition of these and other imping-
ing factors that scholars can manifest the self-reflectivity required to maintain
intellectual integrity. Once these factors are recognized, however, measures can
be taken to at least diminish their tainting influence on research and analysis.
After all, what are post-colonial thought and critical theory if not the attempt to
extricate ourselves—if only partially or imperfectly—from historically inscribed
and contextually defined horizons of thought by critically interrogating and
thereby deconstructing them?

The possibility of mitigating these influences, however, is eliminated once they
are taken to undermine entirely the possibility of empirical falsification. The
acknowledgment that theory is always at one remove from the phenomena we
seek to explain by it can be taken too far. Wendy Brown depicts the precipitous
edge at which theory operates:

> As a meaning-making enterprise, theory depicts a world that does not quite exist,
> that is not quite the world we inhabit. But this is theory's incomparable value, not
> its failure. Theory does not simply decipher the meanings of the world but recodes
> and rearranges them in order to reveal something about the meanings and inco-
> herencies that we live with ... Theory violates the self-representation of things in
> order to represent those things and their relation—the world—differently. Thus,
> theory is never "accurate" or "wrong"; it is only more or less illuminating, more
> or less provocative, more or less of an incitement to thought, imagination, desire,
> possibilities for renewal. (Brown 2005: 81)

Theory does indeed "depict a world that does not quite exist": it selects, organ-
izes, and prioritizes phenomena in ways that are not found in the natural world;
it proposes causative processes that are not immediately apparent; it posits the
existence of orders and patterns that typically do not reveal themselves to naked
observation. This does not, however, excuse theory from the demand for accuracy; provocation and imagination, on one hand, and illumination and insight, on
the other, are different things. While a theoretical claim might be provocative in

its implications and imaginative in its novelty, it is only significant—illuminative and insightful—insofar as it can be shown to be relevant to that to which it refers, insofar as what it claims can be assessed in terms of those phenomena it purports to explain. Illumination must shed light on something, and insight must see into something. If theory consists in explanation—identifying the causes, origins, and/or functions of religion—then it is only relevant insofar as the causes, origins, and/or functions that it proposes can be shown to have some relevant relation with the actual phenomena we identify as religion.

To the extent that a theory fails to account for observed features of those phenomena that it seeks to explain, that theory may be described as incomplete; if it fails to produce any claims at all that withstand empirical falsification (or which are unfalsifiable), that theory may be described as wrong (or empty). Acknowledgment of the fact that theory does not produce an exact representation of the world that it seeks to explain does not imply that the scholar enjoys unconstrained poetic license, but that she is faced with a continual task of revision and refinement. What Bruce Lincoln says about language is equally true of theory:

> Cognizant of the fact that language is neither the world, nor its reflection, but an imperfect instrument with which one engages (and sometimes distorts and sometimes remakes) the world, I struggle to define key terms with a certain precision and rigor, continuing to rethink and revise my usage as its inadequacies and flaws become clear. (Lincoln 2007: 164)

The very possibility that inadequacies and flaws may be recognized and that rethinking and revision may be performed demonstrates that theory, like language, is beholden to something outside itself, accountable to a standard of assessment that is not itself the product of theory. The scholarly text is not "a discourse of free invention, wherein ideological interests escape all controls" (Lincoln 1999: 208), but a discourse that must be grounded in and held accountable to empirics, and where ideological interests are disciplined—as much as they can be—in light of observational, textual, and other kinds of evidence.

In its more extravagant moods postmodern suspicion of claims to objectivity swings the pendulum from the extreme of early modern overconfidence in the powers of Reason to the other skeptical extreme of pure discursive recreation and ungrounded conjecture. On one hand is the likely unattainable ideal of unvarnished and comprehensive truth, a perfect representation of a world taken to be essentially rational in itself; on the other is the concession of any and all claims to empirical relevance and the retreat into a shadowy, solipsistic realm of unaccountable speculation. Theory must strike a balance between these extremes: its inability to satisfy the demands of the former does not justify dissolution into the latter. Theory will always be subject to its own limitations, as the result of a variety of factors, including our inability to transcend history and the limits of our powers of self-awareness. To concede entirely the need for empirical accountability and falsifiability, however, is not only to dissolve the very possibility of academic research, but is simply unnecessary. Through the kind of deliberate and careful self-reflectivity for which many have been calling, as well as peer-review and other ongoing conversations of academic dialogue, we can at least partially rectify the limitations of the theories that we use and our ability to deploy them. Because theories claim to explain empirical phenomena and typically suggest predictable results, they can and should be weighed and measured through observation of the world that they claim to explain. And through multidisciplinary research, the omissions and blind spots of particular theories and disciplines can be ameliorated by deploying the tools of other theories and disciplines.

Recognition of the imperfection of theory—even if that imperfection is inevitable and can never be fully rectified—does not mandate abandoning either theory itself or the demand that a theory's value be determined by its applicability and accountability to the intersubjective world about which it makes claims. The map may not be the territory, but a map that leads you to Knoxville when you're trying to get to Denver is demonstrably inferior to one that brings you at least to the Colorado state line. Recognition of the imperfection of theory acknowledges that theorizing is and likely will remain a work in progress, a project in need of continual revision as the phenomena theory seeks to explain transform through history, as existing tools of investigation (technological and otherwise) are improved and new ones developed, as interdisciplinary cross-pollination produces new and hybrid approaches to research, and as the empirically demonstrated failures of theory's explanatory power are rectified through revision and reflection. By remaining vigilant to when and how our constructed theories and categories misrepresent intersubjectively available facts or fail to account for observed patterns of phenomena, we enable ourselves to revise them when necessary (Strenski under review). Admitting that such revision will in all likelihood always be necessary transforms the "failure" of theory into the opportunity for theoretical innovation and improvement.

Empirics and Interpretation

The kind of theoretical change I describe (dare I call it progress?) is only possible through the self-reflective use of empirics—specifically, empirics that are not themselves the products of theory. If theories are supported or falsified through empirical analysis, then theory cannot itself be the mechanism of that analysis. Otherwise, theories would be validated by their own products and theoretical explanations would be nothing more than self-fulfilling prophecies. Research is therefore in need of another mechanism by which data may be analyzed. Interpretation is one means by which this need is fulfilled. It is a method for analyzing data, the products of which theory then seeks to explain.[3]

This suggests an important distinction between interpretation and theory, and the respective goals of those processes: "interpretations and descriptions ... do not constitute a theory of religion but something more akin to an interpretation of the *meaning* of a religion for the devotee or that member of another religion" (McCutcheon 2003: 209; see also 212). Interpretation—historically grounded and empirically accountable disclosure of the meaning of religious phenomena (experiences, practices, behavior, doctrines, etc.) for the religious subject—neither relies on nor implicates theory; the scholar's interpretation of religious phenomena does not itself propose (or rule out) causes, functions, or origins for those religious phenomena that he studies. Rather, interpretation reveals the meaning of religious phenomena for the religious subject, which the scholar seeks to understand and then to explain.

Interpretation is necessary precisely because the significance or relevance of many religious activities, attitudes, and artifacts does not reveal itself immediately; it is only by discerning the meaning of such phenomena that they may be accurately understood and categorized in (constructed) ways that facilitate comparison and explanation. Interpretation is only necessary in those cases where the meaning of a religious phenomenon (i.e., its significance for religious consciousness) is relevant. For instance, human bodies can often be seen engaging in the following actions: descending from an upright position to a kneeling one; closing the eyes; clasping the hands and/or sometimes bowing from the kneeling position; speaking despite the absence of a publicly observable audience. These actions are often, though not always, performed in predictable patterns, either at certain times of the day or in specific locations.

These are all intersubjectively observable phenomena, and, described as such, neither theory nor interpretation has yet been performed. To label and categorize this set of actions as "prayer" is already to make certain claims about it. Although such categorization is useful (indeed, likely necessary) to facilitate explanation and comparison, that categorization—which implicitly depends on interpretation—cannot itself be carried out through the application of a theory that seeks to explain these actions. For example, historian Maurice Bloch has argued that the form in which some people pray can be explained as the transference of a routinized behavior from the social-political realm of feudal Europe to religious practice. The physical motions of kneeling and folding the hands together mirror the gestures by which feudal vassals pledged fealty to their lords. Bloch suggests that the relation of humanity to divinity is modeled on the feudal relation of vassal and lord, and thereby explains the transference of this practice to the form of (some) prayer (cited in Strenski under review).

That is a plausible explanation. However, using that theoretical explanation as a guide to interpretation is problematic. Doing so would preemptively narrow the range of possible meanings for prayer to those implied by the theory—in this case, meanings such as obedience, loyalty, and a desire for protection. These very well may be the meanings of prayer, but what we commonly describe as "prayer" could also entail a range of other meanings or intentions: propitiation, confession, communion, incantation, thanksgiving, praise, etc. If the activity of prayer is interpreted through the historical explanation offered by Bloch, then the meaning attributed to it is constructed through his theory, and that theory is then "confirmed" in a merely tautological fashion: because the explanation is used to construct the meaning of the activity, the explanation turns out to be perfectly suited and comprehensive. Rather than testing the theory against the empirical data that it seeks to explain, the theory achieves confirmation essentially unchecked because the data against which it could be tested have already been constituted by the theory itself: a self-fulfilling prophecy.

Therefore, it is necessary that data be obtained and analyzed through a mechanism that is independent of theory. The difficulty with fulfilling this methodological requirement with regard to the study of religion is that many of the phenomena in which we are interested become relevant and interesting largely through means that are not publicly observable: the consciousness of the religious subject. In order to disclose the meaning of the observed phenomena—in order to recognize the acts of kneeling and speaking to a non-empirical audience as "prayer" and to discern the meaning of that behavior—the consciousness of the subject who engages in that activity must be brought into the analytical process. In other words, the intersubjectively available data must be interpreted:

> The first goal—and the one that must be included in any academic study of religions—is to *describe* religious beliefs, practices, experiences, and institutions accurately, which is to say, to identify them in a way that captures how they are understood by the practitioners themselves. Since religious phenomena are human phenomena, to describe a religious belief, practice, experience, or institution accurately requires reference to the agents' selfunderstanding. In other words, to describe what the agent holds, does, feels, or joins accurately, one must include what she understands herself to be holding, doing, feeling, or joining. (Schilbrack 2014: 180)

Note Schilbrack's statement that "religious phenomena are human phenomena." Interpretation need not—indeed, cannot—attempt to disclose the meaning of posited non-empirical realities themselves. Assuming that such entities exist (a very large assumption itself), they are not available for the kind of empirically grounded and historically informed investigation that is required for academic analysis. And in any case, such entities are typically experienced in a range of ways, giving rise to a multiplicity of humanly ascribed meanings rather than a single, transcendent meaning. What the religion scholar studies are human phenomena: prayer, pilgrimage, rituals, institutions, beliefs, etc. These are publicly available phenomena (or at least they may be rendered as such) and therefore legitimate subjects of academic analysis precisely because interpretation of them is based on intersubjectively available grounds, and theories that seek to explain them can be weighed and measured against that evidence.

Note also that Schilbrack calls for "accurate" description or interpretation. Interpretive processes are not ungrounded speculations or intuitions about the meanings of religious phenomena; rather, they are historically informed and empirically grounded attempts to disclose the meaning of religious phenomena as they are constructed and experienced by human subjects. Interpretation therefore relies on and is accountable to evidence: the discourse of the religious subject, her observed behaviors and gestures, close textual exegesis, etc. Interpretation reveals the meaning of the religious phenomena as constructed, understood, and experienced by religious consciousness. It ensures that what theory explains is not its own pure creation, but instead the actual phenomena of religion, "actual" in this case referring to the meaning and significance of religious phenomena as they are created and undergone by historically situated religious consciousnesses.

The difference between washing and baptism, killing and sacrifice, traveling and pilgrimage, "turns on the views of the agents" who engage in these behaviors (Schilbrack 2014: 180). In such cases, the necessity of interpretation that reveals the subjective perspective may be aptly demonstrated by considering the difference between a wink and a blink. Gilbert Ryle claimed that there is an "immense but unphotographable difference" between the two (Ryle 2009: 494). Edward Slingerland disputes that claim. Citing the different neural pathways and muscles involved in such subtle but significant differences as that between a spontaneous (authentic) smile and a forced (inauthentic) one, and specific cognitive mechanisms that have evolved over millennia that enable human beings to effectively detect deceit in other human beings, Slingerland argues that the difference between a wink and a blink *is* accessible to third-person analysis. He concedes, however, that "the larger meaning of a particular wink—Why is this person winking at me? What should I do?—is embedded in a set of long, complex stories, and that for the unpacking and analysis of these stories we require the higher-level expertise of anthropologists, novelists, and historians" (Slingerland 2008: 386). In other words: interpretation. It is possible to concede Slingerland's point that there are indeed physical, detectable differences between a wink and a blink while also acknowledging (as Slingerland does) that there is another way in which the two differ: the former has meaning (the subtle communication of some sort of conspiratorial intention) while the latter does not. Recognition of that particular kind of difference—which is certainly not irrelevant—and discerning the meaning of it depend on understanding the consciousness of the agent involved.

This also suggests that while causal explanations employing scientific theories such as those derived from cognitive science are necessary, they do not offer all the tools needed for a comprehensive analysis of religion; what Nancy Frankenberry calls "semantic questions" (or questions of meaning) will have to be explained by theories of a different order—"forms of explanation that make reference to human beliefs, intentions, desires, etc." (Frankenberry 2012: 599). It is specifically research into such semantic questions that depends on interpretation. An art historian researching the materials and methods of ceramics-making in Sub-Saharan Africa likely need not understand the meaning of the symbols carved on the pottery he studies; the religious studies scholar who seeks to explain the perdurance or cross-cultural diffusion of the cosmogonic themes embedded in the myth recounted by those symbols does.

This delegation of duties and the distinction between interpretation and (theoretically driven) explanation does, of course, imply that such a distinction can be drawn. Robert Segal, Craig Martin, and many others have objected that any interpretation already includes an at least implicit explanation, and that therefore this distinction ultimately cannot be sustained (Segal 2014: 1150; Martin under review). It is true that the religious subject's understanding of his own experience, behavior, or practices inevitably includes some at least implicit explanatory claims. For instance, a religious subject might understand his avoidance of shellfish, his rejection of same-sex marriage, or his endorsement of environmentally sustainable energy policy as fulfilling the will of God. In such cases interpretation of religious consciousness will unavoidably refer to explanatory claims on the part of the religious subject—for example, claims that God exists, created the earth, and intended human beings to be stewards of the planet. These explanatory claims cannot be separated from the religious subject's self-understanding without radically altering the belief, practice, or experience that one seeks to study.

In this particular way, interpretation cannot therefore be separated from explanation: a religious explanation is unavoidably embedded in any accurate interpretation of religious consciousness. This is not, however, the stumbling block it is typically taken to be. After all, the religious subject's explanation for his behavior and beliefs is very likely part of what the scholar wants to interpret and explain. Interpretation *must* therefore disclose that emic explanation in order to make it available for theoretical (etic) analysis, which can (and often does) legitimately deploy explanations that contradict those of the religious subject. In this particular manner, the intertwined nature of interpretation and explanation is not a problem for interpretation, but rather an indication of its necessity. The intertwined nature of interpretation and explanation at this juncture also demonstrates why the scholar's own explanatory theory—particularly if it is naturalistic—must be restrained in the interpretive phase of analysis. Precisely because the scholar's explanation is at odds with that embedded in the religious subject's self-understanding, use of the former to interpret the latter inevitably reconfigures the data under analysis, obfuscating or tainting the phenomenon he seeks to study. In other words, the use of theory to interpret the data that theory then seeks to explain not only results in tautological (and therefore meaningless) self-confirmation, it does so by corrupting the data.

Therefore, in interpreting a religious phenomenon the scholar *must* acknowledge the embedded explanatory claims on the part of the religious subject. Acknowledgment is not, however, endorsement. Interpretation only oversteps the boundary into covert theologizing or apologetics when—after having produced a historically and empirically grounded understanding of the meaning of a religious phenomenon—it then goes on to deny the legitimacy of etic explanatory endeavors that reject the explanatory claims embedded in the phenomenon itself. As I have argued elsewhere, this is neither necessary nor legitimate for interpretation (Blum 2012). It is precisely the scholar's intention to study and understand the consciousness of the other—*without* endorsing his (explicit and implicit) explanatory claims—that distinguishes her perspective from that of the religious subject.

Interpretation therefore aids the explanatory endeavor of theory in two regards. First, it keeps theory honest by ensuring that that which theory explains is not merely its own creation. By revealing the emic meaning of religious phenomena including behaviors, practices, and experiences, interpretation facilitates analysis of that which theory seeks to explain. It is a method by which phenomena are analyzed as data. The understanding thereby achieved by interpretation is valuable in itself, merely in virtue of the fact that religious phenomena are now better understood (i.e., their meaning for religious consciousness is grasped). Second, the analysis performed through interpretation serves as a test for the applicability, accuracy, and comprehensiveness of theory. A theory's success or failure is determined by how thoroughly and accurately it explains the data it seeks to explain. Because interpretation analyzes those data independently of theory, it ensures that theory does not descend into circularity by proposing explanations of artifacts that it has itself produced. In this way, theories may be winnowed according to their ability to account for the data they address.

Conclusion

In contemporary engagements in "theory and method," it very well may be that the fate of religious studies hangs in the balance. Recognition of the necessity of theoretical self-reflection, critique, and development is essential for the preservation of the discipline of religious studies and progress in it. Concurrent with this recognition, however, must also be acknowledgment of both the possibilities and limitations of theory. The field of religious studies is currently rife with debate and criticism; it is not only presently better off for it, but will benefit from continued debate and criticism. Rather than seeking for a unified "theory of religion" or even for broad theoretical consensus, religion scholars should instead seek to foster rigorous self-critique and dialogue, and intellectually vibrant multidisciplinarity: the varied nature of the phenomena with which we engage, the development of new tools and techniques for studying them, and the inevitability of historical change in those phenomena all but guarantee that theory will always be a work in progress.

That reflection and self-critique, however, must also be disciplined themselves. Unless theory remains ultimately beholden to empirics—both seeking to explain and being assessed by intersubjectively available evidence—it becomes ungrounded speculation and solipsistic fictionalizing. Self-awareness of the artificial and constructed nature of our theories and categories (including that most basic and controversial one, "religion") serves to improve analytical precision and disciplinary flexibility. Taken too far, however, academic self-analysis becomes lost in a maze of funhouse mirrors. Disciplining theory entails not only self-critique, but empirical accountability. That basic standard of empirical grounding and accountability applies not only to theory as a tool of explanation, but to interpretation as a method of data analysis. Because many of those phenomena we categorize and study as religion become relevant through the medium of consciousness, interpretation is a necessary method of analysis. Like theory, however, interpretation remains grounded in historical, intersubjectively available evidence. Construed as a method for the analysis of data which are then explained through theory, interpretation has an essential role to play in the analytical endeavor we denote "religious studies" by both facilitating and disciplining theory.

Jason N. Blum is a Visiting Assistant Professor at Davidson College. His research focuses on methodology in religious studies and topics at the intersection of philosophy and religion, including the relationship between science and religion, religious experience, and religion, society and ethics.

Notes

1. Interdisciplinarity does not rule out consilience, or the "vertical integration" for which scholars such as Edward Slingerland have called. Depending on how such a model of the interrelations between theories at different levels of analysis is deployed, it could either constrain scholarship or indicate productive paths of research.
2. The predominance of rational choice theory in economics is a foreboding example.
3. In this sense interpretation may be compared to the statistical analysis of datasets or the performance of an experiment in a laboratory.

References

Blum, Jason. 2012. "Retrieving Phenomenology of Religion as a Method for Religious Studies." *Journal of the American Academy of Religion* 80(4): 1025–1048.

Brown, Wendy. 2005. *Edgework: Critical Essays on Knowledge and Politics*. Princeton, NJ: Princeton University Press.

Frankenberry, Nancy. 2012. "A Response to Martin and Wiebe." *Journal of the American Academy of Religion* 80(3): 598–600.

Hughes, Aaron W. 2013. "Theory and Method: Twenty-Five Years On." In Aaron W. Hughes (ed.), *Theory and Method in the Study of Religion: Twenty Five Years On*, 1–17. Leiden: Brill.

King, Richard. 2013. "The Copernican Turn in the Study of Religion." *Method and Theory in the Study of Religion* 25(2): 137–159.

Lincoln, Bruce. 1999. *Theorizing Myth: Narrative Ideology, and Scholarship*. Chicago, IL: University of Chicago Press.

Lincoln, Bruce. 2007. "Concessions, Confessions, Clarifications, Ripostes: By Way of Response to Tim Fitzgerald." *Method and Theory in the Study of Religion* 19(1): 163–168.

Martin, Craig. Forthcoming. "Incapacitating Scholarship: Or, Why Methodological Agnosticism Is Impossible." In Jason N. Blum (ed.), *The Question of Methodological Naturalism*.

McCutcheon, Russell. 2003. *Manufacturing Religion: The Discourse on Sui Generis Religion and the Politics of Nostalgia*. New York: Oxford University Press.

Ryle, Gilbert. 2009. "The Thinking of Thoughts: What Is 'le penseur' Doing?" In Gilbert Ryle, *Collected Essays 1929-1968*, 494–510. New York: Routledge.

Schilbrack, Kevin. 2014. *Philosophy and the Study of Religions: A Manifesto*. Malden, MA: Wiley Blackwell.

Segal, Robert. 2014. "Interpretation and Explanation: A Response to Jason Blum's Defense of the Phenomenology of Religion." *Journal of the American Academy of Religion* 82(4): 1149–1151.

Slingerland, Edward. 2008. "Who's Afraid of Reductionism? The Study of Religion in the Age of Cognitive Science." *Journal of the American Academy of Religion* 76(2): 375–411.

Strenski, Ivan. Under review. "What Can the Failure of Cog-Sci of Religion Teach Us about the Future of Religious Studies?" In Jason N. Blum (ed.), *The Question of Methodological Naturalism*.

3

It's Hard Out Here For a Theorist

Michael J. Altman

It's hard out here for a theorist. On the one hand, the theorists seem to have won the day. There are books on theories of religious studies. There are undergraduate courses on theory and method in the study of religion. *Method and Theory in the Study of Religion* is a successful and venerable journal. We require graduate students to take a seminar or an exam in "theory." But on the other hand, "theory" is often deployed as a pejorative. One must be careful not to be too "theoretical." Tracy Fessenden described this suspicion of theory well:

> As a term of opprobrium, "theory" tends to signal some singular, regrettable thing: an exclusionary and obfuscating patois, an ungenerous spirit of critique, a lengthy list of tomes, most in French or German, that reproach us from the shelf unread. (Fessenden 2012: 378)

Fessenden was describing the situation in the study of religions in America, but I believe it holds true for the larger field of religious studies. Theory is something that we all know we need, but it's something no one wants to have too much of. Just enough, but not too much. As a professor of mine used to say, theory is like underwear: everyone should have it but no one should see it.

Jason Blum's essay (Chapter 2, this volume) speaks to us from this ambivalence. "Theory and theoretical self-consciousness are good things, but one can have too much of a good thing," he writes (p. 21, this volume). A little bit goes a long way, as Jessica Simpson sang. And so Blum calls for restraint lest we "dissolve the object/s of the study of religion" and theory lose its "intellectual integrity" (ibid.). But before we can evaluate Blum's call to protect theory and our object of study, we must first establish exactly what these two things are. What is theory? And what is our object of study? Because when we answer these two questions, I argue, we will see that theory and our object of study are not as fragile as Blum would have us believe. Indeed, we will see that restraint is not only unnecessary but, frankly, irrelevant.

So, to begin with, what is theory? Dr. Blum assumes that theory is explanation. As he renders the work of the scholar of religion, there are religious phenomenon out there in the world that the scholar explains through the application of theory and "to the extent that a theory fails to account for observed features of those phenomena that it seeks to explain, that theory may be described as incomplete" (p. 24, this volume). Furthermore, he writes, "if it fails to produce any claims at all that withstand empirical falsification (or which are unfalsifiable), that theory may be described as wrong (or empty)" (ibid.). This is a deductive-nomological notion of theory. Such a notion rests on two principles:

> First, the idea of logical deduction in axiomatic systems: theorems are deduced from a limited number of axioms. Second, a correspondence criterium of truth: empirical sciences depend on correspondence with facts (sense data), which represents a mind-independent external reality (philosophical realism). (Mjøset 2001: 15641)

While I do not read Blum as searching for universal laws that explain religion, he is looking for regularities that explain the phenomenon at hand. It is both a positivist and realist notion of theory. There is a world out there and we can know it. Religion is out there and we can explain it.

This brings up the second question—though I still haven't answered the first—what is our object of study? For Blum, our object of study is religion. Blum grants that the boundaries of what counts as religion are fluid and changing but, in my reading of him, he still thinks there is stuff out there that is religion. At one point he lists what religion scholars study: "prayer, pilgrimage, rituals, institutions, beliefs, etc." (p. 27, this volume). But why that list? To come at it another way, what is "the difference between washing and baptism, killing and sacrifice, traveling and pilgrimage" (p. 28, this volume)? Blum claims, by way of Kevin Schilbrack, that the difference lies in the views of the agents. But again, why are we paying attention to washing, killing, and traveling or baptizing, sacrificing, and pilgrimage? Because those are "religious!"

And here lies the answer to our first question—what is theory. Theory is not just explanation. Indeed, explanation may be the least of it. Theory is how we decide what our object of study is. Theory is what guides the decision to pay attention to that person slitting the throat of a goat in one part of the world and not to my neighbor skinning a deer in Tuscaloosa, Alabama. To return to Fessenden: "Theory is our case, tacit or explicit, for why *these* materials, why this method, what story our materials tell, why *this* story as we've told it, and what imagined audience we address or seek to conjure thereby" (Fessenden 2012: 378).

So really, the second question—what is our object of study—is a trick question. And it's the answer to the first question. What is theory? It's the question "what is our object of study?" And what is our object of study? Well, that depends on your theory.

Theory is a process of knowledge production, not an explanation of external realities (Mjøset 2001: 15645). Blum argues that we must protect our object of study from being dissolved or tainted, but that seems beside the point. Our object of study is always already *ours*. We choose to call this baptism and that swimming in the creek. We choose to call this a ritual and that a neurosis. There is no reason to "keep theory honest by ensuring that that which theory explains is not merely its own creation" because everything theory explains is always already the theorist's creation. So, theory is not only the explanation of what the theorist has taken an interest in, but it is also the analysis of why a theorist chose that object of study to begin with. This is what Richard King means when he writes, and Blum quotes, "The kind of object one considers 'religion' to be and the kinds of claims one makes about that object is significantly determined by the disciplinary lens and formative assumptions that ground that analysis in the first place" (King 2013: 142).

When the theorist realizes that her object of study is always hers and never a given out there in the world, the positivism and realism of Blum's notion of theory fall aside. So too does the fear that "what theory explains is not its own pure creation." Rather than restraining theory, I call for a letting go. Theorists of religion must let go of positivism and realism and they must embrace their construction of their own object of study.

But what about meaning? Meaning plays an important role in Blum's essay. It is supposed to provide the check, the empirics, against theory. But having rendered theory as knowledge production and not explanation, the need for meaning dissolves. Theorists of religion must let go of meaning because meaning has become the newest form of essentialism in the study of religion. Blum claims that the "religion as essence" party is over. I disagree. Where Eliade once argued for the sacred as the essential center of religion, we now have meaning. The numinous is dead, long live meaning.

Throughout his paper, Blum refers to "the meaning of a religious phenomenon." What he describes as "its significance for religious consciousness." Leaving aside the question of what makes a phenomenon "religious," a question of theory, I am surprised by Blum's use of the singular noun and the definite article: the meaning. Is there only one? And is it definitive? The meaning of x religious phenomenon is y? And how do we get at this meaning? Blum calls for interpretation through paying particular attention to evidence: "the discourse of the religious subject, her observed behaviors and gestures, close textual exegesis, etc." Interpreting this evidence reveals "the meaning of the religious phenomena as constructed, understood, and experienced by religious consciousness." Here's my question: how is consciousness empirical? How do we get at another person's consciousness? What exactly is consciousness, anyways? And why is the ultimate ground for the interpretation of religion found at the level of consciousness?

Re-read a key paragraph of Blum's paper but substitute "the sacred" for "meaning":

> Interpretive processes are not ungrounded speculations or intuitions about *the sacred* of religious phenomena; rather, they are historically informed and empirically grounded attempts to disclose *the sacred* of religious phenomena as they are constructed and experienced by human subjects. Interpretation therefore relies on and is accountable to evidence: the discourse of the religious subject, her observed behaviors and gestures, close textual exegesis, etc. Interpretation reveals *the sacred* of the religious phenomena as constructed understood, and experienced by religious consciousness. It ensures what theory explains is not its own pure creation, but instead the actual phenomena of religion, "actual" in this case referring

to *the sacred* of religious phenomena as they are created and undergone by historically situated religious consciousness. (Blum, p. 28, this volume)

Like the old "sacred," "meaning" exists somewhere altogether different from the
empirical object of study. The bloody corpse of a chicken is only a "sacrifice" at
the level of meaning. Rather than locate the essence of religion in the sacred or
the numinous, Blum locates it in meaning. But where is meaning? Somewhere
in the "religious consciousness." How do we get access to that? Where is that
exactly? And how is it "empirical?" Is that the new *homo religiosus*? And why does
that dead chicken mean sacrifice, anyway? And who determines that "sacrifice"
is *the* meaning?

As Talal Asad warned Clifford Geertz, "he also appears, inadvertently to be
taking up the standpoint of theology. This happens when he insists on the pri-
macy of meaning without regard to the processes by which meanings are constructed" (Asad 1993: 43). Blum makes a similar mistake. Like Geertz, for Blum,
"there must be something that exists beyond the observed practices, the heard
utterances, the written words, and it is the function of religious theory to reach
into, and to bring out, that background by giving them meaning" (ibid.: 43–44).
Interpretation and meaning are not empirical checks on theory. Rather, they are
potential data themselves. I would argue they are part of our object of study. As
Asad wrote to Geertz, so I say to Blum here:

> The connection between religious theory and practice is fundamentally a matter
> of intervention—of constructing religion in the world (not in the mind) through
> definitional discourses, interpreting true meanings, excluding some utterances
> and practice and including others. Hence my repeated question: how does the-
> oretical discourse actually define religion? What are the historical conditions in
> which it can act effectively as a demand for the imitation, or the prohibition, or
> the authentication of truthful utterances and practices. How does power create
> religion? (Asad 1993: 44–45)

And here we come to the biggest weakness of deductive-nomological theory and
the demand to find "the meaning" of religion: it effaces power. I can think of no
greater monument to deductive-nomological theory and the search for meaning
than Daniel L. Pals's *Nine Theories of Religion* (2015). In this compendium of dead
white men, "theory" is explanation. This rendering of "theory" is great for the
undergraduate classroom. I have used the book many times in my REL 100 class.
But the book's focus on how these Europeans explained religion misses another
story about each of these men. It is a story I try to get my students to think about
in the very first chapter, when we read about E. B. Tylor. Why was Tylor interested in "the primitive?" Was there always a "primitive?" Primitive to whom?
You see, the positivism and realism of deductive-nomological theory try to evade
its own construction. Tylor never thought about how his own theories of human
development were not universal laws but historically situated social construc-
tions that supported white supremacy and European imperialism. He thought he
was simply applying theory to explain religion.

So, theory does not need to be restrained. Rather, theory that seeks only to explain religious phenomena is already far too restrained, unable to move beyond its quest for meaning and explanation to understand the discourse of its own possibility.

Michael J. Altman is Assistant Professor in the Department of Religious Studies at the University of Alabama. He researches and teaches on religion in colonial empire, Asian religions in America, and critical theory. His first book, *Heathen, Hindu, Hindoo: American Representations of India, 1721-1893*, is forthcoming from Oxford University Press.

References

Asad, Talal. 1993. *Genealogies of Religion: Discipline and Reasons of Power in Christianity and Islam*. Baltimore, MD: Johns Hopkins University Press.

Fessenden, Tracy. 2012. "The Objects of American Religious Studies." *Religion* 42(3): 373–382.

King, Richard. 2013. "The Copernican Turn in the Study of Religion." *Method and Theory in the Study of Religion* 25(2): 137–159.

Mjøset, L. 2001. "Theory: Conceptions in the Social Sciences." In Neil J. Smelser and Paul B. Baltes (eds.), *International Encyclopedia of the Social and Behavioral Sciences*, 23: 15641–15647. Amsterdam: Elsevier.

Pals, Daniel L. 2015. *Nine Theories of Religion*. New York: Oxford University Press.

4

Signifying "Theory": Toward a Method of Mutually Assured Deconstruction

Richard Newton

Luther H. Martin and Donald Wiebe's 2004 essay "Establishing a Beachhead" (reprinted as Chapter 1 of the present volume) chronicles the precedent for the situation in which we find ourselves today. Thirty years after NAASR's founding, we have seen a great transformation: from a paucity of theory in the academic study of religion to a "time of excess." The context for our discussion suggests that this revolution was not wholly successful. To signify on comedian and cultural critic Paul Mooney, "Everybody wanna do theory, but don't nobody wanna do theory."[1]

Jason Blum's essay (Chapter 2, this volume) sheds light on the struggle many would-be theorists face. "Obsessive self-doubt" and "incessant self-critique" can "dissolve the objects of the study of religion" and "stymie scholarship" (p. 21, this volume). The critical turn of the post-prefix era can lead us into dizzy hermeneutical circles.

In turn he offers a particular kind of restraint: a reveal of "the inherent limitations of [theory's] explanatory power" and an orientation toward the "anchor [of] empirics and philosophically sophisticated methods of analysis" (ibid.). His guidance lays bare the foundations upon which a scholar may construct explanations and interpretations of an object of study.

I take no issue with the course of Blum's argument. Methodologically, I consider myself an anthropologist of scriptures—interested in the discourses mediated through source-texts. This may account for my askew view of Blum's philosophizing. Despite our perspectival differences, I appreciate his essay as a solid primer to religious studies as an analytical discipline.

First and foremost, I offer my thoughts as an honest inquiry of clarification, an attempt to better understand what this approach illuminates about "religion." In the course of my response, I would like to use the language of signification to illustrate the "intellectual integrity" of Blum's theoretical restraint. While my abstraction will highlight the merits of Blum's argument, I contend that it will also embolden some of its critical implications.

When we attend to the dynamics at work in the phenomenon, we must also recognize our own work in constituting that phenomenon. At best, this leads to questions about the definition of knowledge, the politics of its production, and the manner in which it is produced. How would this not lead to a dismembering—and perhaps re-membering—of the scholarly societies that shelter us from the ramifications of our discursive violence?

So I depart from Blum not by way of disagreement but by extension. Theory, I will suggest, prompts us also to take note of the constructed self—especially the scholarly self—and to welcome the inevitable deauthorization of our own epistemological regimes. It signifies an embrace of our own mutually assured deconstruction. What he likens to falling down the rabbit hole into other academic "fields," I see as the chief job of our discipline. Toward this aim, I offer a few possibilities for how NAASR might press onward—specifically through the means we produce and publish knowledge.

Signifying Theory

Blum articulates well the impulse behind those modern intellectual forbears who took our object of study to be a fixed essence. Throughout the paper, he maintains a phenomenological approach, where data comprises "the significance or relevance of many religious activities, attitudes, and artifacts [which] do not reveal themselves to naked observation" (p. 23, this volume). Theory, then, is the gnostic pursuit of that which is occluded by a signifier's confessions, be they timeless values, the strength of an institution, or some ineffable power. He practices an academic asceticism that leads him to a deeper understanding of what Eliade (1987: 163) called "*homo religiosus.*"

But this depends on one's ability to balance two scholarly humors. The first he calls "interpretation." This is where the scholar describes the emic or confessional signifier's own understanding of the significance of signs. The second he calls "theorizing," or the explanation of what that confessional emic signification signifies for the critical etic observer (McCutcheon 2005: 17). If the scholar can harmonize these two dispositions, then a clearer picture of religion will appear.

We can deconstruct these discourses with the assistance of a graphic organizer. The sheet begins as a "blank space." We all recognize that the world is full of potential signs to be signified by signifiers, but Michel de Certeau notes that the scholarly page is a site where choices are made to "delimit a place of production for the subject" (1988: 134). Jonathan Z. Smith makes a similar point in characterizing "religion" as "solely the creation of the scholar's study" (1982: xi). So let us not take for granted that it is on this empty sheet that "religion" happens.

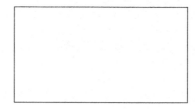

Figure 4.1 "Blank Space" as a Critical Field Site for Religious Studies.

The confessional signifier, or what Blum calls "the object of study" (p. 22, this volume) becomes a horizontal line of three squares: a signifier square, a sign square, a significance square. A right-headed arrow through the squares depicts confessional signification or Blum's understanding of "interpretation." *In toto* it is where we impress a worldview.

Figure 4.2 Interpretation as Confessional Signification.

Blum is clear that the meaning ascribed in the interpretation is not the same as the telos of the scholar: "Acknowledgement is not endorsement." For the critical signifier, the entire horizontal line acts as a "sign" to be explained. Thus we depict theorizing as a diagonal line intersecting that horizontal line (the critic's "sign" or the confessor's interpretive signifying). These explanations take as endpoint a greater understanding of *homo religiosus*—that is, whatever the scholar determines to be critically significant.

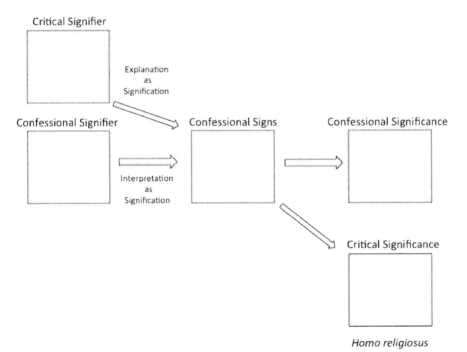

Figure 4.3 Explanation as Critical Signification.

The caricature of postmodern relativism—or even nihilism—is an over sim-plification for Blum because the meaning-making practices of the scholar are restrained by "empirical accountability and falsifiability":

> To the extent that a theory fails to account for observed features of those phe-nomena that it seeks to explain, *that theory* may be described as incomplete; if it fails to produce any claims at all that withstand empirical falsification (or which are unfalsifiable) *that theory* may be described as wrong (or empty) [italics added].

Thus, critical explanations must be bound yet not beholden to the dataset of con-fessional interpretations. Within this tension, Blum attempts to restrain scholars from corrupting their data. When not "grounded in historical intersubjectively available evidence," theory releases us into "fictionalizing and omphaloskepsis." I, too, am concerned that our scholarship will "retreat into a shadowy solipsistic realm of unaccountable speculation" (pp. 21, 24 and 30, this volume).

Signifying "Theory"

On this score, I wonder whether I am more confident in Blum's argument than he is, for I think it not simply possible but essential to widen the parameters of our signification. Charles Long discusses signifying as "worse than lying because it obscures and obfuscates a discourse without taking responsibility for so doing" (1995: 1). This challenges us to recognize that the blank page is now filled with people authorizing themselves to read other people, and that is a task in need of further explanation (see Figure 4.4).

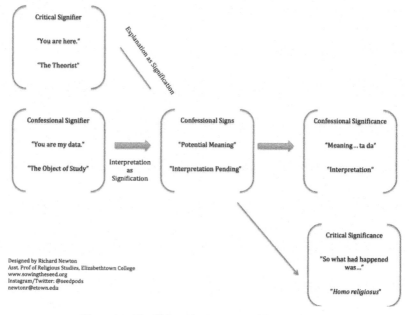

Figure 4.4 Signifying Theory: A Graphic Organizer.

Beyond distinguishing between interpretation and explanation, theory challenges us to become aware that we are always fictionalizing. Roland Barthes says as much in his discussion of "Myth Today" (Barthes 2001: 115). When we realize that the object of study "in no way *signifies* its meaning to me," and "tries very little to tell me something," then "its true and fundamental signification is to impose itself on me as the presence of a certain agreement of the predicate" (ibid.: 116). More bluntly, we are bound to corrupt our data. The prime directive will be violated.[2] Theory reminds us not to confuse "Nature" for "History" (ibid.: 115). This does not make theorizing meaningless. It warns us that scholarship comprises of temporary fictions to be amended by more nuanced accounts.

Blum, I think, agrees with the spirit of my suggestion, but I find myself questioning whether he would return to the bemoaned omphaloskepsis that calls into question the very letters our guild uses to operationalize falsifiability and empiricism. After all, the "modern 'discipline'" of religious studies is an example of what de Certeau calls a "scriptural enterprise," a system that "stocks up what it sifts out and gives itself the means to expand. Combining the power of *accumulating* the past and that of making the alterity of the universe *conform* to its models, it is capitalist and conquering" (de Certeau 1988: 135). This is precisely why navel-gazing is important. It is at least a nod toward a self-awareness that recognizes the scholar's interest in the construction and maintenance of an evaluative system that assigns meaning and worth to persons. For all we know, our heuristic distinctions may be in service of aims unbefitting of a self-proclaimed "observer."

And in this discipline, we have reason to be suspicious of our musings. After all, it was Friedrich Max Müller's orientalist and philological impulse to scholastically "classify and conquer" (Müller 1899: 68) the world's religions that challenged Tomoko Masuzawa to consider

> whether the idea of the diversity of religion is not, instead, the very thing that facilitates the transference and transmutation of a particular absolutism from one context to another ... and at the same time makes this process of transmutation very hard to identify and nearly impossible to understand. (Masuzawa 2005: 216)

Thinking particularly about "the world religions discourse," Masuzawa (2005: 216) questions whether it "can be in anyway enlisted and trusted on this side of historical scholarship." To what extent might that question be raised about any of the approaches we take to studying religion (Newton 2016: 35–37; Tite 2016: 38–39)? Each of the contributors in this volume would confess to take their own work very seriously. Does it not stand to reason that the most critical readers will in kind discover latent significance in our most serious language-games?

Deconstructing Methods

Parsing interpretation and explanation alone does not necessarily ask the difficult question of what scholars are constructing with their sophisticated signifying. When Jonathan Z. Smith invites us into "the historian of religion's workroom" it would be a wasted trip if we asked "how" "why" and "so what" in regard to the data, but failed to ask the same about the scholar's own discursive practices (1982: 44). Thus Smith even advocates that our specialty is a commitment to be "relentlessly self-conscious" (ibid.: xi). In this time of excess, we need theory unrestrained. But as a matter of course, I am convinced that this is not in the best interest of the academy as presently construed.

Consider the rise of the public intellectual. I would hazard to say that some of us have tried to increase our job prospects by crafting a voice that can speak to the modern moment, the "just now" (cf. Latin *modernus, modo*). But what about the slow brewing reflection that Kelly Baker calls "the cold take" (2015)? How little prestige comes with the single, well-thought piece? Bulk and bylines look better on a vita, I am afraid.

Publish or perish is the maxim of yesterday, but I am of a generation of scholars who publish just to birth their way into the professorate. This sort of desperation does not encourage the cold take so often necessary to make sense of the moment. Instead, when crises like the 2015 acts of terror perpetrated in Charleston or Paris occur, throngs of Ta-Nehisi Coates wannabes rush to get their comments on the record.[3] In a 24-hour-news-cycle world, theory should lead us to a greater appreciation of patience and discretion.

At the root of Blum's essay is a commendable call for a richer exchange of ideas. But what are we to make of the means of exchange? Blum writes:

> Through the kind of deliberate and careful self-reflexivity for which many have been calling, as well as peer-review and other ongoing conversations of academic dialogue, we can at least partially rectify the limitations of the theories that we use and our ability to deploy them. (Blum, p. 24–25, this volume)

Systems of credentialing become creative attempts to work around strictures (Ferguson, Marcus, and Oransky 2014). Human practices leave room for human creativity—a virtue of dubious value if we take seriously the restraints of theory.

Yet when the ascetic scholar lets loose the range of explanatory and interpretive motion, the academy itself becomes data demanding investigation. Is there something different about the veil of anonymity when worn while doing fieldwork (Junco 2015)? Can a reader trust a reviewer's bona fide credentials to abbreviate anything more than a willingness to doctor another's work? Editorial anonymity appears a strange practice when compared to the namelessness of comment boards and social media channels begrudged by teacher–scholars. What are the politics of identifying peers? In our self-estrangement, we might take some solace in the precedent of sociologist W. E. B. DuBois, whose own inquiry into "the spiritual strivings" of his own race turned his attention to the question, "How does it feel to be a problem" (1994: 1)? More than many, he understood that a community of interested and invested readers shade the difference in our data. So too is the case when we realize that we are potentially some critic's data.

That is precisely the point that Richard Smith and others raised in the *Journal of the Royal Society of Medicine* in revaluating the role of peer review within their guild (R. Smith 2006; Linkov, Lovalekar, and LaPorte 2006; Schroter 2007). "The most important step on the journey was realizing that peer review could be studied just like anything else ... At the time it was a radical idea, and still seems radical to some—rather like conducting experiments with God or love" (R. Smith 2006: 118). We in religious studies have all the more reason to revisit the god in the machine, unless we are afraid what may be reflected therein.

Toward Theory Less Restrained

We are a bookish lot, and theory prompts us to examine the academy's own scriptural proclivities. Too often we are encouraged to prize an expert's illusory final word instead of appreciating the palimpsest that is scholarship at its best. "Intellectual integrity" requires humility enough to put forth one's best efforts and to look forward to saying "I was wrong." Blum's argument creates a space for the scholar to discover this in conversation with representing the subject of study. The observer is implored to better explain the signifying practices of the confessor. Theory unrestrained demands us (and our peers) to better explain our own interpretive work. We need close readings of our scholarly fictions.

Let us locate our intellectual work in the precarious place that leaves itself vulnerable to corporate navel-gazing—the work we call critical comparison.

In this regard, Kathleen Fitzpatrick's open-source meta-example, *Planned Obsolescence: Publishing, Technology, and The Future of the Book*, is revealing (Fitzpatrick 2009).[4] It is an online digital volume in which readers may comment on the ideas introduced by an author. The ongoing, asynchronous conversation depicts intellectual labor as a "process" of "versioning" rather than established (ibid.: 24). Much as this anthology codifies the back and forth of the 2015 NAASR Annual Meeting, Fitzpatrick's example offers a medium for fostering the rhizomatic reality. New conversations may extend and even supplant the original one. Or the conversation may go untended, withering into refuse.

Perhaps there are many reasons to shy away from such theorizing, but securing the guild's authority should not be one of them. Advocating for an open peer-review process in the academe, Fitzpatrick writes:

> But finally, if the loss of power and prestige are our primary concerns in clinging to closed review, we would be best served by admitting this to ourselves up front. If we enjoy the privileges that obtain from upholding a closed system of discourse sufficiently that we're unwilling to subject it to critical scrutiny, we may also need to accept the fact that the mainstream of public intellectual life will continue, in the main, to ignore our work. This can, of course, be rationalized as the inevitable, unenviable fate of genius in a world of mediocrity. (Fitzpatrick 2009: 11)

If we do our work well, we will inevitably be data for some critical signifier. If this is not the case, then I am not sure what is holding us back besides fear and self-interest. Whatever it is, it stands in significant contrast to the "anchor [of] empirics and philosophically sophisticated methods of analysis" sounding from our profession.

Theory is a space to embrace displacement. It takes empiricism so seriously that the astute scholar is not the one who has the last word, but the one ever-ready to read the next, especially when it circumscribes the very writings to which we are rooted. Titles, honorifics, and pedigree should offer no fast track to legitimacy. To paraphrase the author Ishamel Reed, theorizing is the practice of a "Neo-hoodoo ... where every [hu]man is artist and every artist a priest" (1997: 2298). In the years to come, the academy's theoretical revolution may continue to be signified by many voices (Baram 2014; de Certeau 1988: 135).[5] I simply hope NAASR will spell out our mutually assured deconstruction, restraining us from professing too much.

Richard Newton is Assistant Professor of Religious Studies at Elizabethtown College. He curates the student-scholar media collaborative, Sowing the Seed: Fruitful Conversations in Religion, Culture, and Teaching (sowingtheseed.org).

Notes

1. From *Chappelle's Show*, episode 5, originally aired February 19, 2003. Mooney describes "the black man" as the most copied, fetishized person in late twentieth-century America. Commenting on the limits of this great transformation from Ralph Ellison's *Invisible Man* (1952) to postmodern everyman, Mooney signifies, "Everybody wanna be a nigga, but don't nobody wanna be a nigga." His riff suggests that signifiers find signs (in this case, being a "nigga") most appealing when they can select the parameters of significance—namely those amenable to the signifier. The irony is that wielding such authority stands in stark contrast to the historical reality that brought about the occasion of the sign ("nigga") in the first place. The concomitance of rampant imitation and selective application is similar to the state of theory in religious studies.

2. The prime directive is a reference to an ethical mandate in the *Star Trek* universe that more advanced civilizations should make every effort to refrain from altering the authentic state of more primitive societies upon contact. As a plot device, it provides allegorical opportunity to explore the problematics of ethnographic reflexivity, imperialism, and ethnocentrism. The very nature of the conversation, however, presupposes the existence of a static, free-standing object of study outside of the observer's signification.

3. Ta-Nehisi Coates is a national correspondent for *The Atlantic*. The recipient of a 2015 MacArthur Fellowship, his long-form essays have garnered considerable attention in the United States for a measured discussion of the zeitgeist—especially concerning issues of race in America. His popularity has also given rise to a resurgence in the think-piece and the cachet of the public intellectual.

4. Fitzpatrick's book is available in two major iterations. One is a traditional monograph published by New York University Press in 2009. The other is an openly peer reviewed version via Media Commons which remains available online for open discussion. I will be referencing the latter as its interstitial formatting presages great opportunity for future NAASR publications.

5. Two influences are worthy of mention here to frame my closing remarks. The first is Civil Rights activist and writer Gil Scott-Heron's quotation, "The revolution will not be televised" (Baram 2014). The second is de Certeau's own definition of revolution

as "'that' modern idea, represent[ing] the scriptural project at the level of an entire society seeking to *constitute itself* as a blank page with respect to the past, to write itself by itself (that is, to produce itself as its own system) and to produce *a new history* (*refaire l'histoire*) on the model of what it fabricates (and this will be 'progress')" (de Certeau 1988: 135). Intertextually, they turn theorizing back on the scholar, pointing out that no findings come ex nihilo or exist sui generis.

References

Baker, Kelly J. 2015."Cold Takes: A Sort of Manifesto." October 1. Available at www. kellyjbaker.com/cold-takes-sort-manifesto (accessed December 14, 2015).

Baram, Marcus. 2014. "Why Gil Scott-Heron Wrote 'The Revolution Will Not Be Televised': Finding Inspiration in a World of Unrest and Rage." November 11. Available at https://medium.com/cuepoint/why-gil-scott-heron-wrote-the-revolution-will-not-be-televised-6e298f9d4e2#.4vi02knjt (accessed December 14, 2015).

Barthes, Roland. 2001. *Mythologies* (trans. Annette Lavers). New York: Hill and Wang (first published 1957).

De Certeau, Michel. 1988. "The Scriptural Economy" (trans. Steven F. Rendall). In Michel de Certeau, *The Practice of Everyday Life*, 131–153. Berkeley, CA: University of California Press (first published 1984).

DuBois, W.E.B. 1994. *The Souls of Black Folks*. Chicago, IL: Dover (first published 1903).

Eliade, Mircea. 1987. *The Sacred and the Profane: The Nature of Religion* (trans. William R. Trask). Orlando, FL: Harcourt (first published 1957).

Ferguson, Cat, Adam Marcus, and Ivan Oransky. 2014. "The Peer-Review Scam." *Nature* 515(7528): 480–482.

Fitzpatrick, Kathleen. 2009. "Planned Obsolescence: Publishing, Technology, and the Future of the Academy." Available at http://mcpress.media-commons.org/plannedobsolescence/ (accessed December 14, 2015).

Junco, Rey. 2015. "Yik Yak and Online Anonymity are Good for College Students." *Wired* (March 17). Available at www.wired.com/2015/03/yik-yak-online-anonymity-good-college-students (accessed December 14, 2015).

Linkov, Faina, Mita Lovalekar, and Ronald LaPorte. 2006. "Scientific Journals are 'Faith Based': Is There Science Behind Peer Review?" *Journal of the Royal Society of Medicine* 99(12): 596–598.

Long, Charles H. 1995. *Significations: Signs, Symbols, and Images in the Interpretation of Religion*. Aurora, CO: The Davies Group (first published 1986).

Masuzawa, Tomoko. 2005. *The Invention of World Religions: Or, How European Universalism Was Preserved in the Language of Pluralism*. Chicago, IL: University of Chicago Press.

McCutcheon, Russell. 2005. T. Introduction to Theoretical Background: Insides, Outsides and the Scholar of Religion. In Russell T. McCutcheon (ed.), *The Insider/Outsider Problem in the Study of Religion: A Reader*, 15–22. New York: Continuum (first published 1999).

Müller, Friedrich Max. 1899. "Second Lecture: Delivered at the Royal Institution, February 26, 1870." In Friedrich Max Müller, *Introduction to the Science of Religion: Four Lectures Delivered at the Royal Institution in February and May 1870*, 52–82. London: Longmans Green, and Co. Available at https://archive.org/details/b21782635 (accessed December 14, 2015).

Newton, Richard. 2016. "Signifying on the World Religions Paradigm: My Version of Religion 101." *Bulletin for the Study of Religion* 44(3): 35–37.

Reed, Ishmael. 1997. "Neo-HooDoo Manifesto." In Henry Louis Gates, Jr. and Nellie Y. McKay (eds.), *The Norton Anthology of African American Literature*, 2297–2301. New York: W. W. Norton (first published 1972).

Schroter, Sarah. 2007. "Response to 'Scientific Journals are "Faith Based": Is There a Science Behind Peer Review?'." *Journal of the Royal Society of Medicine* 100(3): 117–118.

Smith, Jonathan Z. 1982. "Introduction." In Jonathan Z. Smith, *Imagining Religion: From Babylon to Jonestown*, xi–xiii. Chicago, IL: University of Chicago Press.

Smith, Richard. 2006. "Peer Review: A Flawed Process at the Heart of Science and Journals." *Journal of the Royal Society of Medicine* 99(4): 178–182.

Tite, Philip L. 2016. "Editor's Corner: Critics or Caretakers? It's All in the Mapping." *Bulletin for the Study of Religion* 44(3): 38–39.

5

On the Restraint of Consciousness

Tara Baldrick-Morrone

Jason Blum's essay "On the Restraint of Theory" (Chapter 2, this volume) sets out to solve the dilemma that many scholars, especially in the North American Association for the Study of Religion, have debated for some time now, namely, how to "do theory" and what to "do" with it, particularly in a time of its overuse (or, as some might prefer to say, its abuse). Blum's position has merit, particularly in his recognition of the social embeddedness of the phenomena that scholars happen to call "religion." Yet, at the end of the day, his approach is one that I find to be less profitable than one might hope. Blum's reliance on consciousness raises major concerns about the role of the scholar in that his appeal to consciousness precludes the scholar from acting as anything other than a reporter, or, as Bruce Lincoln might say, a "collector" (cf. thesis 13 in Lincoln 1996: 227). Before addressing this point, though, I want to focus on what it means to access the consciousness of an agent.

The Inaccessibility and Undesirability of Consciousness

As Blum argues, "religious consciousness" is responsible for constructing and experiencing the meaning of the phenomenon. To get at this meaning, he insists that "the consciousness of the subject who engages in that activity must be brought into the analytical process" (p. 27, this volume). Because this data is that which is "not publicly observable," in order to interpret it the scholar must therefore rely on what the agents understand themselves to be doing. According to Blum, to do otherwise (i.e., to fail to bring in the agent's understanding of the phenomena) would be to create an imperfect representation of reality. This is nothing new, as Wilfred Cantwell Smith argued long ago that "no statement about a religion is valid unless it can be acknowledged by that religion's believers" (1982: 146). But herein lies the predicament with relying on the consciousness of the agent: I do not get a sense from Blum about why an agent's self-understanding is *prima facie* more insightful or more trustworthy than other ways of describing or comprehending the same phenomena. Moreover, to study religion from a critical standpoint means to take into consideration the sociohistorical contexts and discursive strategies of the agents, all of which is ignored if we merely rely on consciousness.

As is explained throughout the essay, the meaning of the phenomena of religion is only able to be obtained by considering what the person understands themselves to be doing; it is then the job of the scholar to interpret that data. If one were to follow this model, then, the agent must be seen as a reliable informant of sorts, one who is fully cognizant and relates the comprehension of their actions truthfully and without embellishment. However, before accepting the self-understanding of the agent at face value, the scholar should be far more rigorous in their collection of data, keeping in mind the questions that Peter Metcalf raises when he writes,

> ethnographies are full of obliging informants, hastening to play Sancho Panza to the ethnographer's Don Quixote. We have to ask ourselves what transactions of power and knowledge underlie their motives. Moreover ... we have to consider the conceptual premises and conversational constraints under which they select what to tell and how to tell it. (Metcalf 2002:1)

In other words, scholars should not abandon the hermeneutics of suspicion so easily, for more is at work than what the agent can observe or know.

In addition to the unreliability of agents, the difficulties of accessing consciousness stand in the way of Blum's projected solution to the shortcomings of theoretical (or theory-heavy) approaches to religion. This requires us to come to terms with the socially embedded nature not only of the phenomena that we study but of consciousness. Blum says as much, but he overestimates the ease with which this can be accessed by scholars. Attempting to gain insight into an agent's consciousness is made all the more unfeasible because, as Lincoln argues, consciousness is not even readily available to the agents themselves. In "Theses on Method," Lincoln writes that to "[u]nderstand the system of ideology that operates in one's own society is made difficult by two factors: (i) one's consciousness is itself a product of that system, and (ii) the system's very success renders its operations invisible" (Lincoln 1996: 226). Thus, the very consciousness we are trying to access is obfuscated by its situatedness, causing it to be comprehended by neither scholars nor the agents themselves. Moreover, to borrow a phrase from literary theory, this approach threatens to introduce the intentional fallacy. As literary scholars W. K. Wimsatt, Jr. and M. C. Beardsley assert in discussing authorial intent in poetry, intent is "neither available nor desirable" (1946: 468). The same, I think, can be said of consciousness. It is neither desirable because of its reliance on the agent (whose interests and motives we are unaware of) nor is it available in that agents are unable to understand the ways in which their consciousnesses have been produced by the world in which they live.

All of this said, I think it would be a mistake to dismiss Blum's arguments without attempting to see how this project works in practice. I had hoped for a detailed example that would illustrate how his approach can be used, but none was given in the version of the essay that I read. However, to give him the benefit of the doubt, and in a bid to demonstrate what accessing an agent's consciousness does for interpreting and explaining phenomena, I decided to use an agent from my own work: Gregory of Nyssa, the fourth-century CE provincial bishop, and his letter on pilgrimage.

Gregory of Nyssa: An Exercise in Accessing Consciousness

Although I have already pointed to some of the issues scholars encounter in accessing an agent's intentions or consciousness, I want to raise another difficulty that arises when trying this method with certain agents, such as Gregory. What does it mean to access a person's consciousness after they have died (and, in this example, someone who has been dead for over 1600 years)? One approach, some might argue, would be to use texts that the agents left behind in order to reveal a window through which to view their reality, which would disclose what they understood themselves to be doing, feeling, thinking, etc. There are a number of problems with thinking about texts in this way, but let me proceed with the example before focusing on them.

Gregory's *Letter* 2, dated to sometime after the Council of Constantinople in 381, is written to a certain Kensitor, who some have speculated is a leader in a monastery (Silvas 2007: 115). The main theme of the letter concerns those who should and should not embark on pilgrimages, such as monks and consecrated women. Take this part of the letter as an example demonstrating how Gregory tries to deter monastics from undertaking pilgrimages (to the Holy Land, in particular):

> Is it that the Lord still lives in the body today in those places and has stayed away from our regions? Or is it that the Holy Spirit abounds among the inhabitants of Jerusalem, but is unable to come to us? Really, if it is possible to infer God's presence from the things that appear, one might more justly consider that he dwelt in the nation of the Cappadocians than in places elsewhere! ... [I]f grace were greater in the vicinity of Jerusalem than anywhere else, sin would not be so entrenched among those who dwell there. But as it is, there is no form of uncleanness that is not brazened among them: fornications, adulteries, thefts, idolatries, drugs, envies, murders ... Well then, where such things go on, what evidence is there that in those places grace abounds more? (Gregory of Nyssa, *Letter* 2.8–10; trans. Silvas 2007: 119–120)

If we are to attempt to extract Gregory's own understanding of what he is doing here, or what he thinks himself to be doing, what might we say? Based on my earlier point, we would no doubt have to take him at his word here. Therefore, as Gregory explains, he is upset that pilgrims travel to areas that are deeply entrenched in sinful behavior. These pilgrims, he argues, should instead stay in Cappadocia, where interaction with the divine is just as available, if not more so. But what else could a scholar say about this letter other than to reiterate what Gregory has already said himself? The text is solely repeated with no real analysis or comprehension of its context or how it might have been used. At this point we should ask ourselves what it is that we are really doing: as I said, it appears as nothing more than mere reporting.

How, then, do we get past the role of scholar-as-reporter? My instinct, as it is so often, is to rely on Lincoln. I turn to a question that I find to be ignored in Blum's discussion of agents and consciousness, namely: "Who speaks here?" (cf. thesis 4 in Lincoln 1996: 225–226). If consciousness is a product of one's environment, whose interpretation and meaning are we privileging by using an agent's consciousness? That is, the appeal to consciousness, to the individual's meaning of the phenomenon, conceals the socially embedded contestations that are always at play. To ignore these stakes and give priority to an agent is to privilege someone or some idea without accounting for the very real interests of the parties involved. In the case of Gregory, asking these questions of his letter (Who is he talking to? What is the immediate and broader context? What are his interests?) allows us to analyze the letter more in light of fourth-century sociopolitical struggles than strictly relying on Gregory's words to reveal reality.

What this amounts to is that this letter, in the wake of Gregory's state-sanctioned trip to Jerusalem, may not solely be concerned with the spiritual welfare of monastics. Instead, his vitriol against Jerusalem may have more to do with the economic boon of the enterprise of pilgrimage. As Peter Brown tells us, "Funds continued to flow out of Rome and the West toward the Holy Places and the monasteries of Egypt. Rome could afford this drain. But in the provinces propaganda for the ascetic movement and the fostering of pilgrimage to the Holy Land threatened to undermine the finances of the less well-endowed local churches" (Brown 2012: 280). Although Brown's example comes specifically from the Western half of the Roman Empire, it is not unreasonable to suggest that circumstances were similar in the imperial East where the province of Cappadocia was situated. The issue is said to have come to a head before the beginning of the fifth century, which lines up with the suggested date of the letter. On my reading, to trust Gregory as a reliable agent would be to divorce him from his context as described by Brown and would not produce this kind of analysis of the letter. Instead, we would be left repeating what Gregory is said to have written, with perhaps no real advancement in understanding the larger social landscape in which Gregory lived and wrote. Furthermore, reading the letter by using the appeal to consciousness undoubtedly turns this text, indeed, perhaps even *all* texts, into confessions that would require us as scholars to see agents as reliable and rational actors whose actions and motives are always transparent, regardless of their intended audiences or historical contexts.

Conclusion

My example above is not meant to discredit Blum's approach. What I aim to draw attention to by using Gregory of Nyssa as an example of an agent is the limited utility of the appeal to consciousness. By no means does it make sense to apply it to all agents or phenomena that scholars classify as "religion"; at the same time, it may not be meant to. Blum in fact criticizes the search for a "single, monolithic theory" to explain the data (p. 22, this volume). Still, even if we were to accept its utility in some instances, I have demonstrated two points of difficulty when attempting to access someone's consciousness, namely, the unreliability of the agents and their—as well as our (i.e., scholars')—inability to tap into their consciousness because of the way that it is embedded in its ideological settings. While Blum's idea that the pendulum has swung so far into theoretical criticism as to have created a neurotic pitch may be an appropriate critique in some cases, he has nudged that same pendulum so far in the opposite direction as to overcorrect the situation by reintroducing approaches that many in previous decades have shown to be lacking critical scholarly rigor.

Tara Baldrick-Morrone is a Ph.D. candidate in Religions of Western Antiquity at Florida State University. Her research focuses on the rhetoric of martyrdom in late antiquity.

References

Brown, Peter. 2012. *Through the Eye of a Needle: Wealth, the Fall of Rome, and the Making of Christianity in the West, 350-550 AD*. Princeton, NJ: Princeton University Press.

Lincoln, Bruce. 1996. "Theses on Method." *Method and Theory in the Study of Religion* 8(3): 225–227.

Metcalf, Peter. 2002. *They Lie, We Lie: Getting on with Anthropology*. New York: Routledge.

Silvas, Anna M. 2007. *Gregory of Nyssa: The Letters: Introduction, Translation, and Commentary*. Leiden: Brill.

Smith, Wilfred Cantwell. 1982. "Comparative Religion: Whither—and Why." In Willard G. Oxtoby (ed.), *Religious Diversity*, 138–157. New York: Crossroad.

Wimsatt, W. K., Jr., and M. C. Beardsley. 1946. "The Intentional Fallacy." *The Sewanee Review* 54(3): 468–488.

6

A Reply

Jason N. Blum

My thanks to Michael Altman (Chapter 3, this volume), Richard Newton (Chapter 4, this volume), and Tara Baldrick-Morrone (Chapter 5, this volume) for their thoughtful remarks on my essay (Chapter 2, this volume). Limitations of space do not allow me to address all of their comments; here, I will respond to the most relevant points of disagreement, identifying divergences in our thinking and clarifying some misunderstandings.

Altman characterizes my approach as assuming that "There is a world out there and we can know it. Religion is out there and we can explain it" (p. 30, this volume). These two claims must be distinguished from each other. While I do endorse the former (with some qualifications), I do not endorse the latter. To begin with the former: yes, I do assume that there is a world "out there" beyond my own consciousness (a term to which I will return) and that scholars not only have access to it, but are in fact beholden to it in important ways. This is not to say that I endorse a naïve ideal of pure objectivity. Intersubjective verification, however, is something of which scholars are capable. While a variety of philosophical problems attend claims concerning "the world out there" and our knowledge of it (some of which are relevant and interesting and others less so), I take it for granted that human subjects can encounter a phenomenon and compare notes on it.

Admittedly, doing so without unintentionally importing implicit theoretical claims or interpretive frames is not easy. I attempt to demonstrate this with my hypothetical example of prayer (p. 26, this volume). To call the action I describe "prayer" is already to imbue that account with a number of assumptions, and so I offer that hypothetical description in order to highlight the range of claims that may be implicitly posited even by use of that seemingly innocuous term. I do take it for granted that other human subjects could observe that activity and agree at least on the very basic physical motions that I describe (i.e., that intersubjective verification is at least possible, even if it requires careful refinement of observational methods and self-reflective bracketing of interpretive and explanatory claims). Unless some sort of intersubjective verification is possible, I don't know how anything resembling scholarship in any discipline could be carried out.

Religion, by contrast, is not "out there." As I acknowledge in my essay, religion is a constructed category (p. 21, this volume)—a concept that scholars bring to those phenomena in which we are interested. The question, therefore, is not whether or not religion exists—insofar as it does, it exists only as an artificial, organizing taxon that facilitates analysis and comparison—but whether and to what degree the concept is useful in terms of furthering our understanding of things that happen out there in the world.[1]

That question cannot be posed, however, unless we are willing to acknowledge that we—and, more importantly, our theories—are in some sort of dialogue with the world. It is for this reason that I am unsure what Altman means when he claims that the scholar is, on one hand, involved in "knowledge production" (p. 33, this volume) and the use of "data" (p. 35, this volume), while, on the other, claiming that "everything theory explains is always already the theorist's creation" (pp. 33–34, this volume). If the latter is true, then theorists are nothing but novelists, spinning yarns that may or may not make for good reading, but whose relevance remains inexplicable. In order for theory to be relevant, it must break out of a coherentist epistemology in order to establish some sort of relationship with the world about which it ought to be making claims, in which case "everything" that theory explains is *not* only the theorist's creation.

"Religion," as a concept, *is* largely the theorist's creation (excepting for the moment the fact that the term is also now a common feature of non-scholarly discourses as well). I heartily agree on the need to continually re-examine the meanings of the term, to reflect on what violence its usage might be doing to those phenomena we employ it to study, and to question whether other concepts might be more (or less) useful. However, I see the deconstructive critique of the term "religion" not as an end in itself, but as a means to facilitating more enlightening interpretations and defensible explanations of things going on out there in the world. Altman therefore misreads me when he claims that my interest in baptism, sacrifice, and pilgrimage as opposed to washing, killing, and traveling is premised on the fact that the former "are religious" (p. 33, this volume). My interest in baptism rather than washing does indicate certain preferences on my part, and it does mirror the discursive practices of the academic institutions of which I am a part; these, however, are not the only or even the primary reasons for my preference. Put simply, there is a more interesting story to be told about baptism than washing. An inquiry into a man's washing would more than likely be rather brief and uninteresting ("I just came back from the gym"), whereas an inquiry into baptism would reveal a complex background of beliefs and behaviors that are themselves worthy of investigation: the man's membership in a particular community, a variety of claims concerning non-empirical realities, related beliefs that impact the man's political and moral positions, etc.

That difference between washing and baptism is not the theorist's own creation: it exists independently of the scholar and her theory. Admittedly, there is no necessity to labelling baptism "religious"; that categorization is an artificial rhetorical move on the part of the theorist, but it is not for that reason obviously illegitimate. The taxon "religion" serves to recognize the link between a particular ritualized practice and the institutions, doctrines, traditions, communities, and texts that constitute the context out of which its meaning is largely derived; acknowledging that context and those linkages helps to make sense of the activity of baptism and the subject's choice to engage in it. The decision to study baptism rather than washing does *not* result from labeling the former rather than the latter "religious." The choice proceeds from the judgment that this is an intriguing behavior that merits study; the "religious" label facilitates recognition of the fact that the practice of baptism is situated in and at least partially understood and explained by its relation to a broad set of other, related phenomena. The label therefore serves to facilitate study, rather than being its impetus.

The difference between washing and baptism, however, can only be acknowledged if it is possible to take into account the perspective of the subject who engages in the activity—in other words, by recognizing that the consciousness of the religious subject is an important factor in many of the phenomena that we seek to study. Both Altman and Baldrick-Morrone question my use of the term consciousness. There are, of course, a number of significant questions to be raised about the term, which is highly contested especially among philosophers of mind. I do not claim to solve those problems, but I do hold that it is possible—even necessary—to bring the religious subject's thoughts, beliefs, emotions, and desires into analysis, and I use the term "consciousness" to denote these and other psychological comportments. Baldrick-Morrone raises a number of questions in this regard, arguing that it is not possible to gain insight into an agent's consciousness because it is "obfuscated by its situatedness, causing it to be comprehended by neither scholars nor the agents themselves" (p. 48, this volume). Baldrick-Morrone is right to point out that consciousness does not immediately present itself for study, but she overstates the point, and her own argument belies her claim that consciousness is beyond the pale of academic discourse. In the midst of dismissing the concept, Baldrick-Morrone refers to Gregory of Nyssa's "vitriol against Jerusalem" (p. 50, this volume).[2] What can the reference to "vitriol" be if not a reference to a psychological attitude—what I call an expression of Gregory's consciousness?

Baldrick-Morrone's concern likely arises from her conflation of my position with that of Wilfred Cantwell Smith. Whereas I claim that a theory must "account for" the data it seeks to explain, Smith argues that any statement about a religion must be acknowledged by that religion's adherents in order to be regarded as valid (p. 47, this volume). These positions are not identical. I argue that expressions of consciousness constitute data, and therefore that it is relevant to question how well a theory accounts for experience or consciousness as reported by a subject. This is typically done by proposing a hypothesis for the cause, origin, or function of that data that rests on an accurate interpretation of it. This is not, however, to install the religious subject as the final arbiter of the truth or accuracy of the researcher's explanations, as Smith seems to suggest. Rather, I contend that theories must be assessed in terms of their ability to offer relatively comprehensive and falsifiable explanations of phenomena "out there" in the world, rather than merely hanging above the intersubjectively experienced world as unmoored abstractions whose authority is simply assumed based on their theoretical prove-nance or *a priori* claims. Nothing in my position militates against reading against the grain or proposing explanations that are at odds with those offered by the religious subject.

This is, in fact, precisely what Baldrick-Morrone proceeds to do when she sug-gests that Gregory's condemnation of pilgrimages to Jerusalem arises not from a sincerely held theological objection (or at least not entirely so), but out of eco-nomic concerns related to the threat pilgrimage represented to less financially secure churches. This is an entirely plausible theory, particularly given the fact that Gregory had made the pilgrimage himself (note that both the economic con-ditions to which Baldrick-Morrone refers and Gregory's pilgrimage are exam-ples of evidence "out there" in the world). Baldrick-Morrone's theory, however, cannot get off the ground without the initial acknowledgement of Gregory's vit-riol. Without recognition of that expression of consciousness, what would her theory be seeking to explain? Her theory responds to the data (Gregory's emo-tional expression) and proposes a plausible explanation that accounts for it and which gains credence through its reliance on empirical evidence.

As Newton notes in his response, my position explicitly allows for this diver-gence between Baldrick-Morrone's explanation and Gregory's self-understand-ing: "Blum is clear that the meaning ascribed in the interpretation is not the same as the telos of the scholar" (p. 39, this volume). This aptly captures the difference between my position and Smith's: whereas the scholar's *interpretation* of a reli-gious phenomenon should accurately capture how that phenomenon was experi-enced by the subject, her *explanation* of a religious phenomenon can and typically does diverge from that offered by the subject herself.[3] However, that explanation is only relevant insofar as it is an explanation of that phenomenon, rather than merely a product of the theory itself. The tricky part, however, is that many reli-gious phenomena exist at least in part through the consciousnesses of religious subjects (i.e., prayer is not only a series of bodily gestures but also a variety of intellectual and emotional comportments). Their meaning or significance is not a brute phenomenon that is readily accessible to empirical observation, and so must be revealed through careful and sophisticated interpretation.

This brings us to the notion of "meaning." Altman asks whether my term "mean-ing" should be singular or plural. Although I do note that the term ought to be understood in the plural (p. 22, this volume), it is worthwhile to underscore that fact as it aids in clarifying one of Baldrick-Morrone's other objections: that con-sciousness is a product of the social system, and is therefore obfuscated from both the scholar's and the subject's understanding. The plural "meanings" gestures to the fact that religion—more specifically, a religious phenomenon (a doctrine, text, tradition, etc.)—does not have a single, monolithic (let alone transcendent) meaning, but rather multiple meanings that are created and experienced by his-torical subjects situated in specific, identifiable social circumstances. Recognition of that fact, however—rather than obfuscating anything—instead makes possi-ble the task of explanation. It is only by referring to Gregory's consciousness (in this case, his expression of anger) that the scholar acknowledges that there is anything at all that is worthy of being explained (in this case, perhaps by citing the economic conditions he faced): his consciousness is thereby rendered as data to be explained. And it is only by distinguishing between the tasks of interpretation and explanation that one may propose that Gregory is ignorant of the ways in which his own consciousness is shaped by those conditions. The distinction between these two tasks is what allows a scholar to retain an accurate account of the phenomena under analysis, including the religious subject's self-understanding (i.e., the meaning the subject attributes to religion) while proposing explanatory theories with which the subject might not agree, thereby avoiding the very error Baldrick-Morrone charges me with committing.

Jason N. Blum is a Visiting Assistant Professor at Davidson College. His research focuses on methodology in religious studies and topics at the intersection of philosophy and religion, including the relationship between science and religion, religious experience, and religion, society and ethics.

Notes

1. My position here is similar to Schilbrack (2014).
2. This isolated example is a relatively simple expression of consciousness, therefore requiring minimal interpretation. Lengthier and more complex expressions of consciousness require greater interpretation.
3. See the distinction between descriptive and explanatory reduction in Proudfoot (1985).

References

Proudfoot, Wayne. 1985. *Religious Experience*. Berkeley, CA: University of California Press.
Schilbrack, Kevin. 2014. *Philosophy and the Study of Religions: A Manifesto*. Malden, MA: Wiley Blackwell.

Part III

7

The High Stakes of Identifying (with)
One's Object of Study[1]

K. Merinda Simmons

For the past handful of years, I have been grappling with the fact that so much of what I had taken for granted in my literary graduate studies and on the MLA job market could not at all be presumed in the disciplinary plane of religious studies, where I now teach and write. Specifically, the critical obituary for the Author did not seem to have circulated in the academic study of religion to quite the extent that it had in literary theory back in the late 1960s. And it's not that English types necessarily had an easy time coping or knew what to do with themselves after the proverbial funeral. In fact, many took the death really hard and became almost belligerent in their staunch denial that the Author could really be gone (I'm looking at you, Harold Bloom). But most critics now accept the death even though they may have been and remain saddened by it. So, by and large, even when scholars are not at all interested in the turns of poststructuralism, they typically cannot get away with rejecting it outright. They must have ready answers for inevitable questions concerning their traditionalist stances. At the *very* least, critics have long been unable to suggest that Shakespeare is worth studying because he is ... well, *Shakespeare*. Instead, they have had to cast his work in relation to and, indeed, as a product of its context. With this turn, academic projects began to sound more historiographical—this or that Shakespearean text suggests something useful about Elizabethan formations and modalities of gender or what-have-you—than exegetical. And with critical theory à la the Frankfurt School in tow, scholars are now remiss not to admit that even historiography was its own interpretive framework. Our own interests as scholars, then, are never off the hook and never out of the picture. Also clear, to a certain degree, are the other scholars to whom we should be talking, as well as those we should simply not engage.

Since shifting from my disciplinary training in literary theory to religious studies, the gaps in who utilizes critical theory,[2] why, and how are simultaneously more than evident and ambiguous in their execution. In other words, there is no shortage of people who claim to be "doing theory," and yet, this glut of critical consciousness has allowed exactly the wrong debate to continue dominating the academic study of religion. What's the wrong debate? To my mind, it is the back-and-forth between theory and theology. And really, casting the disagreement as a "back-and-forth" is, in fact, a misnomer, since theologians seem to care little for what theorists are up to, while we theorists endlessly wring our hands over the ways in which theologians get it wrong. What results is a clamoring of proto-critical voices not really interested in pressing the implications of poststructuralist theory but *very* interested in identifying themselves in contradistinction to the constraints of analyses that start from confessional viewpoints. A central claim in this paper is that defining critical theory as that which is simply *not* theological is not enough. It seems to many that we scholars are about the business of articulating compelling arguments and winning over our readers. But I submit that our job is not to win over the tenacious descriptivist any more than it is to argue with theologians. Implicit in an attempt to move forward the field or advance scholarly discussions is an awareness of the field and discussions on which one is able to have any effect whatsoever. In religious studies, the conflation of something called critical theory with anything not classified as theology makes such awareness difficult to come by.

Developing a research specialization in postcolonial and feminist theories, I went through my graduate studies surrounded by what seemed common knowledge in that context: the only way to engage in a serious consideration of power dynamics and the ways in which race, gender, sexuality, capital, and other identifications intersect with those dynamics was to utilize "critical theory." Where my own locus of identity studies and literary theory were concerned, this meant taking seriously the poststructuralist tools operationalized in the late 1960s and refusing to take for granted a natural or obvious relationship between the labels or concepts we use and what we take them to mean. What seems to dominate identity studies in the academic study of religion, however, is that very explanatory description from which critical theorists have tried to turn away. In so many cases, scholars seem to suggest that a serious engagement of power dynamics and identity is, in fact, predicated upon a *rejection* of poststructuralist critique so as to take stock of "lived experiences" of marginalized groups. What accounts for this inversion, I suggest, is the relationship between scholars and their object of study. If Bruce Lincoln is right that religious studies as a discipline is stacked up to protect its object of study, this is a relationship worth exploring.[3]

Like anything else, academic work is a process of identifying. We identify what interests us and what we implicitly or explicitly suggest is worth analysis. We identify—even if implicitly—our methodologies and approaches. We identify the stakes in whatever discussion we choose to engage in. What too many scholars forget is that this ongoing process is not a series of transitive verbs begging direct objects. It is a formative endeavor. Judith Butler (1993) makes a similar point in a short piece taking on what may seem initially like an unlikely case study to bring up in this essay. But since part of my own claim here is that one's object of study is very much beside the point, I find it fitting indeed. Her brief "Endangered/Endangering: Schematic Racism and White Paranoia," which responds to the verdict in the Rodney King case that acquitted four police officers of excessive force, asks us to think about processes of seeing things. She suggests that the trial and its outcomes demonstrated the following:

that there is no simple recourse to the visible, to visual evidence, that it still and always calls to be read, that it is already a reading, and that in order to establish the injury on the basis of the visual evidence, an aggressive reading of the evidence is necessary. It is not, then, a question of negotiating between what is "seen," on the one hand, and a "reading" which is imposed upon the visual evidence, on the other. (Butler 1993: 17)

In this way, "The visual field is not neutral to the question of race; it is itself a racial formation, an episteme, hegemonic and forceful" (ibid.: 17). Our objects of study are not only not neutral objects hovering somewhere hopelessly external but also not even constituted except through their being seen, identified, and studied. Scholarship is not a secondary text imposed onto a primary source.

Yet the insistence on distinguishing the two at all remains intransigent in the academic study of religion, where "theory courses" continue to be identified as such apart from "subject area" courses in institutional curricula, and where so much of the research that proliferates is intent on bringing to light the experiences of this or that group in an ever-expanding tent of area studies. Indeed, we need only think about how unwieldy and overbearing it would sound to suggest that one is involved in the "academic study of literature" to present the problem with the, well, academic study of religion. Literature is never a thing outside its studies, and thus even the most traditional canon defenders do not mind calling themselves literary *critics*. But religion remains stuck as an object of a preposition. And this object of study continues to be defended by even its more savvy scholars inasmuch as all affiliation roads lead to the AAR, the *JAAR* remains the clearinghouse for scholars looking to gather some publishing capital, and the siphoning off of theory courses from subject area courses is seen simply as an unbroken (even if perhaps a bit unglamorous) machine.

I do not want to appear too nostalgic about literary theory as its own discipline. There are still defenders of a cohesive canon, and there are certainly those whose primary aim is to increase the size of that canon, not realizing that such advocacy work serves only to maintain the structural power inequities that they hope to critique. However, there is no denying the influence of post-Frankfurt School modes of inquiry on that field. Spivak and Foucault have long been just as significant as the New Critics for literary criticism. I was confronted in graduate school with Foucault's claim that "the author's name, unlike other proper names, does not pass from the interior of a discourse to the real and exterior individual who produced it; instead, the name seems always to be present, marking off the edges of the text, revealing, or at least characterizing, its mode of being" (Foucault 1977: 211). This became a necessary starting point, framing any subsequent and feeble attempt to talk about a text or an author as a thing in itself, invested with inherent worth. Another moment from his short "What Is an Author?" reads as downright Durkheimian:

An author's name is not simply an element in a discourse (capable of being either subject or object, of being replaced by a pronoun, and the like); it performs a certain role with regard to narrative discourse, assuring a classificatory function.

> Such a name permits one to group together a certain number of texts, define them, differentiate them from and contrast them to others. In addition, it establishes a relationship among the texts. (Foucault 1977: 210)

The focus here lies productively not in "the author" as an object (i.e., element in a discourse) but as a mode of demarcating. It is the performative role of the author that Foucault is interested in and, as such, we are asked to think about *the act of* grouping together and/or distinguishing texts (i.e., meaning-making exercises) rather than about the texts themselves as things waiting for secondary analysis. Not coincidentally, studies in literature are, of course, called "literary theory" or "literary criticism." The study never gets removed from the method or approach to that study, and the scholar using it.

Within the academic study of religion, however, Durkheim is still a name people think they should know, and they might even read bits of *Elementary Forms* here and there before too long into their careers. But somehow this has not resulted in a subsequent, broad-scale attentiveness to people *doing* things. Too many scholars remain intent on studying *things*. Thus, for some time now, scholars invested in divorcing the academic study of religion from a theological framework have rightly critiqued moves in the field that, while perhaps not advocating for this or that theological vantage point, continue to treat those vantage points as found objects. The discipline is rife with low-hanging fruit on this score. The *JAAR* continues to fill its pages with essays offering an edgy reading of this or that "religion," unconcerned with the implications of leaving the constituents of the category unquestioned. One need look no further than the most recent issue of the *JAAR*. Here are just a couple of the essay abstracts (from the first two pieces, in fact):

> Recent work in religious studies has turned from a long-standing focus on interior expressions of religion to emphasize instead embodied worship and the materiality of religious expression. Yet, for all the worthwhile critique of experience as a theoretical category, in practice various communities have taken up the language of experience as a central term for their own traditions. Scholars of religion have traced the cross-pollination of modern Hindu and Buddhist traditions with the language of "experience"; however, this question has received little attention in the study of Islam. This article addresses that lacuna. Muslim writings on Islam, specifically within the Islamic Republic of Iran, demonstrate a clear engagement with "religious experience." The Muslim writers discussed here, major figures of the Iranian reformist movement of the 1990s and 2000s, attempt to craft an arena of religiosity untouchable by state law and the Islamic Republic's governance of religious action. (Foody 2015: 599)

> In recent years, "mindfulness based psychotherapy" has emerged as a lucrative business with its own brand of tech-savvy, scientific gurus and a literature that relies heavily on psychotherapeutic language for the transformation of Theravāda Buddhist meditation into a secular, Western idiom. My purpose in this article is to take a fresh look at some of the earliest rigorous psychological research on *vipassanā* meditation. I argue first that the perspective articulated in those publications

embodies an understanding of Buddhist meditative practice that is considerably more nuanced than the perspective of contemporary psychotherapeutic discourse aimed at behavioral and affective change. Second, I argue that in conflating *vipas-sanā-bhāvanā* with psychotherapy, we effectively excise the soteriological heart of Buddhist meditation, the great, sacred mystery of the transcendent (*lokut-tara*) embodied in teachings on no-self (*anatta*). When this excision is complete, Buddhism becomes something less than a religion, something less than what it is. (Huntington 2015: 624)

These obvious examples invite easy critique, but what warrants more productive response is the work coming out of domains of religious studies that purports to be advancing theory or social science but that nonetheless treats religion as a found object. Saba Mahmood's work that offers a useful critique of liberal notions of agency while still discussing "embodiment" not as a trope but as a signifier pointing to a clear signified is one example (see Simmons forthcoming). Certainly Ann Taves's take on the category of experience is another.[4] The collection *Bodily Citations: Religion and Judith Butler* (Armour and St. Ville 2006), which takes an add-theory-and-stir approach to identify progressive moves in feminist theology, is another. In fact, Butler's own turn towards ethics in talking about Jewish identity and Zionism could well be another site of such response (see Butler 2013).

The increasingly popular emphasis in studies on material/lived identities and experiences is another space for the kind of critique I am interested in—in the name of new materialism, scholars invoke embodiment and experience rhetor-ically and then proceed to think ontologically. This sleight of hand is how, for example, the Crunk Feminist Collective (www.crunkfeministcollective.com) is able to appeal to an intellectual tradition of scholars and activists who push boundaries of how 'race' has been identified, only to locate blackness experien-tially as a material reality. One can also see the trick operating in the course offer-ings of most religious studies programs across the country. 'Theory' has become successful enough to justify a required course or two in its study, but those courses are distinguished from 'subject area' courses that talk about, presumably, *real stuff*. If this sounds too cynical, we might ask what the 'it' is that students are talking about if not approach/method. Like the scholars who want to continue talking about race as a thing (in the name of 'lived experience'), professors in our discipline want to suggest religion is a rhetorical tool or modern invention and then proceed to teach classes that are about religion (in the name of subject area and thick description).

The same sleight of hand appears in the description for the University of Chicago Press's new Class 200 book series.[5] Claiming to offer "the most innovative works in the study of religion today," editors Kathryn Lofton and John Modern see the series as a cutting-edge offshoot of critical turns in religious studies. But while they do not want to consign scholarship on religion to descriptive or theo-logical motives, they nonetheless suggest that religion is "more than a discursive concept or cultural idiom." Herein lies the problem with "presum[ing] no inaugu-rating definition of religion other than what it is not" and defining by negation (with analyses not too far removed from those asked of students in composition classrooms for the Definition Essay). As NAASR considers its own position in relation to these moves that count for theory right now in religious studies, its members might think about ways to keep the association from becoming an organizational counterpart to the nebulous moniker "theory" as it is currently used in the field (i.e., as a way of distinguishing those scholars who wish to identify themselves as simply not doing theological work).

"Critical theory," after all, does not name a scholar-as-object any more than scholars assign neutral names to objects pre-discursively existing in the world. Just like Butler's take on enterprises of racial formation, these are constitutive rhetorical processes. This is why, despite the ongoing juxtaposition of theorists and theologians, I more and more find unconvincing the idea that there is a camp of critical theory folks who have a specific or categorical denouncement of anything, save theology (though, as described above, many who say they are uninterested in theology appear to use similar turns in logic). And while something called critical theory is the only reason I am able to find myself working within the field of religious studies, I nonetheless find myself profoundly and increasingly alienated from much of the work that is currently identified with it. The definition-by-negation tactics that too many scholars use in order to distinguish theology and theory allow everyone to play the theory game and, in keeping theologians as the only intellectual opposition, allows much of what passes as critical analysis to go unchallenged. Thus, as long as scholars are trying to publish in the *JAAR* or have a significant voice in the AAR, I am not convinced that I have any more in common with them than with the theologians they disparage. This is not a bad thing, necessarily, as I doubt they would find many resonances with my work either. The problem, as I see it, is the seeming refusal by many simply to be clear about and own what kinds of scholarship they are doing. This is decidedly not a problem exclusive to descriptivists and theologians who claim to be doing identity theory. It is just as much a problem—if not more so—on the part of theorists who claim that the AAR is valuable as more than a taxonomic and pragmatic designator at best and, perhaps more aptly, a facilitator of the perpetuation of area studies, a world religions paradigm, a false fight between scholars who have long since abandoned the same ring (if they were ever in the same ring to begin with), and in short, a disciplinary disarray that has cultivated exactly the wrong kind of proliferation of "theory."

In one of his 1976 lectures at the Collège de France, Foucault advocated for what he called "local critiques." These critiques resulted from the "proliferating criticizability of things, institutions, practices, and discourses; a sort of general feeling that the ground was crumbling beneath our feet, especially in places where it seemed most familiar, most solid, and closest [nearest] to us, to our bodies, to our everyday gestures" (Foucault 2003: 6). The discomfort was productive, inasmuch as it shook the foundation of "all-encompassing and global theories"—theories that "provided tools that can be used at the local level only when, and this is the real point, the theoretical unity of their discourse is, so to speak, suspended, or at least cut up, ripped up, torn to shreds, turned inside out, displaced, caricatured, dramatized, theatricalized, and so on" (ibid.). "The local character of the critique," however, "does not ... mean soft eclecticism, opportunism, or openness to any old theoretical undertaking, nor does it mean a sort of deliberate asceticism that boils down to losing as much theoretical weight as possible" (ibid.). For Foucault, "the essentially local character of the critique in fact indicates something resembling a sort of autonomous and noncentralized theoretical production, or in other words a theoretical production that does not need a visa from some common regime to establish its validity" (ibid.). In the study of religion, the AAR has long offered the visa for scholarly validity, and it is high time those taking seriously social theory move away from the totalizing effects of the kind of research it supports.

Bruce Lincoln (1996) gets at this issue in the twelfth of his pithy and incredibly useful "Theses on Method:"

> Although critical inquiry has become commonplace in other disciplines, it still offends many students of religion, who denounce it as "reductionism". This charge is meant to silence critique. The failure to treat religion "as religion"—that is, the refusal to ratify its claim of transcendent nature and sacrosanct status—may be regarded as heresy and sacrilege by those who construct themselves as religious, but it is the starting point for those who construct themselves as historians. (Lincoln 1996: 227)

The failure to treat religion "as religion" is not an affront just to those who identify as religious, sadly. It seems also to alienate those who are able to put "method and theory" as a knowledge base on their CVs and enumerate the things that separate them from theologians. Ultimately, they may not want to call "religion" a stable thing, but they nonetheless maintain an interest in talking about identity as something meaningful so as to further neoliberal awareness projects. If the Author is dead, they create Authors and want the plural form to do substantive analytical work. It doesn't. Eliade is no longer the problem in this context wherein everyone gets to claim theoretical understanding, if not sophistication. The problem lies in continuing to make conversation partners not with self-proclaimed Eliadeans but with those who, while suggesting that *clearly* essentialist notions of the sacred are ridiculous, go on to talk about "religious expression" or "embodied realities" or "lived experiences" of people "on the ground."

It is time finally to let go of the relationship to the academic study of religion as it is currently costumed in its annual meeting and in the pages of its premier journal. I know saying so is perhaps easy from my perch as outsider interdisciplinarian, that doing so perhaps appears difficult—if not impossible—to those shaping their research agendas in their early careers or navigating the academic job market. I think, however, that, like anyone, scholars must take stock of those things over which they do and do not have control. Otherwise, the only end is petulant bickering with people who should never have been in the same conversation to begin with. One can control how one fashions a CV, where one sends an article for review, or what scholarly organizations one chooses to join. Decidedly out of one's control, however, are the degrees to which other scholars employ methodologies and approaches one finds productive. And yet, scholars who call themselves theorists work hard to convince the broader field of religionists to come aboard the theory train. While I find their optimism admirable, I find the work that results ultimately counterproductive. They stop reading *Elementary Forms*, and they start cataloguing all the ways in which theologians get it wrong. Meanwhile, in the field that fancies itself full of theory-savvy non-seminarians, "theory" and "subject area" continue to be separated during courses of study, and up-and-coming scholars understandably naturalize this approach and take it to stand in for the academic study of religion. The relationship to their objects of study, then, becomes closer and closer, while any analytical edge slips further away.

At the 2012 meeting in Chicago, Aaron Hughes made the useful suggestion that NAASR simply stop coordinating its program with the AAR. If we no longer sang to the AAR for our professional supper, he argued, those of us committed to critical approaches might find far better uses for our voices. It seems to me that this is exactly the right direction to take. My anxiety is that the understandable pragmatism that finds the idea too provocative or cumbersome slides into unintentional protectionism all too easily. Too many religionists want to suggest that our primary organizational distinction is between the AAR and the SBL, rather than looking at the enormous gulf between the attention paid to objects of study as things and the attention paid to the scholars identifying their objects of study—setting them apart and implicitly calling them sacred—relating to and with them in the process. And we are thus left with the status quo—a time of nominally theoretical excess without a lot of analytical substance. Being asked to reconsider our conversation partners and our objects of study is a difficult pill to swallow. Hearing about the death of our beloved Author was painful, too, especially after New Criticism had offered a warm blanket of formalist readings during the Cold War. But literary critics had to admit—the Author had had an unusually long life, and plenty of folks will keep putting flowers on his grave. Coming to terms with why it was hard to let go—which had everything to do with scholarly needs and interests and nothing to do with the Author over whom they battled mightily in a match of tug-of-war—ultimately made for better, more considered criticism.

One of the reasons I remain charmed by a Woody Allen-esque brand of jittery fatalism is that I find comforting the logic of what admittedly appears depressing at the outset. Accepting the fact that imminent doom surrounds and that you face near-certain death at every moment helps that airplane not seem so big and scary. Granting that no relationship lets you escape dying alone helps moving on after a particularly bad breakup seem easier. Similarly, self-proclaimed theorists would do themselves a favor by realizing that self-important, at times mind-numbingly vapid, phenomenology isn't going anywhere in the field of religious studies. Trying to make things better by pointing out each instance of academic drivel is a losing game. So too is worrying about how one's work might be received within the ranks of the AAR or within the pages of the *JAAR*. So too is the painstaking attempt at making our work "relevant" to non-specialists in a world continually and maddeningly identified as, unlike academia, *real*. I would hope that understanding that theorists are not in conversation with theologians or descriptive ethnographers, and vice versa, critically minded scholars would find the idea of working through the thorny issues related to discourse analysis and the implications of poststructuralist thought not so very daunting. If "religion" as a taxon should be left to insider participants employing the term—an argument with which I am inclined to agree—we might also consider letting go of the fantasy that we can change the conversations of people speaking a different analytical language that makes heavy use of that very taxon.

K. Merinda Simmons is Associate Professor of Religious Studies at the University of Alabama, and author of *Changing the Subject: Writing Women across the African Diaspora* (Ohio State University Press, 2014). She focuses in her teaching and research on identifications of race, gender, and religion in the Caribbean and the American South.

Notes

1. The reason I have resigned this paper title to appearing reminiscent of so much postmodern stylistic twaddle in contemporary academia is that the preposition does function grammatically to draw attention to two actions that are different, but that remain troublingly intertwined in contemporary studies of religion; namely, identifying an object of study, and identifying *with* that object of study. One suggests scholarly specificity. The other suggests protectionism.
2. What I take this moniker to mean in my own work is a brand of inquiry following from Frankfurt School analysis that invites structural social critique rather than phenomenological or explanatory description.
3. In the sixth of his "Theses on Method," Lincoln (1996) points to some of the causes and manifestations of this mode of protectionism: "Many who would not think of insulating their own or their parents' religion against critical inquiry still afford such protection to other people's faiths, via a stance of cultural relativism. One can appreciate their good intentions, while recognizing a certain displaced defensiveness, as well as the guilty conscience of western imperialism" (ibid.: 226).
4. See McCutcheon (2010), in which he rightly asks whether scholarly focus lies in nouns or verbs.
5. Details of the series available at http://press.uchicago.edu/ucp/books/series/CLA200. html, from which the quotations that follow are taken.

References

Armour, Ellen, and Susan St. Ville (eds.). 2006. *Bodily Citations: Religion and Judith Butler*. New York: Columbia University Press.

Butler, Judith. 1993. "Endangered/Endangering: Schematic Racism and White Paranoia." In Robert Gooding-Williams (ed.), *Reading Rodney King/Reading Urban Uprising*, 15–22. New York: Routledge.

Butler, Judith. 2013. *Parting Ways: Jewishness and the Critique of Zionism*. New York: Columbia University Press.

Foody, Kathleen. 2015. "Interiorizing Islam: Religious Experience and State Oversight in the Islamic Republic of Iran." *Journal of the American Academy of Religion*. 83.3: 599–623.

Foucault, Michel. 1977. "What Is an Author?" In Michel Foucault, *Aesthetics, Method, and Epistemology* (ed. James Faubion, trans. Donald F. Bouchard), 205–222. New York: The New Press.

Foucault, Michel. 2003. *"Society Must Be Defended": Lectures at the Collège de France, 1975-76* (ed. Mauro Bertani and Alessandro Fontana, trans. David Macey). New York: Picador.

Huntington, Jr., C. W. 2015. "The Triumph of Narcissism: Theravāda Buddhist Meditation in the Marketplace." *Journal of the American Academy of Religion* 83(3): 624–648.

Lincoln, Bruce. 1996. "Theses on Method." *Method and Theory in the Study of Religion* 8(3): 225–227.

Mahmood, Saba. 2011. *Politics of Piety: The Islamic Revival and the Feminist Subject.* Princeton, NJ: Princeton University Press.

McCutcheon, Russell T. 2010. "Will Your Cognitive Anchor Hold in the Storms of Culture?" *Journal of the American Academy of Religion* 78(4): 624–648.

Simmons, K. Merinda. Forthcoming. "Politics of Privacy: Distinguishing Religion in Poststructuralist Discourse." In James McClung and Esra Santesso (eds.), *Islam and Postcolonial Discourse.* London: Ashgate.

Taves, Ann. 2010. *Religious Experience Reconsidered: A Building-Block Approach to the Study of Religion and Other Special Things.* Princeton, NJ: Princeton University Press.

8

New Materialism and the Objects of Religious Studies

Martha Smith Roberts

Merinda Simmons's "The High Stakes of Identifying (with) One's Object of Study" (Chapter 7, this volume) offers an important critique of the field, our roles as scholars, and the boundaries of religious studies. She emphasizes that a simple distinction between theory and theology is not enough to define our discipline. Her work encourages instead an engagement with theory that goes beyond a rejection of theology. For Simmons, it is the relationship between scholars and their objects of study—in this case, the protection and preservation of the religious—that creates the possibilities for theological discourses to take hold within the very scholarship that so rigorously rejects theology. The act of distinguishing between theory and object (theory and religion) is one way that this happens in our field, both in classrooms and in research.

Simmons's chapter offers many possibilities for expansion and response. The examples she cites of scholarship from our field's major journals are stark reminders that religious studies and theology remain bound together in their privileging of the categories of religion and religious experience. She also cautions us to be wary of "edgy" theory that functions ontologically. There are many ways that the scholar/object relationship is negotiated in our field to both subtly and overtly replicate a theological essentialism.

My response will focus on one in particular: the critique of material religion, lived religion and experience-centered scholarship. As Simmons notes, "in the name of new materialism, scholars invoke embodiment and experience rhetorically and then proceed to think ontologically" (p. 63, this volume). This is a particularly important critique for my work, and so I want to think about the nuance of material studies of religion, the body, and lived experience. What are the possibilities for engaging the material world? And haven't we been doing this for a long time? If so, what is new about new materialism? I wonder if we can't think through the constructivist-materialist distinction as well, as a way to better understand the aims and limits of new materialism.

I think that at its best, the move to recognize religion "on the ground" is one that seeks to reflect on the negotiations of power that happen between scholars and their objects of study. The idea behind some lived religious scholarship was to let marginalized voices speak, to move away from institutional forms as the final word on religion (a critique of the field itself), as well as to avoid forcing theory from above onto the experiences of insiders. Thus, lived religion is often described as a "bottom-up" instead of "top-down" theory. Material religion was also looking to up-end previous histories, power relations, and ways of knowing, by positing that religion was "more than belief" or at least, not to be limited by a scholarly tradition in which belief, texts, and ideas are central.

Simmons's critique does not seem to be about these egalitarian goals, but rather perhaps, the practices of lived religion scholarship: the emphasis on experience, materiality, and embodiment as the final word and occupying space of an existing, really real, religion. This is an interesting moment of theological thinking in otherwise very "anti-theological" scholarship. Insider accounts are privileged; religion is a given. It is just in a different location.

However, perhaps there are ways to think about bodies, objects, and materials as interactive moments of meaning making that can tell us about how the world works for certain groups, at certain times, in certain places. Sara Ahmed, in her work on new materialism's claims in feminist theory, notes that there is a "routinized" gesture toward constructionism as anti-biologism, in which constructivist scholarship is dismissed as not dealing with the body as a real, living, physical entity, or as reducing everything to language, signification, and culture (Ahmed 2008: 25). And thus new materialism is a call for a turn to the body, the material. This gesture is not limited to feminist theory. In religious studies, we can also speak of a move against the linguistic/cultural turn, referred to in several ways: a participatory turn (which highlights method), a move toward lived experience, vernacular religion, embodied spirituality, and of course, as a material turn.

In religious studies, much like Ahmed's critique in feminist studies, this turn is not exactly new. Many scholars have been thinking about materiality for a very long time. So what is new materialism? Sonia Hazard describes new materialism as a conscious break from three other dominant approaches in the material turn, which focus on symbolism, material disciplines, and phenomenological experience, respectively, all of which, she argues "continue to privilege the human subject while material things themselves struggle to come into sharp focus, that is they remain anthropocentric and beholden to the biases against materiality deeply entrenched in the study of religion" (Hazard 2013: 58).

New materialism, here, places "things" on the same level as ideas and humans. The "assemblages of meaning" in new materialism intensify materialism's critique of constructivism. The material has been ignored, and now, it must be seen as just as important as ideas and humans. The culture-centrism of religion must be overthrown. Where new materialism and Simmons seem to disagree is in her assertion that we still "study *things*," not "people *doing* things" (p. 62, this volume). New materialism would argue that studying people doing things has left out the things.

What Simmons's critique shares with new materialism is a push to recognize the fabricated nature of the subject/object divide (and the theory/religion divide). The problem she sees is a misapprehension of scholars' work as somehow separate from what they are studying, in other words, Simmons critiques the idea that religion is there, in the material world, to be found and studied. If religion is an object that exists outside of our theorizing of it, or if the material is simply a manifestation of the religious, then there is nothing that isn't theological going on here. This is essentializing.

Many new materialism/embodiment studies draw attention to a similar critique of subject/object distinctions—of the ways that materiality is, as Simmons mentions, not an object waiting to be read. Instead, religion is constructed in the very positing of its existence out there.

Perception and interpretation are inseparable. As Nikki Sullivan argues "visuality is the effect and vehicle of sedimented contextual knowledges, rather than a neutral process that provides access to empirical objects/facts" (Sullivan 2012: 303). Simmons uses Butler to point to "the visual field ... itself" as not simply calling to be read, but also always, already, a reading (p. 61, this volume). Hazard tells us that "new materialism ... refuses any ontological difference" between subject and object, "human and nonhuman things" (Hazard 2013: 72, note 17). However, as Sullivan points out, to call for a return to, or turn toward, the material is a gesture that can also "presuppose something called matter—albeit some 'thing' whose substance, whose boundaries are relational, undecidable, and constantly in flux—and in doing so, constitute 'it' (matter) as *a priori*... thus giving matter an ontological priority" as something "more than or other than culture" (Sullivan 2012: 309). This move, this gesture, is itself constitutive.

Again, citing Sullivan, "while on one hand new materialist optics present us with a vision of becoming as always-already inter/intra-relational, on the other hand, such an optics functions in and through the rearticulation of a culture/matter split and by association the constitutive appropriation of both. Thus we remain imprisoned in the limits of a universalizing optics" (ibid.: 309–310). Simmons characterizes new materialism, embodiment, lived religion, and experience as "edgy" objects of study. Her worry, I believe, is that they use the material turn to grant objects subjectivity and agency that mimics a theological reading of matter—as alive, vibrant, and calling to be read by the scholar.

Understanding our use of materiality in our work, field, and discipline is important. Not just that it is there, but how we create it, draw upon it, fashion it. In this sense, broader surveys of the ways in which scholars of religion have utilized materiality can prove helpful. In my own work, I am interested in the body, in the uses of race, in the interpretations of phenotypical features that create race, religion, and racialized religion. And to better understand how race and religion function in U.S. culture, bodies are central. My questions are about how bodies are read, and thus created in the readings, as meaningful in certain ways.

Perhaps the critique here is not that material and biological are *more real* than the social (whatever that might mean), but that material and social are entangled, non-separable, not two independent, discrete systems (Davis 2009: 67). Is there a way to be a materialist and not be pushing against a social constructivist framework, but against the essentializing expressions of it? For example, materialism might be an important corrective to individualist etiologies of neoliberal colorblind racism. In trying to think of other examples where calls for materiality were useful correctives, and perhaps because of the use of visuality and ocularity, Michael Omi and Howard Winant's work on racial formation comes to mind.

Omi and Winant (2015) critique what they call the "ethnicity paradigm" (an attempt to reduce race to an element of ethnicity), which developed out of an insurgent movement against the biological essentialism of race science. The view of race as socially constructed was and is an important critique of dominant racist paradigms (racial biologism, eugenics, and white nationalism); however, it developed into its own hegemonic framework that rejected the reality of race (the corporeal, and ocular dimensions of raciality) while also constructing ethnicity as more real than race (ibid.: 39). One result of this can be seen in (neo-conservative and neoliberal) colorblind theories of race that are so disembodied that they can claim to "not see race" despite also actively working to uphold structural racism (e.g. abolishing affirmative action as a racist policy).

The same move we see in the ethnicity paradigm, the move against race as essential and toward a constructivist "theory" that continues to uphold racism (and race) even as it claims to be post-racial, might be comparable to the scholarship that Simmons is calling out. In this religious studies scholarship, essentialism (as theology) is rejected. But it is replaced by a "theoretical orientation" that may simply be locating that essence somewhere else; thus continuing to uphold essentialism even as it claims to be post-theological.

Omi and Winant offer a corrective to the ethnicity paradigm in racial formation theory, the idea that race can be understood as socially constructed and still very much an embodied phenomenon, through the notion of racial projects. "The task for theory is to capture this situation and avoid both the utopian framework that sees race as an illusion we can somehow 'get beyond' as well as the essentialist formulation that sees race as something objective and fixed, a biological given" (ibid.: 112). And perhaps we can imagine a theory of religious formation that offers a similar corrective to our own field's essentialist paradigms.

The important questions of materialism are not about how matter exists *as such*, or how it manifests something else (like real race or religion), but how matter comes to matter. I remain optimistic that there are thoughtful treatments of materiality, that there are rigorous dismantlings of paradigms, and that there is a way to also answer the criticisms of materialism. There are some good criticisms. However, let us come back to Simmons's title, "The High Stakes of Identifying (with) One's Object of Study." Her work is not only about new materialism, but about a larger gesture that dismisses theology and yet essentializes religion (as "religious expression" or "embodied realities"; p. 65, this volume). As a discipline united by an object of study, how can religious studies develop a challenge to the AAR framework that Simmons illuminates? What are the methods and theories of *this* religious studies? Or is it religious studies at all? Would leaving the AAR be a "routinized gesture"? Or could it be a dismantling of a paradigm? I look forward to continuing this conversation, from our vantage point here (at the NAASR conference), both inside and outside of the AAR.

Martha Smith Roberts is a Ph.D. Candidate at the University of California, Santa Barbara and sits on the Board of Directors for the Institute for Diversity and Civic Life in Austin, Texas. She researches diversity and pluralism in North America.

References

Ahmed, Sara. 2008. "Imaginary Prohibitions: Some Preliminary Remarks on the Founding Gestures of 'New Materialism.'" *European Journal of Women's Studies* 15(1): 23–39.

Davis, Noela. 2009. "New Materialism and Feminism's Anti-Biologism: A Response to Sara Ahmed." *European Journal of Women's Studies* 16(1): 67–80.

Hazard, Sonia. 2013. "The Material Turn in the Study of Religion." *Religion and Society: Advances in Research* 4: 58–78.

Omi, Michael and Howard Winant. 2015. *Racial Formation in the United States* (3rd edition). New York: Routledge.

Sullivan, Nikki. 2012. "The Somatechnics of Perception and the Matter of the non/human: A Critical Response to the New Materialism." *European Journal of Women's Studies* 19(3): 299–313.

9

Killing the Scholar: Critical Theory, Relevance, and Objects of Study

Thomas J. Whitley

As I prepared my response to Simmons's provocative essay (Chapter 7, this volume), I could not help but think of my own identity—or at least how I conceive of my academic identity as contrasted with how some others seem to conceive of my academic identity. I am a historian of early Christianity. At least, this is what I tell people who ask what I do and this is how I frame myself in the numerous research statements I have prepared as part of job applications. I am not someone who *does theory*, and this was my initial response to the invitation to be part of this forum. Theory and method is not a competency that I list on my CV. I feel woefully out of place in a volume like this, and I wonder when the curtain will be pulled back and I will be outed any minute now as one of *them*.

And yet clearly some think I do *do theory*. I was, after all, invited to be part of this forum for what I hope are reasons beyond my serving as an example of what not to do. I am also a fan of Bruce Lincoln and Pierre Bourdieu, for instance. This comes out quite clearly in my "academic" work (read: peer-reviewed journal articles, conference presentations, and my dissertation) as well as what I write for public consumption in outlets such as the University of Alabama department blog, *Religious Studies News*, and *Marginalia Review of Books*. But this fandom—if that is the right word, and though I think it may not seem academic or analytical enough to some, I do think that "fandom" aptly describes my fondness for and use of Bruce Lincoln and Pierre Bourdieu and that "fandom" aptly describes others' adherence to other theorists as well—this fandom, I recognize, exists largely as a result of my being able to halfway understand them and the fact that I happen to agree with them. I have a suspicion that I am not alone in how my theoretical loyalties have been forged. This does not, I admit, seem appropriately analytical. But if "fake it till you make it" works for Alcoholics Anonymous, it just may work for me too. So, here it goes.

There are two main points on which I would like to engage Simmons's suggestions: the act of identifying our objects of study and the relevance, or lack thereof, of critical theory, both in the academy and in the so-called *real* world. These points are tightly intertwined in Simmons's essay and I will treat them in that manner too. For how we conceive of one affects how we understand the other, and vice versa.

Simmons's most forceful comment regarding the act of identifying our objects of study comes toward the end of her essay as she asks us to "reconsider our conversation partners" (this volume, p. 66).

> Too many religionists want to suggest that our primary organizational distinction is between the AAR and the SBL, rather than looking at the enormous gulf between the attention paid to objects of study as things and the attention paid to the scholars identifying their objects of study—setting them apart and implicitly calling them sacred—relating to them and with them in the process. And we are thus left with the status quo—a time of nominally theoretical excess without a lot of analytical substance. (Ibid.)

Simmons is concerned that much of what passes for critical theory is not actually critical theory. The debate has for too long been theory versus theology, but according to Simmons this system of classification is not adequate. Instead, and at the risk of vastly oversimplifying Simmons's argument, it appears that she is calling for yet a further division of all that falls in the not-theology camp at least once more between that which views its objects of study as *things*, still uses "religion" as a taxon, and understands identity as a stable category, on the one hand, and true critical theory, which pays attention to the moves that scholars make when they identify their objects of study, on the other hand. This classificatory scheme itself seems worth our study. Indeed, Lincolnians might be inclined to ask: Of what would Simmons persuade her audience? What are the consequences if her project of persuasion should happen to succeed? Who wins what, and how much? Who, conversely, loses (Lincoln 1996)? Simmons has already answered some of these questions for us. She wishes to persuade her audience that critical theorists are simply having a different conversation than those she classes as non-critical theorists, and that they should come to terms with that reality and stop trying to convince others of their relevance. This would potentially lead to even less of a tie between NAASR and AAR, as she points out. But it would also lead to the continued siloing of the field. Some will see this as positive and necessary; others will not.

Then there remains this question of who wins, who loses, and what is to be won. I have struggled to decide what I think is the right answer here, but it seems to me that what is to be won is academic capital. Even if only in small circles, this subordinate form of capital carries with it power and prestige (Bourdieu 1988: 36). And besides, these small circles are the only ones that matter to some us anyway. Cultural capital in the groups about which we care that also carries with it justifications of our status as marginalized truth-tellers remains a tempting and precious prize to be won. After all, Simmons does lament the problem as she sees it, namely, "the seeming refusal by many simply to be clear about and own what kinds of scholarship they are doing" (this volume, p. 64). In other words, critical theorists are more honest about their scholarship, and thus better academics. Some modern progressive Christians are fond of a similar tactic by claiming their superiority because they recognize their hermeneutic while their conservative counterparts are blind to the hermeneutical processes that lead them to their interpretations of a text (see, e.g., Beck 2015). I think it goes without saying that a popular caricature of critical theorists from corners of the academy that may tend to look down on a volume such as this and those involved is that critical theorists think they are better academics than everyone else because they view their enterprise as true critical scholarship while they view the work of so many others as nothing more than protective services for their objects of study, a charge on which many are indicted unknowingly. Thesis six of Lincoln's "Theses on method" should suffice as representative here. I mean not to attack Simmons. In fact I agree with most of her analysis. But with an eye toward taking stock of the field of critical theory in such a time as this, some self-reflection is in order. I hope that what follows will be read in this vein of self-reflection, as I attempt to wrestle myself with the field of critical theory and my place in it.

This battle for academic capital, in which I see us engaging, is not being fought one-sided. We are quite familiar, I would imagine, with the critiques of the work of many critical theorists because they are not formally part of the area studies which they are critiquing. "How can one presume to come into my area and critique my work when they do not have the requisite background which I possess?" This is the question many ask. Others are dismissed because they are perceived as having no area of study at all, and thus, according to their critics, no solid foundation from which to conduct their work. Academia is, as Bourdieu put it, a "locus of struggle to determine the conditions and the criteria of legitimate membership and legitimate hierarchy, that is, to determine which properties are pertinent, effective and liable to function as capital so as to generate the specific profits guaranteed by the field" (Bourdieu 1988: 11).

Whether we are bound to engage in this struggle, I do not know. But it is a battle we have joined, for better or worse. And all battles have casualties and this battle's chief casualty, in my estimation, is the relevance of critical theory. Simmons laments that " 'theory courses' continue to be identified as such apart from 'subject area' courses" in our curricula, yet she believes it is a "fantasy" to think that critical theorists "can change the conversations of people speaking a different analytical language" (this volume, pp. 67). I would like to think that I am proof that such conversations can be changed. If we truly believe that scholarship can be better by going beyond an "add-theory-and-stir approach," then I have to wonder why we are trying to draw our boundaries tighter. To be fair, Simmons is wary of sliding into "unintentional protectionism," but I'm not sure how different "unintentional protectionism," on the one hand, is from the call for us to simply recognize that we are having a different conversation and so should not be concerned with how we might be received at the AAR or the SBL or in the pages of the *JAAR* or the *JBL*, on the other hand. That is, do they function the same and/ or bring about the same result? Might our motivations—if we could adequately identify such things—be different but the outcome the same? If we think the rest of the field is sick and we have the cure, ought we not at least try to offer our theoretical balm? We will not see critical theory spread in our field if we simply offer an assist to those who would cloister critical theory off into one or two courses per program, an affiliated meeting at the Annual Meeting, and a separate journal or two. Or maybe we are content with this separation, for it is a classification onto which we can project a hierarchy, namely, one that views our faction as having won and that allows—nay, demands—that we act as arbiters of academic capital.

But, put plainly, some of us cannot yet afford to be content with such a posture. I am involved with NAASR as a direct result of senior scholars making a concerted effort to include their junior colleagues. For this I am thankful, but this does not erase the reality that I do not yet have the luxury of tenure, or even a tenure-track job, a luxury which Simmons and others calling for such a demarcation in conversations do enjoy. I may never be so lucky. And so my positionality comes into focus. I, and many others, cannot afford to write off the AAR and SBL. Relevance is not just an academic concern. For many it is a political and economic concern as well. As good critical theorists, we will recognize the *Sitz im Leben* that makes it easier for Simmons and Aaron Hughes, for instance, to issue such calls as well as the *Sitz im Leben* that would disallow me and others from heeding such a call, were we so inclined.

Further, donning blinders to what is sometimes referred to as the *real* world will not improve the situation of critical theory, either. I believe the exact opposite is needed. If we cannot be bothered to at least attempt to communicate to those who hold power over our jobs and to those social actors who have out-sized public influence why critical theory is relevant, we cannot rightly lament when it is not taken seriously and when this has negative economic consequences for us, our colleagues, our students, and our field as a whole. Beyond the economic implications, I do actually think that critical theory is relevant to the non-academic world. Our news coverage of our elections and of events like the Paris Attacks could certainly stand to take a more analytical approach. We should not resign ourselves to seeing an educated and analytically minded *hoi polloi* as a "losing game," or even to seeing non-academics as the *hoi polloi*. We can and should have conversations which are utterly foreign to non-academics, but that need not be our sole endeavor.

For both Simmons and me, the relevance of critical theory is intimately tied to our objects of study—how we choose them, how we conceive of them, how we analyze them, etc. We may be most vulnerably relevant if we would subject our choices to the same analysis to which we have unreservedly subjected our colleagues'. Let us take, for instance, Simmons's main contention that critical theory is different largely because it takes as its object of study the scholars themselves—a contention which seems to be shared by a number of others as well. Why is taking scholars as one's object of study to be preferred? Surely we do not mean to say that everyone must be interested in what we are interested in. And surely we could see the analytical benefit of turning our gaze around and asking, for instance, what affect the ubiquity of Foucault, Lincoln, and Bourdieu, to name just a few of my favorites, has had on our ranks. We pride ourselves on having moved past Eliade, but have we asked what happens when we move beyond Foucault? Can we not recognize similar rhetorical moves being made by those who fancied themselves as Christians a few millennia ago as are made by many scholars today, claims of normativity, heresy, orthodoxy, etc.? If Simmons is right that "one's object of study is very much beside the point" (this volume, p. 60), then why do we care so what one's object of study is? I ask not just because I still very much consider myself a historian who does not simply use theory to bookend my work, but also because if "scholarship is not a secondary text imposed onto a primary source" (this volume, p. 61), as Simmons asserts, then isn't our critical theory scholarship just another instance of a primary source? That is, if we can (and should) take the work of academics who take their objects of study as *things* as primary sources worth studying, then might *we* also be worth studying? Have we simply replaced phenomenology with discourse analysis in our attempts to explain and analyze the world? Why have we chosen *scholars* as our objects of study and have we succumbed to the temptation to treat them as *things*?

I am fully aware that we can, as Simmons calls us to, work "through the thorny issues related to discourses analysis and the implications of post-structuralist thought" without taking scholars as our objects of study (this volume, p. 67). But why do we then so often take scholars as our objects of study? Are we too insistent that scholars are necessary and intrinsically interesting objects of study? Have we fallen victim to Maslow's law of the hammer (Maslow 1966: 15)? Everything is data; from this we are not immune. If anyone is in a position to take critical theorists as data, it is critical theorists. And if we take Bourdieu seriously in *Homo Academicus*, we know this will be a painful process. For "in choosing to study the social world in which we are *involved*, we are obliged to confront, in *dramatized* form as it were, a certain number of fundamental epistemological problems" (Bourdieu 1988: 1). We are our own sort of insiders now, and this means that we too must at some point break with inside experience and learn how to "reconstitute the knowledge which has been obtained by means of this break" (ibid.). To do this, we cannot forget that simply choosing scholars as our objects of study, as opposed to 'religion,' does not allow us to "escap[e] the work of constructing the object, and the responsibility that this entails" (ibid.: 6). Even in taking French academics as his object of study Bourdieu knew that "there is no object of study that does not imply a viewpoint, even if it is an object produced with the intention of abolishing one's viewpoint ... the intention of overcoming the partial perspective that is associated with holding a position within the space being studied" (ibid.: 6). What is the viewpoint implied in our construction of the Scholar as object of study? In choosing the Scholar as our object of study, are we the children whom Lincoln mentions in his sixth thesis who would not insulate their parents against critical inquiry? Some of us, it seems, rather relish in the opportunity to take the Scholar as our object of study just so we can tear it down, though of course in doing so we simultaneously reify it and reinforce its authority (Martin 2012: 127).

Viewing our own work as primary source material, it seems, is just the sort of "local critique" Foucault and Simmons would endorse (Foucault 2003: 6). Such a critique that analyzes our complicated relationship with the Scholar may shake our foundation, but it may be our best move yet. Indeed, if the long-overdue death of the Author led to "better, more considered criticism" (this volume, p. 66), might it now be time for us to start the long and painful process of killing the Scholar?

Thomas J. Whitley earned his PhD in Religion from Florida State University in 2016. His research focuses on the creation and maintenance of "heresy" and "orthodoxy" in early Christianity, primarily through the means of sexual slander.

References

Beck, Richard. 2015. "Emotional Intelligence and Sola Scripture." 22 October. Available at http://experimentaltheology.blogspot.com/2015/10/emotional-intelligence-and-sola.html (accessed November 15, 2015).

Bourdieu, Pierre. 1988. *Homo Academicus* (trans. Peter Collier). Stanford, CA: Stanford University Press.

Foucault, Michel. 2003. *"Society Must Be Defended": Lectures at the Collège de France, 1975-76* (ed. Mauro Bertani and Alessandro Fontana, trans. David Macey). New York: Picador.

Lincoln, Bruce. 1996. "Theses on Method." *Theory and Method in the Study of Religion* 8(3): 225–227.

Martin, Craig. 2012. *A Critical Introduction to the Study of Religion.* Sheffield: Equinox Publishing.

Maslow, Abraham. 1966. *The Psychology of Science*. Chicago, IL: Chicago Gateway.

10

The Rhetoric of Disinterest for Authorizing our Critical Position: Historicizing Critical-Theory in Religious Studies

Stephen L. Young

The wielding of critical theory has become itself a form of symbolic capital in some arenas. This point, of course, accords with how critical theorists interrogate the ideological, discursive, and social dynamics of knowledge production.[1] In my limited space I use Merinda Simmons's suggestive paper, "The High Stakes of Identifying (with) One's Object of Study" (Chapter 7, this volume) as an opportunity to historicize our uses of critical theory in religious studies. I will briefly identify several aspects of her paper that can serve as jumping off points for my reflections. But before proceeding, I wish to signal my deep appreciation of Simmons's points about the variegated landscape of theory in religious studies. Among other things, she intriguingly maps the terrain of how others map this landscape. And Simmons does so in a way that creates productive distinctions for us to think with.

Simmons's characterization of a recent volume (Armour and St. Ville 2006) as taking "an add-theory-and-stir approach" caught my attention. Beyond the creative playfulness of that classification, it resonated with me. My own academic formation has resulted in a strong allergy to add-theory-and-stir, or to what I call the "decoder ring" approach to theory. In this approach we reach into our bags of impressive-sounding tricks and pick out a decoder-ring of theory to "apply" to a text or practice. The usefulness of such theoretical performances is often itself untheorized, especially in my primary historical fields of specialization, early Jewish and Christian studies. The chosen theory exists as a canonical or unquestioned entity, and the productivity of its application is treated as self-evident.[2]

Simmons's map of theory in religious studies offers a vantage point for interrogating add-theory-and-stir or decoder ring approaches. To quote her argument:

> In other words, there is no shortage of people who claim to be "doing theory," and yet, this glut of critical consciousness has allowed exactly the wrong debate to continue dominating the academic study of religion. What's the wrong debate? To my mind, it is the back-and-forth between theory and theology. A central claim in this paper is that defining critical theory as that which is simply *not* theological

is not enough ... In religious studies, the conflation of something called critical theory with anything not classified as theology makes such awareness difficult to come by. (Simmons, pp. 59–61, this volume; emphasis original)

Thus, when one's conceptual map of religious studies, the American Academy of Religion (AAR), or the Society of Biblical Literature (SBL) creates a landscape of conversation partners populated by theologians or exegetes interested primarily in describing texts and inhabiting their ideologies, one can achieve distinction by "adding theory and stirring;" by self-representing as, for example, "I'm not just an exegete, I use theory." Theory becomes something that is *other*. One can then simply add it into her or his primary scholarly pursuit, but without recon-figuring or reorienting that pursuit itself. The dispositions of the "theorists" in such a landscape are, furthermore, shaped by it. They, and to quote Simmons again, "stop reading [Durkheim's] *Elementary Forms*, and start cataloging all the ways in which theologians get it wrong" (p. 66, this volume). Indeed, while writing an article that socially theorizes Evangelical scholarly practices (Young 2015), I found the field wide open. This was because most researchers who cover Evangelical scholarship critique them as though they are all participating in the same conversation.[3]

In what follows I want to work with or extend Simmons's points about the "wrong" versus fruitful academic debates. Simmons rightly emphasizes the inter-relation between the debate performed and the dialogue partners recognized, and thus the importance of attending to who the dialogue partners are. I conceive of my short essay as an interaction between myself, Simmons, and others within the orbit of the North American Association of the Study of Religion (NAASR).[4] And I urge us to theorize with two of Simmons's points. First, that "our own inter-ests as scholars, then, are never off the hook and ever out of the picture" (p. 59, this volume); and second, "Like anything else, academic work is a process of iden-tifying. We identify what interest us and what we implicitly or explicitly suggest is worth analysis" (p. 60, this volume).

So what, at least for the purposes of this paper, interests me? Simmons and her colleagues at the University of Alabama are appropriately fond of encouraging people to "always historicize." I thus propose that we use Simmons's paper as an opportunity to historicize our own critical theorizing practices in NAASR. In other words, I want us to experiment with becoming our own data. I will investi-gate, to quote Simmons's paper again, "people *doing* things" as opposed to simply "things" (p. 62, this volume). More specifically, I interrogate our critical prac-tices in dialogue with Pierre Bourdieu's social theorizing about what he terms the rhetoric of disinterest and also his concept of the dominant versus dominated poles of fields. And to clarify in a way that aligns with emphases thus far, this will not be an add-theory-and-stir or decoder ring invocation of Bourdieu. I will not simply list a few of his concepts in a decontextualized manner and then pretend to discover a one-to-one correspondence between them and that to which I want to draw our attention. Rather, my goal is to leverage Bourdieu's theorizing in a way that facilitates our exploration of our own theoretical practices. What are our practices doing, and for whom? Or to continue with Simmons's framing, what happens when we *do* theoretical practices?

Throughout Bourdieu's work, but especially in his writings collected in *The Field of Cultural Production*, he stresses that a hierarchy of positions characterizes each field, spanning those on the dominating pole to those on the dominated pole (Bourdieu 1993: 37–73, 82–86, 131–141). He often refers to the dominating pole as the "heteronomous" principle or position, and the dominated as the "autonomous" (ibid.: 38). One's position in the field shapes not only one's dispositions and tastes, but also one's strategies for establishing distinction and accumulating the forms of capital available in that field.[5] To use one of Bourdieu's signature examples, in an artistic field, the dominating actors are the art dealers, museum administrators, and artists patronized by them. They have the given, institutional status and associated capital. They, accordingly, have the primary access to material and economic capital. Their discourses reflect their dominant positions and tend to naturalize the arbitrary distribution of power and capital (which favors them) through promoting misrecognition of the legitimacy of the status quo. The artists not associated with such institutions, however, occupy the dominated positions. In order to accumulate forms of capital, especially symbolic or cultural capital, their strategies for distinction reflect the practical options available to the dominated.[6] Bourdieu highlights in particular the common rhetoric of disinterest among the dominated, whereby they make a virtue of necessity (i.e., their lack of access to the dominating institutions and their associated capital) and represent themselves as not doing art for business or money or other interested reasons, but instead art for art's sake. They do not produce art for the curators of the dominant institutions and positions, but only for other legitimate (read: disinterested) people.

To what extent do we, through our institutional mythmaking about NAASR, construct ourselves as inhabiting something analogous to what Bourdieu terms a dominated position? And correspondingly, to what extent does our discourse at least structurally approximate the dynamics and social effects of what Bourdieu terms the rhetoric of disinterest, which characterizes those inhabiting dominated positions? My contention is not that Simmons, myself, or others at NAASR represent ourselves as actually disinterested or that our practices correspond in a one-to-one way with Bourdieu's examples. Indeed, some of the scholarly production in NAASR circles is among the most critically reflexive work I have encountered. I doubt most of us would, to quote Bourdieu on the rhetoric of disinterest among the dominated,

> Assert ... the irreducibility of the values of truth and justice and, by the same token, the absolute independence of the guardians of these values, the intellectuals, explicitly defined as such in opposition to the constraints and seductions of economic and political life. (Bourdieu 1993: 54)

Again, I suggest instead a structural similarity between the dynamics of fields as Bourdieu explicates them and those of the study of religion according to how we map it. Our mapping of the field of religious studies creates a discursive territory in which we distinguish and legitimate ourselves through kinds of discourse that approximate the strategies available to the dominated in Bourdieu's rubric. In comparison with how we represent the interests of the dominant class of participants in the contested field (or is it fields?) of religious studies, in our mythmaking we appear as, relatively speaking, disinterested. In the short space remaining I briefly examine the cosmology of religious studies as constructed by Simmons's critical theorizing. I attend in particular to the interplay between the type of theorizing she advocates and how she constructs the relative positions between herself and others. This permits us to socially theorize or, at least in a limited way, historicize some of our critical theorizing practices.

At one point Simmons writes, "And while something called critical theory is the only reason I am able to find myself working within the field of religious studies, I nonetheless find myself profoundly and increasingly alienated form much of the work that is currently identified with it" (p. 64, this volume). Throughout the paper she identifies this opposing "much of the work that is currently identified with ... [the] field of religious studies" with the broader institutional apparatus of AAR and its key component (and credentialing) parts, such as the *Journal of the American Academy of Religion* (*JAAR*). Simmons accordingly populates this opposing but most sizable classification of people and practices with two groups. First, "the theologians." Second, other scholars who critique theologians but still implicitly treat theologians as dialog partners through defining theory as that which is not theology, or, as Simmons describes this move, defining theory by negation. In addition to configuring the *JAAR* as "the premier journal" of "the academic study of religion" and associating it with this largest and opposing classification of scholars, Simmons appropriately magnifies its credentialing and legitimating significance. Simmons furthermore emphasizes what we can redescribe as the interests of this majority class of people who dominate AAR and *JAAR* in her cosmology of religious studies. For example, they seek to make their "work 'relevant' to non-specialists in a world continually and maddeningly identified as, unlike academia, *real*" (p. 66, this volume). And their construal of a world that could be "real" similarly fashions them as distinct from the post-structuralist form of subjectivity (if you will) that Simmons performs throughout her essay. This numerically prevalent class of other scholars, with their interests, thus also dominates the institutional apparatus and dominant forms of academic capital (e.g., publication in *JAAR*) in the oppositional field identified by Simmons. And Simmons repeatedly makes her relative position explicit. For example: "Thus, as long as scholars are trying to publish in the *JAAR* or have a significant voice in the AAR, I am not convinced that I have any more in common with them than with the theologians they disparage" (p. 64, this volume).

Simmons constructs herself as an outsider relative to the AAR establishment. She is distinguished from those whose participation marks them as seeking to "have a significant voice in the AAR." Finally, given the relative positions Simmons has mapped and their (at least by implication) opposing sets of interests, she calls for the dominated faction to separate; to cease producing work for the established apparatus:

It is time finally to let go of the relationship to the academic study of religion as it is currently costumed in its annual meeting and in the pages of its premier journal. I know saying so is perhaps easy from my perch as an outsider interdisciplinarian ... If we no longer sang to the AAR for our professional supper, [Hughes] argued, those of us committed to critical approaches might find far better uses for our voices. It seems to me that this is exactly the right direction to take. (Simmons, p. 66, this volume)

My suspicion is that many in the orbit of NAASR resonate with how Simmons maps religious studies and understands the import of critical theory. So to elaborate on some of my questions above, by identifying with and inhabiting such a mapping of religious studies, are we not taking up positions that could be translated into or redescribed as the dominated pole of a contested field? Do our ways of representing or producing distinction between ourselves and broader scholars at AAR align, at least in structural position and effect, with the rhetoric of disinterest as elucidated by Bourdieu? Again, I am emphatically not claiming that Simmons or most others of us at NAASR myth-make about our practices as though we are actually disinterested – quite the opposite. But just as most of us struggle to help our students understand – when it comes to social or structural analysis, "conscious" intention or explicit claims should often take a backseat in our gaze to social or discursive effect. Accordingly, when it comes to how our classifications both fix different groups of scholars in relative positions and construct the interests characterizing different classes of scholars, have we not positioned ourselves in a manner analogous to the disinterested party who, ideally, produces critical scholarship for others in our (dominated) position? I pose these probing questions not simply for rhetorical effect, but to invite conversation. This is something of a playful and tentative proposal. I find this route for historicizing our critical theorizing potentially productive, but am curious what others think about this way of configuring ourselves as data.

Stephen L. Young has a PhD in Religious Studies from Brown University. His research focuses on the intersections between mythmaking, discourses about deities, and textuality and sacred books in the ancient Mediterranean.

Notes

1. See, for example, Bourdieu (1988) and Foucault (1972). Foucault's discussion of discourse about sexuality as a conduit of relational power is also an on-point analogy (Foucault 1978).
2. Especially for the purposes of reflexivity, it may be important to note that similar critiques of Frankfurt School and other critical theorists, and of scholars who use their theories, have been made by those who position themselves among other camps of scholarship. For example, Pascal Boyer, who identifies with "cognitive science" approaches to cultural anthropology and religious studies, criticizes what he terms the "Salient Connections" mode of using critical theory, including the Frankfurt School with which Simmons identifies (Boyer 2012: 120–124).

3. Little social-theoretical work has been published about Evangelical scholarship. The reader can consult Barr (1977) and Grabbe (1987, 1988) for classic examples of scholarship about Evangelical scholarship. Barr and Grabbe implicitly treat their object of study as a dialogue partner precisely through their forms of direct critique.

4. This is not to say that I consider scholars associated with NAASR to be the only legitimate dialogue partners, but simply that for the purposes of this brief reflection I confine myself to recent topics of interest in NAASR discourses.

5. To offer an example from Bourdieu, "Those in the dominant positions operate essentially defensive strategies, designed to perpetuate the status quo by maintaining themselves and the principles on which their dominance is based. The world is as it should be, since they are on top and clearly deserve to be there; excellence therefore consists in being what one is ... The dominant are drawn towards silence, discretion and secrecy, and their orthodox discourses, which is only ever wrung from them by the need to rectify the heresies of the newcomers, is never more than the explicit affirmation of self-evident principles which go without saying and would go better unsaid ... The dominated producers ... have to resort to subversive strategies which will eventually bring them the disavowed profits only if they succeed in overturning the hierarchy of the field without disturbing the principles on which the field is based. Thus their revolutions are only ever partial ones, which displace the censorships and transgress the conventions but do so in the name of the same underlying principles. This is why the strategy *par excellence* is the 'return to the sources' which is the basis of all heretical subversion and all aesthetic revolutions, because it enables the insurgents to turn against the establishment the arms which they use to justify their domination, in particular ... disinterestedness. The strategy of beating the dominant groups at their own game by demanding that they respect the fundamental law of the field, a denial of the 'economy,' can only work if it manifests exemplary sincerity in its own denial" (Bourdieu 1993: 83–84; emphasis original). While Bourdieu's publications do not often focus on "religion," terminology long associated with religion suffuses his discussions of other topics, as is evident from the language of orthodoxy and heresy in this quotation. For discussion of Bourdieu's use of such "religious" language, see Rey (2007).

6. Bourdieu conceives of different types of capital operating in different fields, writing most frequently about economic capital, cultural capital, social capital, and their interrelationships (e.g., Bourdieu 1986).

References

Armour, Ellen, and Susan St. Ville (eds.). 2006. *Bodily Citations: Religion and Judith Butler.* New York: Columbia University Press.

Barr, James. 1977. *Fundamentalism.* London: SCM.

Bourdieu, Pierre. 1986. "Forms of Capital." In J. Richardson (ed.), *Handbook of Theory and Research for the Sociology of Education,* 241–258. New York: Greenwood Press.

Bourdieu, Pierre. 1988. *Homo Academicus* (trans. P. Collier). Stanford, CA: Stanford University Press.

Bourdieu, Pierre. 1993. *The Field of Cultural Production: Essays on Art and Literature.* New York: Columbia University Press.

Boyer, Pascal. 2012. "From Studious Irrelevancy to Consilient Knowledge: Modes of Scholarship and Cultural Anthropology." In Edward Slingerland and Mark Collard (eds.), *Creating Consilience: Integrating the Sciences and the Humanities*, 113–129. New York: Oxford University Press.

Foucault, Michel. 1972. *The Archaeology of Knowledge and the Discourse on Language* (trans. A. M. Sheridan Smith). New York: Random House.

Foucault, Michel. 1978. *The History of Sexuality, Volume 1: An Introduction* (trans. R. Hurley). New York: Random House.

Grabbe, Lester L. 1987. "Fundamentalism and Scholarship: The Case of Daniel." In Barry P. Thompson (ed.), *Scripture: Meaning and Method*, 133–152. Pickering: Hull University Press.

Grabbe, Lester L. 1988. "Another Look at the *Gestalt* of 'Darius the Mede.'" *Catholic Biblical Quarterly* 50: 198–213.

Rey, Terry. 2007. *Bourdieu on Religion: Imposing Faith and Legitimacy*. Bristol, CT: Acumen.

Young, Stephen L. 2015. "Protective Strategies and the Prestige of the 'Academic': A Religious Studies and Practice Theory Redescription of Evangelical Inerrantist Scholarship." *Biblical Interpretation* 23: 1–35.

11

A Reply

K. Merinda Simmons

The rejoinder as a writing genre tends to begin with an obligatory statement of gratitude at the opportunity to give some closing comments or to clarify particular remarks that the respondents have taken up. That such a statement has become expected tends to make the first few lines in a response such as this easy to skim or skip completely. I do hope I can slow down that temptation for whoever reads this, however. This panel in which I was fortunate enough to participate was the most generative for me in recent memory, and I am deeply indebted to Stephen Young, Martha Smith Roberts, and Thomas Whitley for their careful and thought-provoking work (I am also extremely grateful to NAASR for hosting the discussion and to Aaron Hughes for moderating it). I particularly appreciate the sustained attention in all three papers to the power dynamics that animate any discussion on the state or future of a field, this one being no exception. The questions they ask of my paper are important ones indeed, and I am glad for the productive challenge of considering and engaging with them.

A clarification of critical interlocutors should make the field—as well as professional opportunities and job prospects—appear broader, not more restricted. I do understand, though, how my approach might come off as a sort of self-indulgent disinterestedness. It is easy to play the scholar-meets-James-Dean rebel who is too cool for school but who shows up to all the classes to make sure everyone else knows it. It is especially easy if doing so with tenure. But of course I am as invested and situated as they come. So does my approach run the risk of isolating itself, touting a kind of defensive disinterestedness along the lines of what Bourdieu—and Stephen Young, in his response—describe? Almost certainly. I think the way to avoid creating (or perpetuating) a description of the field wherein "traditional" studies and "theoretical" ones present two opposing poles—thus stacking up a dominant/dominated binary—is to retheorize the very parameters of the field to which one refers. That is, as long as theorists cast themselves solely in opposition to theologians or descriptivists, there is an easy temptation to argue theory's analytical superiority by virtue of its marginalized status in the field. However, such an argument situates theory always in relation to the theology it antagonizes, only reifying the very dominance of theological discourses that critical analysis would seek to deconstruct.

My own approach to the question of how something called critical theory might be situated in the field of religious studies attempts to change the goalposts on that field such that theory is not cast always in relation to theology or descriptivism. There is much to Young's phrase, then, that identifies "the study of religion *as we tend to map it*." It is that very mapping—or those mapping tendencies—that I think deserve serious consideration. My own sense is that letting go of theology, as well as the strand of descriptive ethnography with no interest in the stakes present in its mode of analysis (an important qualifier, as there are certainly elements of that methodology that can offer useful historiographic examination and critique), would open up a broader landscape rather than restrict scholars to a smaller one. And since the boundaries we draw are indicative of our operative anxieties regarding the means by which we identify a this from a that, I will make plain that my own anxieties have to do with the ease with which critical theory gets conflated with a methodological approach that takes for granted the importance of a scholar's object of study.

Martha Smith Roberts helpfully reminds us that a term or approach often used in the service of the kind of phenomenological descriptivism I critique—like new materialism—should not be made its own analytical monolith. "At its best," she states, "the move to recognize religion 'on the ground' is one that seeks to reflect on the negotiations of power that happen between scholars and their objects of study." I agree with Roberts's account that "New materialism would argue that studying people doing things has left out the things." I would ask those scholars, however, in what ways the people doing things do not qualify as, well ... things worth studying. The naïve optimism that entertains a fantasy of materials hovering separate from their contexts is what I see as an intellectual nonstarter. If new materialists and I share an emphasis on "the fabricated nature of the subject/object divide (and the theory/religion divide)," I do not know why there should remain an emphasis on material culture, as though the phrase demarcates something specific. I would think we could, then, agree that the phrase is a redundant one.

That said, I find Roberts's own claims and the work she is doing in relation to something called new materialism very insightful indeed. Her important question, "Is there a way to be a materialist and not be pushing against a social constructivist framework, but against the essentializing expressions of it?," as well as her reference of the work done on racial formation by Omi and Winant, are welcome indeed. Butler's contention in *Senses of the Subject* (in an essay considering Descartes) comes to mind: "I think it must be possible to claim that the body is not known or identifiable apart from the linguistic coordinates that establish the boundaries of the body—*without* thereby claiming that the body is nothing other than the language by which it is known" (Butler 2015: 20). That Roberts incorporates Omi and Winant, Sara Ahmed, and Nikki Sullivan into her own analytical framework is what I find so potentially useful about a theoretical reframing of what it means to study religion in the first place. This is also exactly why listing "method and theory" on a CV does not a critical theorist make. Likewise, one need not list these terms to have important things to say about either or both of them. Stated even more bluntly, I have come to wonder if identifying something called critical theory *as* something particular or special is, perhaps, part of its undoing. When invoked as a destination rather than a roadmap (or a vehicle?), critical theory becomes an echo chamber rather than a way in to a more productive conversation. It is the potential for the echo chamber effect, I think, that all the responses deftly address.

In one of his incisive ways in to thinking through the problems of this echo chamber, Thomas Whitley reasonably asks, "If we think the rest of the field is sick and we have the cure, ought we not at least try to offer our theoretical balm?" I am not entirely sure that the rest of the field is sick (or at least, I'm not as interested as I probably used to be in diagnosing it as such) ... It seems robust, indeed, but has simply honed a very different set of strengths than those attempted by critical theorists. The same training and kind of fitness honed to make an excellent weightlifter will likely not make an excellent long-distance runner. Meanwhile, even if some might call part of the field sick, I am convinced that the palliative effects of critical thinking's proverbial medicine are not of much use since they deal with a very different set of ailments. Antihistamines will not alleviate a broken bone, just as a cast or splint will not help hay fever. The arrogant or isolating move, to my mind, would be for scholars of religion to continue insisting upon a theology/theory dichotomy that reduces each to its relation to the other and, in the process, making the field very small indeed.

In this way, I think clarifying our terms of critical engagement opens up, rather than closes down, what it means to be a scholar of religion. Or, if my approach is guilty of drawing tighter boundaries, I would not for a moment consider myself to be suggesting that this makes our respective circles of scholarship smaller. I have colleagues who engage with my work and vice versa who are scholars of Southern studies, Africana studies, English, and women's and gender studies. Our challenging and constructive interactions have shaped me as a scholar in significant ways. Indeed, that the kind of questions I think are worth asking are applicable across a host of different datasets is what separates "method and theory" from traditional area studies. What's more, the ability to see one's scholarship as relevant across various sites also situates an early-career scholar more effectively on the job market.

Whitley is quite right to bring up the pragmatic issues of situating oneself in a discipline with the job market (and all its attendant power dynamics) in mind. An important part of the work in transitioning from literary studies to religious studies for me was figuring out what part(s) of the latter discipline I could reasonably engage with my own interests and approach. I was a literary theorist, after all. Matters of the English job market, which were presented as bleak at best, were not lost on me. And it certainly is no secret that area studies are still quite popular within the MLA and its list of job descriptions. My attention to theoretical questions seemed to make me difficult to "place." Yet, that same attention also gave me the conceptual tools to answer more effectively the various forms of the "so what?" question in relation to my work. I was not pitching myself as an interdisciplinarian or critical theorist on the job market. My dissertation dealt specifically with analyses of women's migration narratives at the nexus of the Caribbean and the American South. But the occasion for that study—namely, my critique of authenticity claims that I read within those scholarly analyses—provided applications for my work across datasets. Those applications are what brought me into the unlikely field of religious studies despite my relative lack of emphasis in that area (at least, in the area as I had previously conceived of it).

There is certainly no denying that I was incredibly fortunate to be introduced— very much by happenstance—to a religious studies department at all and, what's more, a department that cared about modes of analysis more than particular areas of study. In the effort not to pitch itself so much in relation to theology or area studies, the department in which I now work has not limited itself but instead has become more expansive by incorporating other disciplinary backgrounds and methodologies. The unifying thread among my colleagues and me is an interest in seeing the people and texts we study as illustrative of broader themes and issues. I know that mine is not necessarily a typical story, and I know what kinds of pressures the job market presents to candidates. Those should not be underestimated, and Whitley brings productive attention to them. I would like to think, however, that, while occasional resignation to attending an expensive conference for the sake of an interview or attempting to publish in the JAAR will sometimes be deemed worth the opportunity cost, there are additional ways to respond to those pressures. To suggest as much should not reflect the retrospective naivety that can inflict professors once they secure stable jobs, but rather the entrepreneurial necessity on the part of graduate students and early-career scholars that I know is too often overlooked by those very same professors. One way to think toward such entrepreneurship is to tackle more directly the theoretical implications of one's work. Emphasis on critical theory can be, then, not a petulant form of isolation but rather a pragmatic way of positioning oneself more broadly on the market.

There is, necessarily, a tension between perceived inclusions and exclusions in my approach. What should constitute "critical theory"? What counts as the kind of descriptive ethnographies and historical analyses I critique, and how are those boundaries drawn? Are there elements of such approaches that still resonate with theoretical questions? And what constitutes theology as a field or subfield within this large organization called the American Academy of Religion. I have my own answers to these questions. But mine are not at all universal, so questions of power and politics that decidedly attend these questions are important to consider. Any "inclusion" always excludes. Looking at the inevitable limits of the AAR's ever-growing tent is a worthwhile endeavor. My own take on what should be included when using the moniker of critical theory excludes, too. And it is quite right to think through the potential shortfalls of these exclusions. My hope, however, is that, rather than glibly resorting to Frost's adage that "good fences make good neighbors," we might be able to emphasize the ways in which any process of building fences gives the occasion to think about our own analytical processes. In suggesting that we not keep picking fights with theologians, I wish to suggest a greater mode of scholarly self-reflection—one that Young, Roberts, and Whitley have all demonstrated in their responses, and one that broadens prospective contributions by those invested in critical theory at any career stage, whether in print or on the market.

K. Merinda Simmons is Associate Professor of Religious Studies at the University of Alabama, and author of *Changing the Subject: Writing Women across the African Diaspora* (Ohio State University Press, 2014). She focuses in her teaching and research on identifications of race, gender, and religion in the Caribbean and the American South.

Reference

Butler, Judith. 2015. *Senses of the Subject*. New York: Fordham University Press.

Part IV

12

What the Cognitive Science of Religion Is (and Is Not)

Claire White

Over the past decade or so there has been an exponential growth in research in the cognitive science of religion (CSR). Yet despite this, there continues to be a lack of understanding, and sometimes blatant misunderstanding, about what characterizes the field. This state of affairs is due, in part, to the reluctance of those within the field to commit to a precise definition. CSR is broad in scope. It is also a relatively young academic approach to the study of religion and, con-sequentially, is ever-expanding and often in a state of flux. Scholars have often characterized CSR by what it is not rather than what it is. In this chapter, I argue that at the heart of CSR is a theory that human cognition is necessary (but not sufficient) to explain the persistence and prevalence of human ideas and behav-iors deemed "religious." It is thus distinguished from its often atheoretical aca-demic counterparts in the study of religion by the attempt to explain, rather than describe, religion and because of the centrality of the role of the human mind in this explanation. The fruitfulness of this approach is demonstrated by what it has explained since its inception.

Introduction: What This Chapter Is (and Is Not)

The cognitive science of religion (CSR) is a relatively new approach to the study of religion and in recent years has been gaining scholarly momentum. This growth is showcased by: the large number of academic publications, such as edited vol-umes, journal editions, and individual articles; panels in conferences (like this one); the creation and growth in membership of specialized journals and schol-arly associations (such as the Cognitive Science of Religion group at the American Academy of Religion and the International Association for the Cognitive Science of Religion); the growing number of institutes and programs dedicated to such research and the increased allocation of funding to CSR projects. As Harvey Whitehouse exclaimed in his opening address during a transnational videocon-ference sponsored by the American Academy of Religion, "these are exciting times for the scientific study of religion."[1]

The enthusiasm of scholars within CSR, however, is not always paralleled by those outside it. As with any "new kid on the block," the theories and methods of

CSR are often met with bewilderment, skepticism, and sometimes outright antagonism from those who study religion or have vested interest in the epistemic status of religious belief. The target audience of this chapter is not those who are outright dismissive of the field (they are unlikely to be convinced by what I have to say anyway), but rather, those who are relatively new to the approach and open to engaging in methodological and theoretical pluralism. Further, this chapter will not entail a comprehensive overview of CSR (these exist elsewhere; see for example Barrett 2011; Geertz 2015; Pyysiäinen 2001). Rather, the aim of this chapter is twofold. First, to outline what—in 2015—minimally constitutes CSR (what it is) and second, to discuss how and why common misunderstandings of CSR still exist (what it is not).

I am grateful for the opportunity to present this approach to the wider religious studies community. My current appointment, as the first cognitive science of religion professor in a Religious Studies Department in the United States,[2] has given me practice in articulating to others outside the area what, precisely, CSR entails; especially my undergraduate students who ask me (usually with gaping mouths) to define what exactly *is* CSR? Their confusion is understandable. First, the term "cognitive science of religion" is vague at best and convoluted at worst. I realized this when students showed up to my class expecting to learn only about the history of the alleged conflict between science and religion (they had overlooked the "cognitive" part). As a result, I renamed the class "cognitive approaches to the study of religion," but even then the phrase remained ambiguous. After all, you would be hard pressed to find a discipline that does not deal, in some way, with how humans think. Furthermore, scholars have been dealing with the mind in religion, broadly speaking, for centuries—so it becomes less clear how CSR is different from other disciplines, such as the psychology of religion. Thus, CSR can seem like an umbrella term under which almost any discipline or theory can fall, rather than a distinct approach.

These misnomers are compounded by a general lack of willingness from those within CSR to commit to a concise or precise definition. Rather, a common strategy to communicate what it entails is to point to particular projects, especially:

- sensitivity toward detecting human-like beings in the environment (see Guthrie 1980, 1993);

- minimal counterintuitiveness (MCI) theory of religious transmission (e.g., Barrett and Nyhof 2001; Boyer 1994; Boyer and Ramble 2001); and

- discrepancies between theological correctness—the official theological doctrine of a given tradition—and theological incorrectness—deviations from official religious dogma which often emerge during real-time cognitive processing (Barrett 1998; Barrett and Keil 1996; Slone 2004).

These examples showcase the scope and breadth of research and key ideas but may contribute to the sense that CSR is piecemeal and lacks core theoretical commitments.

The reluctance of scholars to define the field is understandable in light of the fact that CSR is a relatively new approach to the study of religion. Correspondingly, it is expanding and in a state of flux. Theories and research are open to revision in light of new evidence. Prominent examples include the extent to which theories concerning transmission biases such as a hypersensitive agency detection device (HADD; i.e., the cognitive system deemed responsible for detecting human-like beings in the environment; e.g., see Atran 2002; Boyer 2013a), or MCI theory, explain belief in supernatural agents (e.g., Barrett 2008; De Cruz and Smedt 2010; Gervais and Henrich 2010; Purzycki and Willard in press); the relationship between theological correctness and folk concepts of religion (e.g., De Cruz 2014); and the cognitive mechanisms and structure of common representations of the afterlife and supernatural agents (Bering 2002; Bloom 2009a; Cohen et al. 2011; Hodge 2008; 2011; Richert and Harris 2006). Indeed, one of the most vigorous debates in CSR is currently taking place. This concerns the theory, proposed by Norenzayan and colleagues, about the relationship between the cultural prevalence of moralizing gods and the transition to large-scale societies (e.g., Baumard and Boyer 2013a; McKay and Whitehouse 2014; Norenzayan et al. 2014; Watts et al. 2015).

Further, there are disagreements within the field over the exact details of ideas and theories, especially: the evolutionary origins of religious ideas and behaviors (e.g., Bering 2006; Bloom 2009b; Bulbulia 2008; Sosis 2009; Wilson 2008); including the mechanisms of cultural change (e.g., Henrich and McElreath 2003; Richerson and Boyd 2008; for an overview, see Geertz 2015); and even models of cognition involved in religious thought (Barrett 2004; Baumard and Boyer 2013b; McCauley 2011; Oviedo 2015). These disagreements strengthen rather than diminish the approach, as the burden of proof is upon scholars to defend and provide evidence for their theory among alternatives. Likewise, the continuous revision of theories is not a weakness, but rather, the hallmark of a true scientific approach to the study of religion. As Barrett (2011: 232) put it, reassessment places emphasis on "empirical fortification and/or falsification of claims" in CSR.

What Is the Cognitive Science of Religion?

Although there is no singular period in time to which we can point and say that CSR came to be, it is fair to say that until around the 1990s there was no such thing as a cognitive science of religion as it has come to be known today. While a cognitive approach to the study of religion was foreshadowed by Sperber as early as 1975, and proposed by Guthrie in 1980, it was not until 2000 that the approach was well enough established for the term "cognitive science of religion" to be used (Barrett 2000; Lawson 2000). CSR thus emerged gradually in the 1990s as an amalgamation of multiple works that were happening at around the same time and largely independent from one another. The most notable of these included:

- *Rethinking Religion: Connecting Cognition and Culture* (Lawson and McCauley 1990);

- *Faces in the Clouds: A New Theory of Religion* (Guthrie 1993);

- *Inside the Cult* (Whitehouse 1995);

- *Explaining Culture* (Sperber 1996); and

- *The Naturalness of Religious Ideas* (Boyer 1994).

Despite the diversity in topics, these works were unified by a general dissatisfaction with the current assumptions and explanations of how cultural concepts (especially concerning religion) were acquired and transmitted in a culture. Broadly speaking, the basic problem was that previous research tended to be centered on principles of cultural relativism.[3] In particular, while few would seriously deny that we acquire religion from culture, models at the time examined the environmental inputs (culture) and largely ignored how the mind processed those inputs into (religious) outputs. Further, existing models privileged religious diversity over cross-cultural patterns, thus exaggerating the differences between religions (and thereby justifying the "area studies" approach to religious studies). Given that there are discernible patterns of religiosity across cultures and eras, and given the problem that Chomsky dubbed the "poverty of the stimulus" (Chomsky 1980), scholars in CSR sought to integrate work in cognitive science with work being done in the cultural study of religion. Most importantly, they advocated a scientific approach to study the phenomena.

Five general areas of discontent in particular were expressed in these works, and have since been elaborated upon by subsequent scholarship. Even though there is no single explanation for a religious phenomenon that is CSR, the acceptance of five key ideas minimally constitutes the field.

Commitment 1: There Is No Single Entity That Constitutes Religion, but There Are Discernible Patterns of Thought and Behavior That Can Be Called "Religion"

One basic claim that CSR scholars subscribe to is a commitment to the idea that there is no singular naturally occurring phenomenon that constitutes religion. That is to say, there is no single coherent category of thoughts and behaviors around the world that scholars can point to and say that *this* demarks religion (e.g., see Atran 2002; Boyer 2013b). Rather, the term religion is a convenient, general-purpose label that enables scholars to understand particular systems of thought and patterns of behavior. This idea is not unique to CSR and has been expressed throughout the history of religious studies, often in more radical forms (e.g., see Lindeman and Svedholm 2012; Smith 2004; Taylor 1998). CSR scholars accept that what we term religious is a useful starting point because it appears to characterize a cluster of recurring features (see Taves 2011).

While this perspective is not unique to a cognitive approach to religion, it demarks the field from other so-called big theories in the study of religion that sought to explain religion more-or-less as a single or coherent entity (most notably Durkheim 1976; Freud [1930] 1989; Marx 1970; Tylor 1871). From the perspective of the cognitive sciences, what constitutes religious systems is an assortment of recurring psychological predispositions and behaviors, expressed in a myriad of ways with differential environmental inputs. Correspondingly, we can expect these panhuman tendencies to express themselves in other cultural domains such as sport, art, music, and so on. In this respect, although these psychologically meaningful units may join together in ways to form distinctive religious systems, the units that constitute religion are not, in themselves, unique to it, because they are present in other cultural domains. Going against the grain of some historical figures in the study of religion (e.g., Eliade 1996), according to CSR, religion is not *sui generis*. Nor do all religious systems represent a unique cluster of phenomena. This point may seem obvious, but it is often overlooked in modern research agendas. As Slingerland and Bulbulia (2011: 3) put it, "much of the scholarly study of religion has been largely a project of documenting religious diversity," which can be seemingly endless, without any yardstick upon which to measure how these systems are similar, or even, different when compared to others. By contrast, scholars in CSR take some similarities, such as the representation of non-visible agents, as their starting point. As it turns out, when we survey the flora and fauna of beliefs and practices deemed "religious" across the world there are a number of recurring features.

More importantly, these theoretical tenets inform the methodological bedrock and theoretical foundations of the approach. If there is no single thing deemed religion then CSR scholars do not waste their time trying to capture or explain it as such. Conversely, if what constitutes religious systems is the assortment of various psychological propensities—reassembled in culturally contingent ways—then the aim of CSR is to identify both the psychological predispositions and cultural environments that give rise to them.

Commitment 2: Religion Can Be Explained Scientifically

Early pioneers of the newly emerging cognitive science of religion sought to put an end to the penchant of religious studies scholars, who, like other humanistic disciplines, engaged in seemingly endless interpretative thick descriptions which were vague, lacked explanatory power and, therefore, were unable to be empirically assessed among competing interpretations (Lawson and McCauley 1990; Slone and Mort 2004; Sperber 1996). Further, as these early proponents of a cognitive approach argued, interpretation usually requires explanation, and scholars were already proposing explanations of religion, often using outdated models of human cognition or a "black box" theory of human psychology that lacked discussion of underlying psychological mechanisms. Consider, for instance, Salins and Obeyesekere's explanation of Hawaiian rituals performed in response to the arrival of Captain Cook in 1779 (for a discussion of this, see Cohen et al. 2008),

Obeyesekere's explanation of the prevalence of reincarnation beliefs as wish ful-fillment that kin would return to the human world (see White in press for a dis-cussion of this) or most famously, Durkheim's theory of collective effervescence in communal rituals (for evidence of mechanisms involved, see Fischer et al. 2014; Konvalinka et al. 2011). The aim of the new cognitive approach to the study of religion, therefore, was not simply to produce a better interpretation of religion but to explain it by applying contemporary theories of how the mind works and using scientific methods to test these ideas (Lawson and McCauley 1990).

One question that naturally follows from this characterization of the field is what, exactly, does CSR purport to explain? To date, CSR has focused on explain-ing two broad aspects of religion in particular, and I refer to these as the two "P"s for convenience. First, CSR focuses on the question of why particular kinds of ideas (and corresponding behaviors) *persist* in relatively stable forms throughout history and across different cultural environments when there may be many ver-sions of the idea that can be constructed (see Sperber 1996). The second question of interest is why some ideas are especially *prevalent* over others within and across traditions. As it turns out, despite the potential for diversity in religious ideas across cultures, some concepts—such as representations of supernatural agents—are remarkably stable. As Boyer (2003:119) put it, there is a "limited catalogue of the supernatural." The goal of CSR is to explain this limited repertoire by appeal-ing to what is known about how humans tend to think.

Of course, it would be naïve to suggest that CSR has succeeded in explaining these aspects of religion, and in some respects we have only scratched the sur-face of the vast repertoire of such phenomena. Even as an objective, however, these aims demark CSR as a discipline that is distinct from others, especially the psychology of religion, which tends to focus more on individual differences in acquiring and representing religious concepts than accounting for cross-cultural patterns; and the sociology of religion, which tends to focus more on how social dynamics shape religious ideas and behaviors than specifying the interaction between the environment and cognitive mechanisms to account for such varia-tion (see Barrett 2011).

CSR is distinctive in its broad interdisciplinarity and diversity of methodolo-gies. To address questions about the distribution and stability of religious con-cepts, CSR scholars often collaborate with—or leverage upon existing research by—other specialists, especially: anthropologists, historians, psychologists, phi-losophers, sociologists and religionists. Additionally, CSR researchers use methods that are most appropriate to the types of questions they tend to ask concerning the persistence and prevalence of so-called "religious" ideas and behaviors. Some popular research designs include comparative research with children and adults and large-scale cross-cultural and historical surveys.

CSR researchers have relied upon—and conducted—research with children and adults, both within and across cultures, to understand early cognitive biases that facilitate or constrain the acquisition of religious ideas. Cultures are often selected for comparison on the basis of prior ethnographic fieldwork and because they differ meaningfully from the western sample (e.g., Astuti and Harris 2008; Cohen

2007; Emmons and Kelemen 2014; Malley 2004; White in press b; Whitehouse 1995). From this research, we now have a better understanding of how and why children reason about—and respond to—phenomena that are staples of religion, such as:

- gods and supernatural agents (e.g., Barrett and Richert 2003; Richert and Barrett 2005; Knight 2008; Piazza et al. 2011);

- the design and origin of the natural world (e.g., Evans 2001; Kelemen 2004); and

- life before, or after death (e.g., Astuti and Harris 2008; Bering and Bjorklund 2004; Bering et al. 2005; Emmons and Kelemen 2014; Richert and Harris 2006).

Research has also demonstrated how adults represent and respond to a variety of religious concepts, including:

- the transmission of religious ideas (Boyer and Ramble 2001);

- gods and supernatural agents (Barrett 1998; Bering 2002; McKay et al. 2011; Purzycki 2013);

- supernatural causes of illness (e.g., Legare and Gelman 2008; Legare et al. 2012);

- the origins of the natural world, and a creator deity (Järnefelt et al. 2015);

- prayer (Barrett 2001);

- teleological reasoning about life events (Heywood and Bering 2014);

- continued existence in the afterlife (e.g., Astuti 2007; Bering 2006);

- representations of the self and others during spirit possession (e.g., Cohen 2007; Cohen and Barrett 2008);

- continued personal identity in reincarnation (e.g., White 2015, 2016, in press; White et al. 2015); and

- ritualized actions (e.g., Atran 2002; Cohen et al. 2014; Fischer et al. 2014; Watson-Jones et al. 2016; Xygalatas et al. 2011).

CSR scholars may also draw upon existing archaeological, historical, ethnographic data and large scale social surveys to test goodness-of-fit with their theories (e.g., see Baumard and Boyer 2013a; Norenzayan 2013; Norenzayan and Shariff 2008; Purzycki 2013). Others conduct secondary analyses of existing ethnographic and historical databases, such as the Standard Cross-Cultural Sample (SCCS) and the Human Relations Area Files (HRAF) (see Slingerland and Sullivan in press for an overview of survey research). Such databases make possible analyses of aspects across cultures and throughout time, while controlling for effects of historical contact between societies (i.e., Galton's problem). These databases also enable scholars to formally test probabilistic models of aspects of religious ideas and behaviors, such as physical contact with the corpse by kin during ritual preparation for disposal (White et al. in press) or the co-occurrence of ritual dynamics and particular socio-political arrangements (Atkinson and Whitehouse 2011), and the representation of high gods (Johnson 2005). Analyses of large datasets is likely to flourish in CSR research agendas, due to the emergence of new databases specifically tailored for questions concerning cognition, the environment and religion, such as the Historical Database of Sociocultural Evolution (Turchin et al. 2012) and the Database of Religious History (DRH), which is collecting data directly from historians and other specialists (see Slingerland and Sullivan in press).[4]

Other methods are likely to proliferate in CSR in the coming years as evidenced by the development of external funding for research projects. These include: the neurosciences, where researchers are employing the latest brain imaging technologies to understand the neural correlates activated in religious cognition and experiences (such as projects in the Institute for the Bio-Cultural Study of Religion's lab at Boston University; see also Andersen et al. 2014; McNamara 2009); and computer modeling, where researchers are developing large-scale agent-based models to predict and explain religious dynamics both past and present (such as the Institute for the Bio-Cultural Study of Religion's "Modeling Religion Project"; Masaryk University's "Generative Historiography of Religion Project"; and see also Whitehouse et al. 2012).

Although methodologically diverse, CSR researchers are bound together by a commitment to a scientific approach to the study of religion. Thus, CSR scholars formulate testable hypotheses about religious ideas and behaviors and make predictions about the past, present or future state of affairs. Such predictions are subject to verification or revision based on the principles of testability and goodness-of-fit of existing data. Scholars do not merely pay lip service to such principles but have actively endorsed them. For example, scholars will often propose a general theory to explain some aspect of religion and then invite critique from an array of specialists in multiple disciplines (e.g., on topics such as rituals: Boyer and Liénard 2006; Schjoedt et al. 2013; on gods: Norenzayan et al. 2014; on the afterlife: Bering 2006). Perhaps the best example of this commitment is Harvey Whitehouse's theory of ritual dynamics (Whitehouse 2000, 2004). Whitehouse openly invited scholars from multiple disciplines to critique his theory in order to improve it. For instance, he sought out religious historians to apply his theory to prehistorical, Greco-Roman, and Christian religions to test the goodness-of-fit (Whitehouse and Martin 2004), and has since modified his theory in light of existing evidence (Whitehouse and McCauley 2005). Like others in CSR, he also teamed with experimental psychologists and other specialists to formulate his theory in empirically testable ways and to test it against competing alternatives (e.g., Atkinson and Whitehouse 2011; Barrett 2005; Barrett and Lawson 2001; Cohen and Barrett 2008; Richert et al. 2005).

Commitment 3: To Explain Religion, We Must First Fractionate and Reduce It into Meaningfully Constituent Parts

CSR scholars would happily admit that they, like all scientists, are in the business of reduction (see McCauley 2000; Slingerland 2008).[5] CSR takes a bottom-up approach, fractionating religion into cross-culturally recurrent forms of ideas and practices, such as concepts of non-visible agents as punitive deities, continued consciousness in the afterlife, and ritualized behavior (e.g., see Boyer 2003). By fractioning religious systems into empirically tractable units of analyses, rather than trying to top-down define and then explain religion as a whole, CSR scholars believe they have a better chance of eventually reconstructing, and explaining, these religious systems in their entirety; namely, as distinct socio-cultural packages of ideas and practices (see Boyer 2003; McKay and Whitehouse 2014). Although this approach has led some to the impression that CSR is narrow in scope (see Cohen et al. 2008), this represents a misunderstanding of the field, since it is also characterized by general theories of aspects of religion, such as the relationship between ritual dynamics and socio-political arrangements (e.g., Whitehouse 2004) and the rise of large-scale prosocial religions and moralizing gods (Norenzayan 2013).

To successfully explain religion, therefore, involves two things. The first draws on what is known in the cognitive and evolutionary sciences about panhuman cognition—that is, how humans attend to, process and remember information—to explain why these patterns persist (e.g., content biases). The second draws on specialist understanding of particular socio-cultural environments in which these ideas and behaviors operate, to explain how these predisposed patterns of thinking and behaving manifest themselves in particular contexts (e.g., context biases; see Gervais and Henrich 2010; Henrich and McElreath 2003). These are complementary because one cannot say much about how ideas tend to be similar if one does not understand the ways in which these ideas and behaviors are modified (i.e., the extent to which they vary).

Commitment 4: Religious Ideas and Practices Are Actively Processed by the Human Mind

The most significant of all commitments, and what most distinguishes CSR from other approaches to the study of religion is the active role attributed to human cognition in the formation and transmission of religious ideas. What unifies the diversity of the various research projects in CSR is the basic idea that the mind is not a blank slate, sponge, or a Xerox machine, but that we actively filter and shape information (including religious ideas) in the world around us. Due to biases in the content of religious ideas, some ideas are encoded, stored and recalled better than others. This theory has been characterized as the epidemiology of representations, presented by Sperber (1996), and its implications are simple: to account for the persistence and prevalence of religious ideas, one must take account of panhuman cognitive predispositions. Such dispositions comprise corresponding intuitions that emerge in all human beings with minimal instruction, even though their expression may be modified by cultural input (McCauley 2011).

CSR is sometimes accused of neglecting the role of the socio-cultural environment and historical factors in affecting the forms and transmission of religious ideas, but this is inaccurate (see Cohen et al. 2008). As Trigg and Barrett put it (2014: 4), the cognitive science of religion "draws upon the cognitive sciences to explain how pan-cultural features of human minds, interacting with their natural and social environments, inform and constrain religious thought and action." It was, from the beginning, cognition *and* culture—never cognition *not* culture. The historic and culturally situated character of religion is, correspondingly, emphasized even by early works in the area, such as those by Whitehouse (1995) and Guthrie (1993). More importantly, scholars have continued to demonstrate a deep commitment to understanding how these biases manifest themselves in particular socio-cultural contexts, often by drawing on their specialist knowledge and spending years in the field (e.g., Cohen 2007; Whitehouse 1995; Whitehouse and Martin 2004; Xygalatas 2014). Others within the field have gone to pains to emphasize the meshing of both cognition and culture to produce religious ideas and behaviors[6] (for example, the "Religion, Cognition and Culture Research Unit" at Aarhus; see Geertz 2015).

From its inception, CSR was a reaction against strong social constructionist accounts of religion. The impression that the field has neglected historic and cultural pressures may therefore be due in part to a contrast effect between the emphasis placed on socio-cultural factors by works of CSR scholars and other accounts of religion that focus more or less exclusively on the role of culture. In addition, there has also been a tendency from those within the field to promote the approach by emphasizing the cognitive component, and perhaps even a bias from those who first encounter it to remember the novel features—which tend to be the cognitive aspects. A related consideration is pragmatic. In academic discourse, it is often easier to give examples of what CSR can deliver by appealing to broad cognitive theories than to discuss how these biases are shaped by historic and cultural particulars.

Commitment 5: Religion Is Cognitively Natural

The final claim is that religion is cognitively natural. This entails two things. First is the commitment to methodological naturalism, which is the basic idea, shared broadly in religious studies, that the "human side" of religious ideas and experiences can be studied in naturalistic terms. CSR scholars are interested in understanding how and why humans respond to ideas that are deemed religious, rather than to decipher the ontological status of those ideas, which is clearly outside of the scope of CSR research both methodologically (how would we test it?) and theoretically (why would we test it?). Second, if the cognitive resources that psychologically underpin religious concepts are not distinct from those that underpin their non-religious counterparts, then there is no need to posit a special domain that is religious cognition. Regardless of metaphysical claims, and attempting to bracket their personal epistemic commitments about the status of religion, CSR scholars claim that religion is cognitively natural. Given what we know about the persuasiveness of particular forms of thought which underpin much of religion in different contexts, religious ideas are part and parcel of our normally developing cognition and rapidly spread when introduced in social environments; much like music, art, or language, religion is natural.

A related question concerns the source of this naturalness. One response, already highlighted, is to point to the early emergence of ideas as indication of cognitive naturalness. That is to say, given minimal instruction, humans are predisposed to represent the world in certain ways that are showcased by how people tend to think about concepts that we associate with religion, even though they can be tuned by cultural environments (McCauley 2011). One account could simply point to these intuitions and predispositions as criteria of what makes certain features of religious representations and behaviors natural. Another response goes further by locating the source of these intuitions to early emerging predispositions to evolved domain-specific systems. Thus the systems themselves, which are a product of human evolution, are responsible for these early emerging biases. The latter is of course an evolutionary account of religion. Even though there is an ongoing debate about the origin, function and exact role of evolution in religious ideas and behaviors (especially whether it enhanced survival and the unit of selection; e.g., see Bering 2006; Bloom 2009b; Bulbulia 2008; Henrich and McElreath 2003; Richerson and Boyd 2008; Sosis 2009; Wilson 2008), all evolutionary accounts attempt to get at the ultimate causality behind the origins and persistence of religious ideas. Most assume that evolutionary sciences are, or should be, essential to a cognitive explanation of religious phenomena (see Wilson 2008) while others, (most notably Barrett 2011) have argued the case that it is distinct and complementary, often referring to "cognitive and evolutionary approaches to the study of religion" to capture both (e.g., see Trigg and Barrett 2014; Watts and Turner 2014). As I have briefly alluded to here, although it is possible to propose a cognitive explanation of religion that does not draw upon an understanding of evolutionary processes, engagement with the evolutionary sciences offers a broad theoretical framework for organizing facts about pan-human tendencies, greatly enriches the explanatory potential of CSR and clearly demarks it from other approaches.

The idea that religion is natural often causes controversy for those outside the field. This "naturalness-of-religion" thesis (coined by Barrett 2000) has provoked controversy from both sides of the religion debate. On the one hand, some argue that we are essentially "explaining religion away," with the associated claim that a natural explanation of religion makes the existence of anything supernatural superfluous (e.g., for an overview see Barrett 2007; Leech and Visala 2011). On the other hand, some have interpreted the idea that religion is natural as meaning that religion is true (for further treatment on this issue see De Cruz and Smedt 2015; Jong 2013; Trigg and Barrett 2014). As Boyer (2008: 1038) put it, "some people of faith fear that an understanding of the processes underlying belief could undermine it. Others worry that what is shown to be part of our evolutionary heritage will be interpreted as good, true, necessary or inevitable."

To date, most researchers have responded by not engaging in debates about the philosophical or theological implications of their findings in lieu of getting on with the science, but this has created the unfortunate effect of leaving some suspicious of deep-seated commitments and religious agendas, especially when research is funded by donors who have been traditionally sympathetic to religious concerns (e.g., see Leech and Visala 2011; Martin and Wiebe 2012). While I cannot testify to the research agenda of every CSR scholar, the unifying feature of CSR research is a commitment to the scientific process. Namely, if the methodological hallmarks that designate good scientific research (e.g., design validity, probabilistic testing, replication, etc.) are employed in all sciences, then they can and should be used to distinguish poor from strong scientific research in CSR. Regardless of personal commitments, methodologically sound research is good research.

Conclusion

Although relatively new and developing, CSR is underpinned by a commitment to five tenets, that: there is no single entity that constitutes religion; religion can be explained scientifically; to explain religion we must fractionate and reduce it into meaningfully constituent parts; religious ideas and practices are actively processed by the human mind; and religion is cognitively natural. At the core, CSR is a theory about the spread and prevalence of religious phenomena and the active role that human cognition, in addition to the socio-cultural environment, plays in this process. The ultimate goal of CSR is to identify, and then explain, how and why some ideas and practices that are labeled religious are cross-culturally recurrent, and how they are modified by cultural input.

One of the hallmarks of the new cognitive approach to religion is that it is interdisciplinary and scholars engage in, and encourage, methodological pluralism. As a scientific approach to religion, CSR scholars have been keen to refine compelling ideas that stem from both the humanities and social sciences into scientifically tractable theories and then test them. This inclusivity offers scholars of religion everywhere an opportunity to refine existing ideas in the spirit of the pursuit of knowledge. Yet rather than beating down the doors of CSR researchers, mainstream religious studies scholars have watched the field grow from a distance, often with skepticism for what we can show, sometimes with scornful disdain for any scientific approach to the study of religion. Yet as Lawson put it:

> A cognitive approach to ... religion is capable of arousing intense suspicion ... the standard assumption in the social sciences and the humanities has been that only social and cultural methods can explain social and cultural facts. Of course the possibility of a cognitive science of religion depends *upon showing that cognitive explanations of socio-cultural facts are not only possible but have already happened.* (Lawson 2000: 47; emphasis added)

Although CSR scholars do not claim to have explained religion (provocative book titles aside), in the past fifteen years or so the field has made tremendous progress in understanding the cognitive basis of religious ideas and behaviors. Armed with an empirical toolkit and cutting-edge theories on how the mind works, CSR researchers will continue to attempt to explain the stability and diversity of religious ideas and behaviors across the world and throughout history, and perhaps even make predictions about the future of the religious landscape. These are exciting times indeed.

Claire White is Associate Professor in the Department of Religious Studies at California State University, Northridge. She is also Co-Chair of the Cognitive Science of Religion Group at the American Academy of Religion.

Acknowledgements

An earlier version of this chapter was presented at the annual meeting of the North American Association for the Study of Religion, November 2015, Atlanta. It was written during release time awarded by The College of Humanities at California State University, Northridge. Thanks to Justin Barrett, Joseph Bulbulia, Mitch Hodge, Ted Slingerland, Jason Slone, and James Van Slyke for commenting on earlier drafts, and to Armin Geertz, Justin Lane, and Wesley Wildman for providing me with information about their research.

Notes

1. See Harvey Whitehouse's welcome and introduction to New Scientific Approaches to the Study of Religious Experience, held Friday, May 22, 2009, at https://vimeo. com/5129309.
2. This is to the best of my knowledge. Although other religious studies professors are active in CSR research, my position was advertised (in 2012) explicitly as a tenure-track position for a specialist in CSR.
3. Whitehouse's work (1995) was not an explicit treatment of current approaches to the study of religion but showcased the potential of findings from cognitive psychology to enhance explanation in traditional ethnography.
4. These methods are not meant to be exhaustive. Others include: textual analyses (see Slingerland 2013); experimental and quasi-experimental fieldwork (see the "Experimental Anthropology Lab" at the University of Connecticut); and the philosophical, historical/archaeological and/or theological treatment of CSR theories (e.g., De Cruz and Smedt 2010; Geertz and Jensen 2014; Hodge 2011; Nichols 2007; Nicholson 2014; Pyysiäinen 2001; Schloss and Murray 2011; Whitehouse and Martin 2004).
5. To date, CSR has focused most on explaining common representations of, and responses to, supernatural agents. The focus to date is likely a product of two factors. First is the influence of scholars such as Guthrie (1980). Second is the ubiquity and accessibility of the phenomena and the comparative ease with which scholars can investigate these phenomena. This focus may be interpreted as a Tylorian minimalist view of religion *as* supernatural agents but it does not adequately characterize the field, since CSR researchers have addressed other phenomena. Indeed, some have studied phenomena

that may be considered outside of what mainstream scholars would classify as religion, such as atheism (Lanman 2012) and magic (Sørensen 2007).

6.   This also includes the interaction between the brain, body and environment in the formation of, and reception to, religious ideas and behaviors. Often referred to as situated or distributed cognition (for example see Geertz 2010).

References

Andersen, M., Schjødt, U., Nielbo, K. L., and Sørensen, J. 2014. "Mystical Experience in the Lab." *Method and Theory in the Study of Religion* 26(3): 217–245. doi: 10.1163/15700682-12341323.

Astuti, Ritta. 2007. "Ancestors and the Afterlife." *Quaderns de l'Institut Català d'Antropologia* 23: 61–78.

Astuti, Ritta and Paul L. Harris. 2008. "Understanding Mortality and the Life of the Ancestors in Rural Madagascar." *Cognitive Science* 32(4): 713–740. doi: 10.1080/03640210802066907.

Atkinson, Quentin D. and Harvey Whitehouse. 2011. "The Cultural Morphospace of Ritual Form: Examining Modes of Religiosity Cross-Culturally." *Evolution and Human Behavior* 32(1): 50–62. doi: 10.1016/j.evolhumbehav.2010.09.002.

Atran, Scott. 2002. *In Gods We Trust: The Evolutionary Landscape of Religion*. Oxford: Oxford University Press.

Barrett, Justin L. 1998. "Cognitive Constraints on Hindu Concepts of the Divine." *Journal for the Scientific Study of Religion* 37(4): 608–619. doi 10.2307/1388144.

Barrett, Justin L. 2000. "Exploring the Natural Foundations of Religion." *Trends in Cognitive Sciences* 4(1): 29–34. doi: 10.1016/S1364-6613(99)01419-9.

Barrett, Justin L. 2001. "How Ordinary Cognition Informs Petitionary Prayer." *Journal of Cognition and Culture* 1(3): 259–269. doi: 10.1163/156853701753254404.

Barrett, Justin L. 2004. *Why Would Anyone Believe in God?* Walnut Creek, CA: Rowman AltaMira.

Barrett, Justin L. 2005. "In the Empirical Mode: Evidence Needed for the Modes of Religiosity Theory." In Harvey Whitehouse and Robert N. McCauley (eds.), *Mind and Religion: Psychological and Cognitive Foundations of Religion*, 109–126. Lanham, MD: Rowman & Littlefield.

Barrett, Justin L. 2007. "Is the Spell Really Broken? Bio-psychological Explanations of Religion and Theistic Belief." *Theology and Science* 5(1): 57–72. doi: 10.1080/14746700601159564.

Barrett, Justin L. 2008. "Coding and Quantifying Counterintuitiveness in Religious Concepts: Theoretical and Methodological Reflections." *Method and Theory in the Study of Religion* 20(4): 308–338. doi: 10.1163/157006808x371806.

Barrett, Justin L. 2011. "Cognitive Science of Religion: Looking Back, Looking Forward." *Journal for the Scientific Study of Religion* 50(2): 229–239. doi: 10.1111/j.1468-5906.2011.01564.x.

Barrett, Justin L. and Frank C. Keil. 1996. "Conceptualizing a Nonnatural Entity: Anthropomorphism in God Concepts." *Cognitive Psychology* 31(3): 219–247. doi: 10.1006/cogp.1996.0017.

Barrett, Justin L. and E. Thomas Lawson. 2001. "Ritual Intuitions: Cognitive Contributions to Judgments of Ritual Efficacy." *Journal of Cognition and Culture* 1(2): 183–201. doi: 10.1163/156853701316931407.

Barrett, Justin L. and Melanie A. Nyhof. 2001. "Spreading Non-natural Concepts: The Role of Intuitive Conceptual Structures in Memory and Transmission of Cultural Materials." *Journal of Cognition and Culture* 1(1): 69–100. doi: 10.1163/156853701300063589.

Barrett, Justin L. and Rebekah A. Richert. 2003. "Anthropomorphism or Preparedness? Exploring Children's God Concepts." *Review of Religious Research* 44(3): 300–312. doi: 10.2307/3512389

Baumard, Nicolas and Pascal Boyer. 2013a. "Explaining Moral Religions." *Trends in Cognitive Sciences* 17(6): 272–280. doi: 10.1016/j.tics.2013.04.003.

Baumard, Nicolas and Pascal Boyer. 2013b. "Religious Beliefs as Reflective Elaborations on Intuitions: A Modified Dual-Process Model." *Current Directions in Psychological Science* 22(4): 295–300. doi: 10.1177/0963721413478610.

Bering, Jesse M. 2002. "Intuitive Conceptions of Dead Agents' Minds: The Natural Foundations of Afterlife Beliefs as Phenomenological Boundary." *Journal of Cognition and Culture* 2(4): 263–308. doi: 10.1163/15685370260441008.

Bering, Jesse M. 2006. "The Folk Psychology of Souls." *Behavioral and Brain Sciences* 29(5): 453–462. doi: 10.1017/s0140525x06009101.

Bering, Jesse M. and David F. Bjorklund. 2004. "The Natural Emergence of Reasoning about the Afterlife as a Developmental Regularity." *Developmental Psychology* 40(2): 217–233. doi: 10.1037/0012-1649.40.2.217.

Bering, Jesse M., Carlos Hernandez Blasi, and David F. Bjorklund. 2005. "The Development of Afterlife Beliefs in Religiously and Secularly Schooled Children." *British Journal of Developmental Psychology* 23(4): 587–607. doi: 10.1348/026151005x36498.

Bloom, Paul. 2009a. *Descartes' Baby: How the Science of Child Development Explains What Makes Us Human.* New York: Basic Books.

Bloom, Paul. 2009b. "Religious Belief as an Evolutionary Accident." *The Believing Primate: Scientific, Philosophical, and Theological Reflections on the Origin of Religion*, 118–127. doi: 10.1093/acprof:oso/9780199557028.003.0006.

Boyer, Pascal. 1994. *The Naturalness of Religious Ideas: A Cognitive Theory of Religion.* Berkeley, CA: University of California Press.

Boyer, Pascal. 2003. "Religious Thought and Behaviour as By-products of Brain Function." *Trends in Cognitive Sciences* 7(3): 119–124. doi: 10.1016/s1364-6613(03)00031-7.

Boyer, Pascal. 2008. "Being Human: Religion: Bound to Believe?" *Nature* 455(7216): 1038–1039. doi: 10.1038/4551038a.

Boyer, Pascal. 2013a. "Why 'Belief' Is Hard Work: Implications of Tanya Luhrmann's When God Talks Back." *HAU: Journal of Ethnographic Theory* 3(3): 349–357. doi: 10.14318/hau3.3.015.

Boyer, Pascal. 2013b. "Explaining Religious Concepts: Lévi-Strauss the Brilliant and Problematic Ancestor." In Dimitris Xygalatas and William W. McCorkle (eds.), *Mental Culture, Classical Social Theory and the Cognitive Science of Religion*, 164–175. Durham: Acumen.

Boyer, Pascal and Pierre Liénard. 2006. "Precaution Systems and Ritualized Behavior." *Behavioral and Brain Sciences* 29(6): 635–641. doi: 10.1017/s0140525x06009575.

Boyer, Pascal and Charles Ramble. 2001. "Cognitive Templates for Religious Concepts: Cross-Cultural Evidence for Recall of Counter-intuitive Representations." *Cognitive Science* 25(4): 535–564. doi: 10.1207/s15516709cog2504_2.

Bulbulia, Joseph (ed.). 2008. *The Evolution of Religion: Studies, Theories, and Critiques.* Bakersfield, CA: Collins Foundation Press.

Chomsky, Noam. 1980. *Rules and Representations*. Oxford: Basil Blackwell.

Cohen, Emma. 2007. *The Mind Possessed: The Cognition of Spirit Possession in an Afro-Brazilian Religious Tradition*. New York: Oxford University Press.

Cohen, Emma and Justin Barrett. 2008. "When Minds Migrate: Conceptualizing Spirit Possession." *Journal of Cognition and Culture* 8(1): 23–48. doi: 10.1163/156770908x 289198.

Cohen, Emma, Jonathan A. Lanman, Harvey Whitehouse, and Robert N. McCauley. 2008. "Common Criticisms of the Cognitive Science of Religion—Answered." *Bulletin of the Council of Societies for the Study of Religion* 37(4): 112–115.

Cohen, Emma, Emily Burdett, Nicola Knight, and Justin Barrett. 2011. "Cross-Cultural Similarities and Differences in Person-Body Reasoning: Experimental Evidence from the UK and Brazilian Amazon." *Cognitive Science* 35(7): 1282–1304. doi: 10.1111/ j.1551–6709.2011.01172.x.

Cohen, Emma, Roger Mundry, and Sebastian Kirschner. 2014. "Religion, Synchrony, and Cooperation." *Religion, Brain and Behavior* 4(1): 20–30. doi: 10.1080/2153599x. 2012.741075.

De Cruz, Helen. 2014. "Cognitive Science of Religion and the Study of Theological Concepts." *Topoi* 33(2): 487–497. doi: 10.1007/s11245-013-9168-9.

De Cruz, Helen and Johan Smedt. 2010. "Science as Structured Imagination." *Journal of Creative Behavior* 44(1): 29–44. doi: 10.1002/j.2162-6057.2010.tb01324.x.

Durkheim, Emile. 1976. *The Elementary Forms of the Religious Life*. New York: Routledge.

Eliade, Mircea. 1996. *Patterns in Comparative Religion*. Lincoln, NE: University of Nebraska Press.

Emmons, Natalie A. and Deborah Kelemen. 2014. "The Development of Children's Prelife Reasoning: Evidence from Two Cultures." *Child Development* 85(4): 1617–1633. doi: 10.1111/cdev.12220.

Evans, E. Margaret. 2001. "Cognitive and Contextual Factors in the Emergence of Diverse Belief Systems: Creation versus Evolution." *Cognitive Psychology* 42(3): 217–266. doi: 10.1006/cogp.2001.0749.

Fischer, Ronald, Dimitris Xygalatas, Panagiotis Mitkidis, Paul Reddish, Penny Tok, Ivana Konvalinka, and Joseph Bulbulia. 2014. "The (Fire) Walker's High: Affect and Physiological Responses in an Extreme Collective Ritual." *PLoS One* 9(2): e88355. dio: 10.1371/journal.pone.0088355.

Freud, Sigmund. [1930] 1989. *The Future of an Illusion*. The Standard Edition of the Complete Psychological Works of Sigmund Freud (ed. James Strachey), vol. XXI. New York: W. W. Norton.

Geertz, Armin W. 2010. "Brain, Body and Culture: A Biocultural Theory of Religion." *Method and Theory in the Study of Religion* 22 (4): 304–321.

Geertz, Armin W. 2015. "Religious Belief, Evolution of." In James D, Wright (ed.), *International Encyclopedia of the Social and Behavioral Sciences* (2nd edition), vol. 20, pp. 384–395. Oxford: Elsevier.

Geertz, Armin W. and Jeppe Sinding Jensen. 2014. *Religious Narrative, Cognition and Culture: Image and Word in the Mind of Narrative*. New York: Routledge.

Gervais, Will M. and Joseph Henrich. 2010. "The Zeus Problem: Why Representational Content Biases Cannot Explain Faith in Gods." *Journal of Cognition and Culture* 10(3): 383–389. doi: 10.1163/156853710x531249.

Guthrie, Stewart. 1980. "A Cognitive Theory of Religion." *Current Anthropology* 21(2): 181–94. doi: 10.1086/202429.

Guthrie, Stewart. 1993. *Faces in the Clouds*. New York: Oxford University Press.

Henrich, Joseph and Richard McElreath. 2003. "The Evolution of Cultural Evolution." *Evolutionary Anthropology: Issues, News, and Reviews* 12(3): 123–135. doi: 10.1002/evan.10110.

Heywood, Bethany T. and J. M. Bering. 2014. "'Meant to Be': How Religious Beliefs and Cultural Religiosity Affect the Implicit Bias to Think Teleologically." *Religion, Brain and Behavior* 4(3): 183–201. doi: 10.1080/2153599x.2013.782888.

Hodge, K. Mitch. 2008. "Descartes' Mistake: How Afterlife Beliefs Challenge the Assumption That Humans Are Intuitive Cartesian Substance Dualists." *Journal of Cognition and Culture* 8(3): 387–415. doi: 10.1163/156853708x358236.

Hodge, K. Mitch. 2011. "On Imagining the Afterlife." *Journal of Cognition and Culture* 11(3–4): 367–389. doi: 10.1163/156853711x591305.

Järnefelt, Elisa, Caitlin F. Canfield, and Deborah Kelemen. 2015. "The Divided Mind of a Disbeliever: Intuitive Beliefs about Nature as Purposefully Created among Different Groups of Non-religious Adults." *Cognition* 140: 72–88. doi: 10.1016/j.cognition.2015.02.005.

Johnson, Dominic D. P. 2005. "God's Punishment and Public Goods." *Human Nature* 16(4): 410–446. doi: 10.1007/s12110-005-1017-0.

Jong, J. (2013). "Explaining Religion (Away?)." *Sophia* 52(3): 521–533.

Kelemen, Deborah. 2004. "Are Children 'Intuitive Theists'? Reasoning about Purpose and Design in Nature." *Psychological Science* 15(5): 295–301. doi: 10.1111/j.0956-7976.2004.00672.x.

Knight, Nicola. 2008. "Yukatek Maya Children's Attributions of Belief to Natural and Non-natural Entities." *Journal of Cognition and Culture* 8(3): 235–243. doi: 10.1163/156853708x358164.

Konvalinka, Ivana, Dimitris Xygalatas, Joseph Bulbulia, Uffe Schjødt, Else-Marie Jegindø, Sebastian Wallot, Guy Van Orden, and Andreas Roepstorff. 2011. "Synchronized Arousal between Performers and Related Spectators in a Fire-Walking Ritual." *Proceedings of the National Academy of Sciences* 108(20): 8514–8519.

Lanman, Jonathan. 2012. "On the Non-evolution of Atheism and the Importance of Definitions and Data." *Religion, Brain and Behavior* 2(1): 76–78. doi: 10.1080/2153599x.2012.667950.

Lawson, E. Thomas. 2000. "Towards a Cognitive Science of Religion." *Numen-Leiden* 47(3): 338–348. doi: 10.1163/156852700511586.

Lawson, E. Thomas and Robert N. McCauley. 1990. *Rethinking Religion: Connecting Cognition and Culture*. Cambridge: Cambridge University Press.

Leech, David, and Aku Visala. 2011. "The Cognitive Science of Religion: Implications for Theism?" *Zygon* 46(1): 47–64.

Legare, Cristine H. and Susan A. Gelman. 2008. "Bewitchment, Biology, or Both: The Co-existence of Natural and Supernatural Explanatory Frameworks across Development." *Cognitive Science* 32(4): 607–642. doi: 10.1080/03640210802066766.

Legare, Cristine H., E. Margaret Evans, Karl S. Rosengren, and Paul L. Harris. 2012. "The Coexistence of Natural and Supernatural Explanations across Cultures and Development." *Child Development* 83(3): 779–793. doi: 10.1111/j.1467-8624.2012.01743.x.

Lindeman, Marjaana and Annika M. Svedholm. 2012. "What's in a Term? Paranormal, Superstitious, Magical and Supernatural Beliefs by Any Other Name Would Mean the Same." *Review of General Psychology* 16(3): 241–245. doi: 10.1037/a0027158.

McNamara, Patrick. 2009. *The Neuroscience of Religious Experience*. Cambridge: Cambridge University Press.

Malley, Brian. 2004. *How the Bible Works: An Anthropological Study of Evangelical Biblicism.* Walnut Creek, CA: Rowman AltaMira.

Martin, Luther H. and Donald Wiebe. 2012. "Religious Studies as a Scientific Discipline: The Persistence of a Delusion." *Journal of the American Academy of Religion* 80(3): 587–597. doi: 10.1093/jaarel/lfs030.

Marx, Karl. 1970. *Introduction to A Contribution to the Critique of Hegel's Philosophy of Right.* Collected Works, volume 3. New York: Cambridge University Press.

McCauley, Robert N. 2000. "The Naturalness of Religion and the Unnaturalness of Science." In F. Keil and R. Wilson (eds.), *Explanation and Cognition*, 61–85. Cambridge, MA: MIT Press.

McCauley, Robert N. 2011. *Why Religion Is Natural and Science Is Not.* New York: Oxford University Press.

McKay, Ryan and Harvey Whitehouse. 2014. "Religion and Morality." *Psychological Bulletin* 141(2): 447. doi: 10.1037/a0038455.

McKay, Ryan, Charles Efferson, Harvey Whitehouse, and Ernst Fehr. 2011. "Wrath of God: Religious Primes and Punishment." *Proceedings of the Royal Society of London B: Biological Sciences* 278(1713): 1858–1863. doi: 10.1098/rspb.2010.2125.

Nichols, Shaun. 2007. "Imagination and Immortality: Thinking of Me." *Synthese* 159(2): 215–233. doi: 10.1007/s11229-007-9205-6.

Nicholson, Hugh. 2014. "Social Identity Processes in the Development of Maximally Counterintuitive Theological Concepts: Consubstantiality and No-Self." *Journal of the American Academy of Religion* 82(3): 736–770. doi: 10.1093/jaarel/lfu029.

Norenzayan, Ara. 2013. *Big Gods: How Religion Transformed Cooperation and Conflict.* Princeton, NJ: Princeton University Press.

Norenzayan, Ara and Azim F. Shariff. 2008. "The Origin and Evolution of Religious Prosociality." *Science* 322(5898): 58–62. doi: 10.1126/science.1158757.

Norenzayan, Ara, Azim F. Shariff, Will M. Gervais, Aiyana K. Willard, Rita A. McNamara, Edward Slingerland, and Joseph Henrich. 2014. "The Cultural Evolution of Prosocial Religions." *Behavioral and Brain Sciences*, 1–86. doi: 10.1017/s0140525x14001356.

Oviedo, Lluis. 2015. "Religious Cognition as a Dual-Process: Developing the Model." *Method and Theory in the Study of Religion* 27(1): 31–58. doi: 10.1163/15700682-12341288.

Piazza, Jared, Jesse M. Bering, and Gordon Ingram. 2011. "'Princess Alice Is Watching You': Children's Belief in an Invisible Person Inhibits Cheating." *Journal of Experimental Child Psychology* 109(3): 311–320. doi: 10.1016/j.jecp.2011.02.003.

Purzycki, Benjamin Grant. 2013. "The Minds of Gods: A Comparative Study of Supernatural Agency." *Cognition* 129(1): 163–179. doi: 10.1016/j.cognition.2013.06.010.

Purzycki, Benjamin Grant, and Aiyana K. Willard. In press. "MCI Theory: A Critical Discussion." *Religion, Brain and Behavior.* doi: 10.1080/2153599x.2015.1024915.

Pyysiäinen, Ilkka. 2001. *How Religion Works: Towards a New Cognitive Science of Religion.* Leiden: Brill.

Richerson, Peter J. and Robert Boyd. 2008. *Not by Genes Alone: How Culture Transformed Human Evolution.* Chicago, IL: University of Chicago Press.

Richert, Rebekah A. and Justin L. Barrett. 2005. "Do You See What I See? Young Children's Assumptions about God's Perceptual Abilities." *International Journal for the Psychology of Religion* 15(4): 283–295. doi: 10.1207/s15327582ijpr1504_2.

Richert, Rebekah A. and Paul L. Harris. 2006. "The Ghost in My Body: Children's Developing Concept of the Soul." *Journal of Cognition and Culture* 6(3): 409–427. doi: 10.1163/156853706778554913.

Richert, Rebekah A., Harvey Whitehouse, and Emma Stewart. 2005. "Memory and Analogical Thinking in High-Arousal Rituals." In Harvey Whitehouse and Robert N. McCauley (eds.), *Mind and Religion: Psychological and Cognitive Foundations of Religiosity*, 127–145. Lanham, MD: Rowman & Littlefield.

Schjoedt, Uffe, Jesper Sørensen, Kristoffer Laigaard Nielbo, Dimitris Xygalatas, Paganiotis Mitkidis, and Soseph Bulbulia. 2013. "Cognitive Resource Depletion in Religious Interactions." *Religion, Brain and Behavior* 3(1): 39–55. doi: 10.1080/2153599x.2012.736714.

Schloss, Jeffrey P. and Michael J. Murray. 2011. "Evolutionary Accounts of Belief in Supernatural Punishment: A Critical Review." *Religion, Brain and Behavior* 1(1): 46–99. doi: 10.1080/2153599x.2011.558707.

Slingerland, Edward. 2008. "Who's Afraid of Reductionism? The Study of Religion in the Age of Cognitive Science." *Journal of the American Academy of Religion* 76(2): 375–411.

Slingerland, Edward. 2013. "Body and Mind in Early China: An Integrated Humanities–Science Approach." *Journal of the American Academy of Religion* 81(1): 1–50. doi: 10.1093/jaarel/lfs094.

Slingerland, Edward and Joseph Bulbulia. 2011. "Evolutionary Science and the Study of Religion." *Religion* 41(3): 1–23. doi: 10.1080/0048721x.2011.604513.

Slingerland, Edward and Brenton Sullivan. In press. "Durkheim with Data: The Database of Religious History (DRH)." *Journal of the American Academy of Religion*.

Slone, D. Jason. 2004. *Theological Incorrectness: Why Religious People Believe What They Shouldn't*. New York: Oxford University Press.

Slone, D. Jason and Joel G. Mort. 2004. "On the Epistemological Magic of Ethnographic Analysis." *Method and Theory in the Study of Religion* 16(2): 149–163. doi: 10.1163/1570068042360233.

Smith, Jonathan Z. 2004. *Relating Religion: Essays in the Study of Religion*. Chicago, IL: University of Chicago Press.

Sørensen, Jester. 2007. *A Cognitive Theory of Magic*. Walnut Creek, CA: Rowman AltaMira.

Sosis, Richard. 2009. "The Adaptationist-Byproduct Debate on the Evolution of Religion: Five Misunderstandings of the Adaptationist Program." *Journal of Cognition and Culture* 9(3): 315–332. doi: 10.1163/156770909x12518536414411.

Sperber, Dan. 1996. *Explaining Culture*. Oxford: Blackwell Publishers.

Taves, Ann. 2011. *Religious Experience Reconsidered: A Building-Block Approach to the Study of Religion and Other Special Things*. Princeton, NJ: Princeton University Press.

Taylor, Mark C. (ed.). 1998. *Critical Terms for Religious Studies*. Chicago, IL: University of Chicago Press.

Trigg, Roger and Justin L. Barrett (eds.). 2014. *The Roots of Religion: Exploring the Cognitive Science of Religion*. Farnham: Ashgate Publishing.

Turchin, Peter, Harvey Whitehouse, Pieter Francois, Edward Slingerland, and Mark Collard. 2012. "A Historical Database of Sociocultural Evolution." *Cliodynamics: The Journal of Theoretical and Mathematical History* 3(2): 271–273.

Tylor, Edward Burnett. 1871. *Primitive Culture: Researches into the Development of Mythology, Philosophy, Religion, Art, and Custom*, vol. 2. London: Murray.

Watson-Jones, Rachel E., Harvey Whitehouse, and Cristine H Legare (2016). "In-Group Ostracism Increases High Fidelity Imitation in Early Childhood." *Psychological Science* 27(1): 34–42.

Watts, Fraser and León P. Turner (eds.). 2014. *Evolution, Religion, and Cognitive Science: Critical and Constructive Essays*. Oxford: Oxford University Press.

Watts, Joseph, Simon J. Greenhill, Quentin D. Atkinson, Thomas E. Currie, Joseph Bulbulia, and Russell D. Gray. 2015. "Broad Supernatural Punishment but Not Moralizing High Gods Precede the Evolution of Political Complexity in Austronesia." *Proceedings of the Royal Society of London B: Biological Sciences* 282(1804): 20142556. doi: 10.1098/rspb.2014.2556.

White, Claire. 2015. "Establishing Personal Identity in Reincarnation: Minds and Bodies Reconsidered." *Journal of Cognition and Culture* 15(3–4): 402–429. doi: 10.1163/15685373-12342158.

White, Claire. 2016. "Cross-Cultural Similarities in Reasoning about Personal Continuity in Reincarnation: Evidence from South India." *Religion, Brain and Behavior* 6(2): 130–153.

White, Claire. In press. The Cognitive Foundations of Reincarnation. *Method and Theory in the Study of Religion.*

White, Claire, Robert Kelly, and Shaun Nichols. 2015. "Remembering Past Lives: Intuitions about Memory and Personal Identity in Reincarnation." In Helen De Cruz and Ryan Nichols (eds.), *The Cognitive Science of Religion and Its Philosophical Implications*, 169–196. London: Bloomsbury Academic.

White, Claire., Maya Marin, and Daniel M.T. Fessler. In press. "Not Just Dead Meat: An Evolutionary Account of Corpse Treatment in Mortuary Rituals." *Journal of Cognition and Culture.*

Whitehouse, Harvey. 1995. *Inside the Cult: Religious Innovation and Transmission in Papua New Guinea.* New York: Oxford University Press.

Whitehouse, Harvey. 2000. *Arguments and Icons: Divergent Modes of Religiosity.* New York: Oxford University Press.

Whitehouse, Harvey. 2004. *Modes of Religiosity: A Cognitive Theory of Religious Transmission.* Walnut Creek, CA: Rowman AltaMira.

Whitehouse, Harvey and Luther H. Martin (eds.). 2004. *Theorizing Religions Past: Archaeology, History, and Cognition.* Walnut Creek, CA: Rowman AltaMira.

Whitehouse, Harvey and Robert N. McCauley. 2005. *Mind and Religion: Psychological and Cognitive Foundations of Religiosity.* Walnut Creek, CA: Rowman AltaMira.

Whitehouse, Harvey, Ken Kahn, Michael E. Hochberg, and Joanna J. Bryson. 2012. "The Role for Simulations in Theory Construction for the Social Sciences: Case Studies Concerning Divergent Modes of Religiosity." *Religion, Brain and Behavior* 2(3): 182–201. doi: 10.1080/2153599x.2012.691033.

Wilson, David Sloan. 2008. "Evolution and Religion: The Transformation of the Obvious." In Joseph Bulbulia, Richard Sosis, Erica Harris, Russell Genet, Cheryl Genet, and Karen Wyman (eds.), *The Evolution of Religion: Studies, Theories, Critiques*, 23–30. Bakersfield, CA: Collins Foundation Press.

Xygalatas, Dimitris. 2014. *The Burning Saints: Cognition and Culture in the Fire-walking Rituals of the Anastenaria.* New York: Routledge.

Xygalatas, Dimitris, Ivana Konvalinka, Joseph Bulbulia, and Andreas Roepstorff. 2011. "Quantifying Collective Effervescence: Heart-Rate Dynamics at a Fire-Walking Ritual." *Communicative and Integrative Biology* 4(6): 735–738. doi: 10.4161/cib.17609.

13

"Show Me the Money": Big-Money Donors and the Cognitive Science of Religion

Brad Stoddard

In 2003, a scholar at the Graduate Theological Union reviewed two new books—*Religion Explained: The Evolutionary Origins of Religious Thought* by Pascal Boyer, and *How Religion Works: Towards a New Cognitive Science of Religion* by Ilkka Pyysiäinen—for the *Journal of the American Academy of Religion*. The reviewer dismissed both the authors and their books, lamenting that "the high social prestige enjoyed by cognitive scientists" would ensure that the authors' ideas were "likely to be taken more seriously than their intellectual substance should merit" (Bulkeley 2003: 671). These authors, the reviewer decried, were "unapologetically hostile ... toward religion" (ibid.) and their cognitive theories were unnecessarily reductionist and otherwise dismissive of religion. To correct this, he argued, "Religious Studies scholars would do well to apply their critical skills to the task of refuting the grandiose generalizations and simplistic denunciations of religion that fill the pages of [these] books" (ibid.). Instead of dismissing religion, the reviewer concluded, cognitive science should help illumine "the rich and colorful diversity of human religious life" (ibid.: 674).

I open this essay by citing this exchange, as it exposes an interesting rift in the cognitive science of religion (CSR). For some scholars (like the authors of the aforementioned books), cognitive science helps explain, reduce, and ultimately invalidate religion. Other scholars argue the opposite, as they believe that cognitive science justifies religion, as it authenticates religion as a natural and healthy component of human cognition. In other words, CSR is not a united field; rather, it consists of various parties with competing and conflicting interests.

In "What the Cognitive Science of Religion Is (and Is Not)" (Chapter 12, this volume), however, Claire White attempts to move beyond these two modes of thinking as she articulates a defense of the field as consistent with the larger scientific study of religion.[1] White offers a valuable and well-written introduction to CSR, where she briefly summarizes the history of the field and itemizes the key ideas that constitute it. She concludes, "The ultimate goal of CSR is to identify, and then explain, how and why some ideas and practices that are labeled religious are cross-culturally recurrent, and how they are modified by cultural input" (p. 106, this volume). For White, CSR combined with cultural studies help explain the development, evolution, and future of "ideas and practices" commonly labeled as "religion" or "religious."

In opposition to White, however, several scholars have criticized the larger field of CSR (see Day 2007; McCutcheon 2010, 2012; Modern in progress). While I find myself largely sympathetic to many of the issues and concerns they raise, in this paper, I will sidestep these issues and instead outline an alternate (or perhaps an additional) methodology for studying CSR. This methodology stems out of my personal research interests, and ideally, it resonates with the goals of the North American Association for the Study of Religion's (NAASR) executive administrators, who organized this panel to put scholars who are not CSR "experts" in dialogue with scholars who are.

To this end, this chapter does not engage White or the competing truth claims proffered by proponents of CSR. Instead, this essay focuses on the discourse of CSR, as it argues that the rhetoric of "CSR" is an authorizing discourse that a variety of actors deploy to competing and contradictory ends. Specifically, this chapter explores the Templeton Foundation's interest in funding CSR research, paying particular attention to the political, economic, and socio-cultural interests that motivate the research produced by Templeton Foundation-funded studies.

The academic study of religion has always relied to various degrees on private and governmental donors, who beginning in the larger context of the Cold War became interested in funding research and pedagogy that address religion (see McCutcheon 2004). With the end of the Cold War and the demise of the Soviet Union, one might have expected such funding to dissipate, but arguably the opposite occurred as a variety of private donors, philanthropic organizations, and other non-profits have intervened to fund a host of religious research. Organizations such as the Lilly Endowment and the John D. and Catherine T. MacArthur Foundation are among the prominent organizations that provide funding for religious research, in addition to individual donors such as former Senator John C. Danforth, who recently donated $30 million to open the John C. Danforth Center on Religion and Politics at Washington University (Levitt 2009).

In this larger world of big-money donors, however, the John Templeton Foundation is perhaps the largest and most consistent donor, as it annually donates millions of dollars to a variety of scholars who research religion, including scholars interested in CSR. The Templeton Foundation's interest in religion stems from its founder's personal interest, as Templeton fancied himself a *bricoleur* of sorts who attempted to reconcile scientific inquiry and religious pluralism. Sir John Templeton was a former Rhodes Scholar turned businessman and entrepreneur who amassed a large fortune in the second-half of the twentieth century (Herrmann 1998). Throughout his career, he supported various conservative organizations, think tanks, and other proponents of free market capitalism. In 1964 he renounced his U.S. citizenship and moved to the Bahamas, which allowed him to retain over $100 million he would have otherwise paid in U.S. taxes (Bauman 2007: 15).

Religiously, Templeton was a lifelong Presbyterian who served for over four decades on the board of trustees of Princeton Theological Seminary, the largest

Presbyterian seminary. In addition to his commitment to Presbyterianism, however, he was open to receiving religious truths from other religions as well. "I am still an enthusiastic Christian," he said, "but why shouldn't I try to learn more? Why shouldn't I go to Hindu services? Why shouldn't I go to Muslim services? If you are not egotistical, you will welcome the opportunity to learn more" (Fausto 2014). His commitment to religious pluralism would influence the various philanthropic investments he made as founder and president of the John Templeton Foundation. Templeton created the Foundation in 1987, and it has since spent millions of dollars funding the academic study of religion, including research that addresses CSR (Ehrenreich 2007).

I was first exposed to the Templeton Foundation's tremendous influence not only on the academic study of religion, but on religion and public policy more broadly, while researching for my dissertation on faith-based prisons and other faith-based correctional facilities. The architects and proponents of faith-based correctional facilities repeatedly cited Templeton Foundation-funded research when they successfully lobbied state governments to create the nation's first faith-based correctional dormitories.[2] Specifically, they cited the work of Byron Johnson, who in his magnum opus *More God, Less Crime* (published by Templeton Press), argued "that faith-motivated individuals, faith-based organizations, and the transformative power of faith itself are proven keys in reducing crime and improving the effectiveness of our criminal justice system" (Johnson 2005: xi). In the same book, Johnson also boasted that he receives over $1 million annually from private organizations and other donors collectively interested in supporting his research, which consistently advocates for religious solutions to social problems such as a crime and criminality. Judging from the footnotes in his numerous publications, the Templeton Foundation has been a major donor to Johnson's work for some time.

More recently, however, the Templeton Foundation allocated millions of dollars to advance CSR research. As a case in point, the Templeton Foundation allocated up to $3 million for a project they called "God in Minds: The Science of Religious Cognition" (John Templeton Foundation 2013). In 2007 the Foundation donated over $3.8 million to prominent CSR researcher Justin Barrett and his colleagues for their project, "Empirical Expansion in the Cognitive Science of Religion and Theology" (John Templeton Foundation 2007). The Foundation also awarded smaller grants to CSR researchers, such as the $268,000 it awarded to Robert McCauley and the comparably modest grant of $74,000 it awarded to James Jones. Clearly, the Templeton Foundation has a vested interest in promoting CSR research, but the questions remain: Why is the Templeton Foundation interested in CSR? How does CSR relate to the Foundation's broader economic and political goals? And how, exactly, do the Foundation's researchers constitute or conceive of "religion"?

A comprehensive answer would prove longer than the allocated space, but at least a few preliminary conclusions are readily evident. The Templeton Foundation would suggest that their interest in religion stems from its founder's desire to reconcile science and religion. Where many people (including many of the founders of the academic study of religion) see an inherent tension between the two, Templeton apparently believed that religion and science not only can, but should complement each other, as they both address what the Templeton Foundation refers to as "the Big Questions."[3]

Scholars are aware, however, that the world "religion" is an empty or floating signifier, and that people use the word "religion" as a generic term when they actually mean something much more specific.[4] To understand what the Templeton Foundation means when it references "religion," we could examine the specific scholars who receive the Templeton Foundation's research awards and their research projects, where we find people like Miroslav Volf, a prominent theologian at Yale Divinity School who recently secured from the Templeton Foundation a $4.2 million grant for a research project titled "Theology of Joy and the Good Life" (Yale Center for Faith and Culture. 2015). Collectively, Volf and the other recipients of Templeton Foundation research grants—whether they research CSR, crime, or other research projects—advance notions of religiosity that are compatible with the free market, libertarian economic system that the Templeton Foundation champions. "Religion," in this research, functions similarly to what Althusser referred to as an ideological state apparatus insofar as it is a non-government entity that upholds the libertarian economic and political order that Templeton envisioned. Templeton Foundation-funded CSR research can assist in creating this order, as it naturalizes "religion" as a cognitively rooted, natural, and otherwise healthy aspect of social life. Admittedly, this is not the type of CSR research that White and many of the scholars interested in CSR pursue, but this acknowledgement should not detract from the larger points, first, that the field of CSR research is wide and diverse, and second, that people with competing agendas cultivate and deploy CSR discourse to advance political and economic agendas.

In conclusion, this brief summary of the Templeton Foundation's interest in CSR research provides but one case study of the rhetorical (and economic) value of CSR discourse. As the opening vignette suggests, the discourse of CSR serves a variety of competing goals, and analyses that examine these goals are legitimate grounds for academic inquiry. CSR continues to be an authorizing discourse that various parties deploy, often to conflicting ends. When we study the proponents of CSR, whether they are Pascal Boyer, Justin Barrett, or the Templeton Foundation, we can recognize and identify the human, all too human interests that lurk behind this new model of religiosity.

Brad Stoddard is and Assistant Professor of religious studies at McDaniel College.

Notes

1. To this end, White's analysis is seemingly congruent with the vision of the North American Association for the Study of Religion (NAASR) as articulated by its founders (see Chapter 1, this volume; see also Geertz and McCutcheon 2000).

2. For example, the State of Texas created the nation's first faith-based correctional dormitory. As they laid the administrative foundation for this dorm, the Texas Advisory Task Force on Faith-Based Community Service Groups issued a document citing and quoting Byron Johnson (see Advisory Task Force on Faith-Based Community Service Groups 1996).

3. "The Big Questions" is a phrase that the Templeton Foundation repeatedly uses (e.g., see John Templeton Foundation undated a, undated b; see also www.bigquestionsonline.com).

4. For a recent example of the history and critique of the category of religion, see Nongbri (2013).

References

Advisory Task Force on Faith-Based Community Service Groups. 1996. *Faith in Action ... A New Vision for Church-State Cooperation in Texas*. December. Texas: Advisory Task Force on Faith-Based Community Service Groups.

Bauman, Robert E. 2007. *Where to Stash Your Cash Legally: Offshore Havens of the World*. Delray Beach, FL: The Sovereign Society.

Bulkeley, Kelly. 2003. "Review." *Journal of the American Academy of Religion* 71(3): 671–674.

Day, Matthew. 2007. "Let's Be Realistic: Evolutionary Complexity, Epistemic Probablism, and the Cognitive Science of Religion." *The Harvard Theological Review* 100(1): 47–64.

Ehrenreich, Barbara. 2007. "John Templeton's Universe." *The Nation* (October 22). Available at www.thenation.com/article/john-templetons-universe (accessed 10 July 2016).

Fausto, Rose Fres. 2014. "Meet Sir John Templeton." *The Philippine Star* (January 29). Available at www.philstar.com/health-and-family/2014/01/29/1284095/meet-sir-john-templeton (accessed 25 July 2016).

Geertz, Armin W., and Russell T. McCutcheon. 2000. "The Role of Method and Theory in the IAHR." *Method and Theory in the Study of Religion* 12: 3–37.

Herrmann, Robert L. 1998. *Sir John Templeton from Wall Street to Humility Theology*. Philadelphia, PA: Templeton Foundation Press.

Johnson, Byron R. 2011. *More God, Less Crime: Why Faith Matters and How It Could Matter More*. West Conshohocken, PA: Templeton Press.

John Templeton Foundation. 2007. "Empirical Expansion in the Cognitive Science of Religion and Theology." Available at www.templeton.org/what-we-fund/grants/empirical-expansion-in-the-cognitive-science-of-religion-and-theology (accessed 10 July 2016).

John Templeton Foundation. 2013. "Gods in Minds: The Science of Religious Cognition." Available at www.templeton.org/what-we-fund/funding-competitions/gods-in-minds-the-science-of-religious-cognition (accessed 10 July 2016).

John Templeton Foundation. Undated a. "Big Questions Essay Series." Available at www.templeton.org/signature-programs/big-questions-essay-series (accessed 10 July 2016).

John Templeton Foundation. Undated b. "Science and the Big Questions." Available at www.templeton.org/what-we-fund/core-funding-areas/science-and-the-big-questions (accessed 10 July 2016).

Levitt, Aimee. 2009. "Danforth Foundation Gives Wash. U. $30 Million to Study Religion and Politics." *Riverfront Times* (December 19). Available at www.riverfronttimes.com/

newsblog/2009/12/16/danforth-foundation-gives-wash-u-30-million-to-study-religion-and-politics (accessed 10 July 2016).

McCutcheon, Russell T. 2004. "'Just Follow the Money': The Cold War, the Humanistic Study of Religion, and the Fallacy of Insufficient Cynicism." *Culture and Religion* 5(1): 41–69.

McCutcheon, Russell T. 2010. "Will Your Cognitive Anchor Hold in the Storms of Culture?" *Journal of the American Academy of Religion* 78(4): 1182–1193.

McCutcheon, Russell T. 2012. "A Tale of Nouns and Verbs: Rejoinder to Ann Taves." *Journal of the American Academy of Religion* 80(1): 236–240.

Modern, John. In progress. "The Religion Machine, or a Particular History of Cognitive Science." Book manuscript.

Nongbri, Brent. 2013. *Before Religion: A History of a Modern Concept.* New Haven, CT: Yale University Press,

Yale Center for Faith and Culture. 2015. "Yale Center for Faith & Culture Awarded $4.2M Grant to Study Theology of Joy and the Good Life." September 10. Available at http://faith.yale.edu/news/yale-center-faith-culture-awarded-42m-grant-study-theology-joy-and-good-life (accessed 10 July 2016).

14

Of Elephants and Riders: Cognition, Reason, and Will in the Study of Religion

Matt Sheedy

In my own area of critical social theory, expertise tends to take the form of depth-knowledge of a particular thinker, thinkers, or school of thought, and is not always as methodologically rigorous as it could be, nor does it necessarily pay enough heed to the empirical work of the natural and social sciences.[1] Despite the problems that any explanatory definition of religion entails (see Arnal and McCutcheon 2013a), the search for a common ground is inevitable, and can lead to many interesting (and unexpected) cross-pollinations. In this respect, having "outsiders" such as myself appraise some of the claims of CSR strikes me as a useful exercise in testing both its clarity and its ability to communicate with other "critical" scholars in the study of religion, who will have likely been exposed to a limited number of books and essays that were recommended as *central*, or at least representative examples for preliminary engagement. Such a vantage point may even help underscore what is lacking in more popular iterations of the field, regardless of how many CSR scholars may purport to have already "addressed" this or that critique. Ultimately, if such critiques have not been adequately understood, taken seriously, and incorporated, then sub-disciplinary tensions will likely remain at a stalemate, like some big emotional elephant in the room with various frustrated riders trying desperately to assert their own reason and will on an uncooperative beast.

Several scholars that I've come across in my brief adventures in CSR point to Lawson and McCauley for having spurred the development of this approach with their 1990 book *Rethinking Religion: Connecting Cognition and Culture*,[2] a point that Justin Barrett (2011: 232) affirms when he writes that what initially distinguished CSR was a desire to bring cognitive and empirical methods to bear on the study of religion, to "science it up," as it were. These methods could then be used to "explain" religious phenomena and not merely "interpret" them, as is common with more hermeneutical approaches, theological or otherwise, and can be seen in certain strains of critical theory.

According to Robert McCauley and Emma Cohen (2010: 779–780), antecedents to CSR include theories of metaphysics and epistemology that raised questions about the plausibility of supernatural agents and their various properties (see Proctor 2005). Where CSR seems to differ from these earlier approaches is in its emphasis on adopting a naturalistic and experimental approach toward ideas and practices that in some way relate to the "supernatural," and to examine those a priori or "built-in" cognitive and evolutionary mechanisms that determine the range of "natural" behaviors and responses in well-functioning human brains.[3]

While I don't want to reduce the evident variety of methods and theories in CSR (see overviews by Barrett 2011; McCauley and Cohen 2010; Geertz 2010), the idea of minimally counter-intuitive agents appears to be a core concept that helps to explain the generation of supernatural ideas as a "natural" by-product of our cognitive make-up, with evolutionary models stepping in to help to explain cultural transmissions and adaptions. Whereas cognitive methods are interested in the supposed content of "religious" ideas (e.g., characteristics of Gods and demons), evolutionary approaches focus on so-called "religious" behaviors, such as rituals.[4] It also seems evident, by the account of several CSR scholars, that this approach is self-consciously reductive, and bares certain similarities to E. B. Tylor's (1871: 8) definition of religion as "the belief in spiritual beings." Herein lies what I take to be a significant challenge for CSR that has not, to my knowledge, been adequately addressed; namely, the implications of using the term "religion" to describe processes that are said to occur in all times and places.

In his recent essay "Has the Cognitive Science of Religion (Re)defined 'Religion'?" (2014), Juraj Franek presents a range of ideas on what constitutes a "cognitive definition of religion," all of which in some way maintain the idea of counter-intuitive agents as the main operating feature (ibid.: 6–9). What I found both interesting and unique about Franek's argument is that he takes up a variety of social constructionist critiques of the category religion, citing Timothy Fitzgerald, Craig Martin, and Russell McCutcheon, among others. While acknowledging a few of their concerns, Franek argues that without an approximate definition of religion, the discipline will be unable to demarcate both its object of study and its basic theoretical premises (ibid.: 4). Franek defines two types of social constructionist approaches. The first follows a "family resemblances" model of polythetic classification,[5] where particular items on a list are grouped together based on similarity (ibid.: 15). In contrast to this model, which Franek terms "power innocent," is a "power-based" social constructionism, following the likes of Nietzsche, Foucault, and Bourdieu. Here the arbitrariness of classification is signaled as "culture-specific and prone to diachronic change," where the "transfer of meaning from one generation to another" is best understood in relation to existing distributions of power.

Against these critiques, Franek argues that CSR shows that the category religion is not entirely arbitrary since its grounding in the idea of counter-intuitive agents is "constrained by our evolved mental architecture," while noting that the "power-based" critique can at least be minimized by adhering to "methodological principles based on the empirical testability of hypothesis" (ibid.: 19). Such a careful approach, he continues, is not "purposefully invented to cement power relations desirable for their inventors," since "they are generated naturally as byproducts of the human brain, with the possibility of political (mis)use as an optional, secondary development" (ibid.: 26).

While there is considerably more to Franek's argument, two problems stand out in particular. First, by consciously reducing a definition of religion to minimally counter-intuitive agents, he does not appear to avoid what he calls the "power-based" social constructionist critique. In a nutshell, by framing MCIs and related cognitive mechanisms as central to a definition of religion, Franek makes them both *primary* and *determinative* of all so-called "religious" social formations. As an example, he draws on the work of Ilkka Pyysiäinen, who argues, contrary to Durkheim, that Buddhism is in fact a religion following a minimal CSR definition. Pyysiäinen writes: "Buddha and the buddhas most clearly belong to the category of counter-intuitive beings, and ... Buddhism thus need not be problematic with regard to a global concept of religion" (quoted by Franek 2014: 24). Here Pyysiäinen privileges a definition of Buddhism that conceives of supernatural beings as central, which not only displaces common perceptions of, say, Theravada and "Western" Buddhism as peripheral, but presumes this definition to be consistent in all times and places. Among other things, this appears to fall into an essentialist trap of proclaiming what religions *are*, rather than what they *do* and are made to do. Such attention to re-describing "religion" need not undermine the explanatory aims of CSR, as scholars like Lawson and McCauley (1993) and Jason Sloan (2004) contend,[6] but rather sharpen our attention to the political nature of the term and its implications (Asad 2003; Fitzgerald 2007; Martin 2014; Masuzawa 2005).

Of all of the critiques of CSR that I have come across, I have found those by Maurice Bloch (2008) and James Laidlaw (2007) to be the most persuasive.[7] For Bloch, placing emphasis on "religion" or the "supernatural" is misguided for at least two reasons. First, such categories are part of what he calls a much larger "transcendental social" network that cannot be neatly divided up between, say, politics, religion, or gender, which are themselves constructed and contingent categories, and rely on ideas that are both natural *and* supernatural. Second, and relatedly, Bloch argues that what counts as intuitive or counter-intuitive is context-dependent, which suggests that so-called supernatural "beliefs" may be conditioned by things like interests and group norms rather than simply emerging "bottom-up" from human brains (Bloch 2005). Here the "imaginative" dimension looms large, where, as the case *may* be, it is the "status function" of supernatural ideas that make them appealing and not their cognitive intuitiveness *per se*.[8]

James Laidlaw, for his part, argues that CSR is important for giving us an account of mental operations involved in some aspects of normative religious thought and action, such as why ideas of gods, ghosts, and magic are so ubiquitous. He is critical, however, of how CSR privileges cognitive mechanisms over contextual interpretations, arguing that "religion" cannot be explained analytically, but only historically (Laidlaw 2007: 212–213). Part of the reason for this is what may be an unresolvable chicken and egg problem that asks whether our thinking is better explained by mental causes or the various *reasons* agents hold,[9] along with the role of *imagination* and *will* in interpretive processes (ibid.: 214–215). For example, when it comes to supernatural beliefs, Laidlaw argues that one cannot determine in advance whether beliefs are primary or even believed in, since what is at stake could just as easily be things like prestige or social advantage, group cohesion, social pressure, etc. (for a related argument, see Habermas 2008). Moreover, such beliefs are always and already constituted through particular practices and institutions, performed in myriad ways, for multiple reasons, and are contingent on multiple ways of knowing (Laidlaw 2007: 224–229).

Claire White begins her paper with what appears to be a fairly standard disclaimer among CSR scholars regarding the hostility they often face from outsiders,[10] which cannot be easy given its propensity to grate against most theologies, along with its striving for a reductionist theory of religion. Among the range of contested theories in CSR, White notes debates about the role of HADDs and MCIs, as well as "the relationship between theological correctness and folk concepts of religion," and the "cultural prevalence of moralizing gods and the transition to large-scale societies" (p. 97, this volume). I mention these latter two examples in particular because they appear to signal attention to the role of language use, narrative, and power dynamics within social formations that are deemed religious, along with a socio-political analysis of the function of moralizing gods as societies evolve over time. In both cases, there would appear to be attention to historicizing "religion," which I hope Dr. White could elaborate on.

Regarding White's five key ideas (or "commitments") that minimally constitute the field, I was struck by a passage in Commitment 1, which she labels under the heading "There is no single entity that constitutes religion, but there are discernible patterns of thought and behavior that can be called 'religion'" (p. 98, this volume). White goes on to note that the term religion is "a convenient, general-purpose label," while advocating for a concept that is both reductive and polythetic at the same time. As she writes:

> From the perspective of the cognitive sciences, what constitutes religious systems is an assortment of recurring psychological predispositions and behaviors, expressed in a myriad of ways with differential environmental inputs. Correspondingly, we can expect these panhuman tendencies to express themselves in other cultural domains such as sport, art, music, and so on. In this respect, although these psychologically meaningful units may join together in ways to form distinctive religious systems, the units that constitute religion are not, in themselves, unique to it, because they are present in other cultural domains. (White, p. 99, this volume)

While I find myself in full agreement with the importance of analyzing and explaining "recurring psychological predispositions and behaviors," and the hypothesis that some of these may constitute "panhuman tendencies," as White contends, one question still looms large for me: who gets to decide which systems are "religious"? This is not an innocent question, since the reference to "sport, art, and music," suggests to me a very particular range of behaviors, which are often stereotypically described as the "collective effervescence" of group solidarity at a football match; feelings of awe and wonder when gazing upon a work of art; or an ineffable "experience" when listening music. While such descriptions may be common features of the rhetoric of many "religious" social formations, the priority they are given here appears to privilege a limited set of behaviors and risks playing into the rhetoric of authenticity as to what constitutes "religion." This bracketing off of religion from other things found in the social world is not unlike varieties of empiricism and even positivism, in the sense that it predetermines its object in advance and robs the pattern from its context (see Arnal and McCutcheon 2013b).

I find myself in full agreement with the opening sentiment in Commitment 2, where White notes the frustration of the pioneers of CSR with the "seemingly endless interpretative thick descriptions" (p. 99, this volume) that have plagued the study of religion and that often inhibited empirical explanations due to their vagueness and overgeneralization—the stock and trade of most introductory textbooks in the field. And while it is certainly valuable research to engage with what children and adults think about things like "gods and supernatural agents," the origins of the world, life after death, or "representations of the self and others during spirit possession" (p. 101, this volume), it is not at all clear to me how a cognitive approach to such questions controls for the contingent and constructed ideas that circulate within a variety of social fields—say, for example, between a lower class, four-year-old evangelical male, and an upper class, six-year-old United Church female, whose habitus includes an emphasis on gender and sexual equality. To put a finer point on it, the "bottom-up" approach that CSR advocates of "fractioning religious systems into empirically tractable units of analyses" (p. 103, this volume) seems to be at odds with the emphasis that White also places on paying attention to the "particular socio-cultural environments in which these ideas and behaviors operate." While I certainly agree with White that cognition and culture must be complementary, as she puts it, I am skeptical when she follows up this point by noting that, "one cannot say much about how ideas tend to be similar if one does not understand the ways in which these ideas and behaviors are modified" (ibid.). Here, again, it would appear that it is culture and context that modify our "built-in" cognitive make-up, rather than being caught up within it, leaving me to wonder whether certain iterations of CSR fall into a similar trap as "blank slate" theories, only here the mind is not blank but rather programmed in certain determinative ways, where culture modifies our base-line cognitive features and not the other way around (or not also, and at the same time). If, for example, a small child living in contemporary Atlanta hears a bump in the night and attributes some sort of agency to it, the explanations that she contrives or is told by her parents may have nothing at all to do with what is conventionally termed "religion." For ideas to be deemed religious requires a particular context within which this child has been socialized, leaving me to wonder whether so-called "religious ideas" arise from what White terms our "panhuman cognitive predispositions?"

Near the end of her paper, White addresses some controversies surrounding the idea that religion is natural, including, on the one hand, the charge that CSR is "explaining religion away," and thereby undermining it, and, on the other hand, suggesting that it is "part of our evolutionary heritage" and therefore inevitable.

What appears to be missing from this picture, not unlike in Franek's argument, is what I take to be the crux of what he calls the "power based" social constructionist critique; namely, that the classification of religion as determined by the existence of supernatural beings or super-empirical ideas, does not account for how the historically shifting category "religion" is conditioned by various legal, social, and political interests. Among other things, this emphasis seems to prioritize certain "folk" practices such as spirit possession, or, say, more literal interpretations of scripture as the *sine qua non* of religion, which thinkers like Dawkins and Dennett have zeroed-in on for certain political ends. If CSR is to meet the challenges of the social constructionist critique of the category "religion," it seems to me that it will need to move away from its operational desire to ground "religion" as a cognitive by-product of human minds, and pay much closer attention to historicizing the concepts that are used in each and every instance, in a phrase, the political uses that it is always and already caught up in.

Matt Sheedy received his Ph.D. (2015) in religious studies from the University of Manitoba, Winnipeg, and is co-editor of the *Bulletin for the Study of Religion* blog and *Religion Compass*. His research interests include critical social theory, theories of secularism, as well as representations of Christianity, Islam, and Native traditions in popular and political culture.

Notes

1. One notable exception is the work of Jürgen Habermas (the focus of my doctoral dissertation), who has attempted to incorporate the natural and social sciences into his broader critical theoretical framework (see Habermas 1990, 2008).
2. I found the first chapter in *Rethinking Religion*, "Interpretation and Explanation: Problems and Promise in the Study of Religion" (Lawson and McCauley 1990: 12–31), to be particularly useful in this regard, as is Lawson and McCauley (1993).
3. Both Geertz (2010) and Jensen (2009) strike me as having offered valuable critiques of what they take to be an overemphasis on human minds in some branches of CSR, by presenting their own social cognitivist approach. Jensen develops these ideas further in his 2014 book, *What Is Religion*.
4. For an extensive argument that seeks to include non-human primates within the category of species that engage in rituals that could be deemed "religious," see Schaefer (2015).
5. For a critique of this approach see McCutcheon (2001).
6. In their critique of prevailing paradigms in the history of religions, Lawson and McCauley spend less than a page on what they term the "romantic rebellion" in anthropology that has been influenced by deconstructionism, with no reference to or analysis of any such claims (Lawson and McCauley 1993: 204–205). While Sloan (2004: 22–45) spends considerably more time addressing what he takes to be problems with the "socioculturalist" (following Clifford Geertz) and "postmodern socioculturalist" critiques (e.g., Asad, Lincoln, McCutcheon, and J. Z. Smith), his analysis fails to actually analyze any of these arguments, save for a few brief remarks on a quote from Bruce Lincoln (ibid.: 31). Similarly, Cohen, Lanman, and Whitehouse (2008) make no reference to any such critiques of CSR in a recent essay purporting to address this very topic.

7. While I recognize that both Bloch and Laidlaw are cultural and social anthropologists by training, their critiques strike me as more "insider" than, say, critical theorists such as myself.
8. Arnal and McCutcheon underline this problem (2013b: 151–162) when they write: "Describing an entity or phenomenon as 'supernatural' or 'spiritual' not only assumes too much about the problematic issue of belief, but also focuses on the phenomenon's supposed actual characteristics, which are not in evidence, rather than on its discursive characteristics" (ibid.: 152).
9. Sloan (2004) addresses part of this problem with the distinction between abductive vs. deductive thinking, though does not, on my reading, seem to get at the crux of these critiques.
10. As a side note, this tendency strikes me as odd given the rather sharp ascendency of CSR as a relevant area within religious studies (e.g., it was the main theme at the 2010 IAHR Congress: Religion: A Human Phenomenon), including its funding opportunities, as discussed by Brad Stoddard in Chapter 13, this volume.

References

Arnal, William and Russell T. McCutcheon. 2013a. "On the Definition of Religion." In William Arnal and Russell T. McCutcheon, *The Sacred Is the Profane: The Political Nature of "Religion"*, 17–30. New York: Oxford University Press.

Arnal, William and Russell T. McCutcheon. 2013b. "The Origins of Christianity Within, and Without, 'Religion': A Case Study." In William Arnal and Russell T. McCutcheon, *The Sacred Is the Profane: The Political Nature of "Religion"*, 134–170. New York: Oxford University Press.

Asad, Talal. 2003. *Formations of the Secular: Christianity, Islam, Modernity*. Stanford, CA: Stanford University Press.

Barrett, Justin L. 2011. "Cognitive Science of Religion: Looking Back, Looking Forward." *Journal for the Scientific Study of Religion* 50(2): 229–239.

Bloch, Maurice. 2005. "Are Religious Beliefs Counter-Intuitive?" In Maurice Bloch, *Essays on Cultural Transmission*, 103–121. Oxford: BERG.

Bloch, Maurice. 2008. "Why Religion Is Nothing Special but Is Central." *Philosophical Transactions of the Royal Society B: Biological Sciences* 363(1499): 2055–2061.

Cohen, Emma, Jonathan Lanman, and Harvey Whitehouse. 2008. "Common Criticism of the Cognitive Science of Religion—Answered." *CSSR Bulletin* 34(4): 112–115.

Fitzgerald, Timothy. 2007. *Discourse on Civility and Barbarity: A Critical History of Religion and Related Categories*. New York: Oxford University Press.

Franek, Juraj. 2014. "Has the Cognitive Science of Religion (Re)defined 'Religion'?" *Religio* 22(1): 3–27.

Geertz, Armin W. 2010. "Too Much Mind and Not Enough Brain, Body and Culture. On What Needs to Be Done in the Cognitive Science of Religion." *Historia Religionum* 2: 21–37.

Habermas, Jürgen. 1990. *Moral Consciousness and Communicative Action* (trans. Christian Lenhardt and Shierry Weber Nicholsen). Cambridge, MA: MIT Press.

Habermas, Jürgen. 2008. "Freedom and Determinism." In Jürgen Habermas, *Between Naturalism and Religion* (trans. Ciaran Cronin), 151–180. Cambridge: Polity Press.

Jensen, Jeppe Sinding. 2009. "Religion as the Unintended Product of Brain Functions in the 'Standard Cognitive Science of Religion Model.'" In Michael Strausberg (ed.), *Contemporary Theories of Religion: A Critical Companion*, 129–155. New York: Routledge.

Jensen, Jeppe Sinding. 2014. *What Is Religion?* Durham: Acumen.

Laidlaw, James. 2007. "A Well-disposed Social Anthropologist's Problems with the 'Cognitive Science of Religion.'" In Harvey Whitehouse and James Laidlaw (eds.), *Religion, Anthropology and Cognitive Science*, 211–246. Durham, NC: Carolina Academic Press.

Lawson, Thomas E. and Robert N. McCauley. 1990. *Rethinking Religion: Connecting Cognitive and Culture*. New York: Cambridge University Press.

Lawson, Thomas E. and Robert N. McCauley. 1993. "Crisis of Conscience, Riddle of Identity: Making Space for a Cognitive Approach to Religious Phenomena." *Journal of the American Academy of Religion* 61(2): 201–223.

Martin, Craig. 2014. *Capitalizing Religion: Ideology and the Opiate of the Bourgeoisie*. London: Bloomsbury.

Masuzawa, Tomoko. 2005. *The Invention of World Religions: Or, How European Universalism Was Preserved in the Language of Pluralism*. Chicago, IL: University of Chicago Press.

McCauley, Robert and Emma Cohen. 2010. "Cognitive Science and the Naturalness of Religion." *Philosophy Compass* 5(9): 779–792.

McCutcheon, Russell T. 2001. "'We're All Stuck Somewhere': Taming Ethnocentrism and Transcultural Understandings." In Russell T. McCutcheon, *Critics Not Caretakers: Redescribing the Public Study of Religion*, 73–84. Albany, NY: SUNY Press.

Proctor, James D., ed. 2005. *Science, Religion, and the Human Experience*. New York: Oxford University Press.

Schaefer, Donovan O. 2015. *Religious Affects: Animality, Evolution, and Power*. Durham, NC: Duke University Press.

Sloan, D. Jason. 2004. *Theological Incorrectness: Why Religious People Believe What They Shouldn't*. New York: Oxford University Press.

Tylor, Edward B. 1871. *Primitive Culture*, vol. 2. New York: Torchbook.

15

A Reply

Claire White

The aim of my target article (republished as Chapter 12 of the present volume) was to provide non-specialists with an overview of what the cognitive science of religion (CSR) is, and, conversely, by addressing common misunderstandings of the field, what it is not. It is therefore highly appropriate that the two commentaries comprising Chapters 13–14 of this volume are from the intended target audience, scholars in the academic study of religion who are new to the approach. Both responses are largely skeptical of CSR as an enterprise, but for different reasons. Stoddard (Chapter 13) maintains that the internal motivations of those who conduct and fund CSR research is to annihilate or promote religion, while Sheedy (Chapter 14) voices concern that the definition of religion adopted in CSR normalizes and privileges some phenomena to the exclusion of others.

I am grateful for the opportunity to elaborate upon some aspects of CSR further. It is, however, apparent that a more formidable barrier to fruitful dialogue between scholars in CSR and those versed in more traditional, humanistic approaches to the study of religion is a mutual understanding, and appreciation of, the role of science in the scientific study of religion. This echoes similar points made by my colleagues elsewhere (e.g., see McCauley 2012; Slingerland 2008, 2012). In what follows, I will review some of Stoddard's claims and then address Sheedy's main points.

Stoddard raises concerns about the motivations of CSR scholars and those (especially the John Templeton Foundation) who fund the research. Stoddard begins and ends his critique by dichotomizing the motivations of CSR scholars as either "helping to explain, reduce, and ultimately invalidate religion" (p. 115, this volume) or to authenticate religion as a "natural and healthy component of human cognition" (ibid.). This characterization of CSR is the antithesis of a scientific approach to the study of religion. As I pointed out (Commitment 5: "religion is cognitively natural"; p. 104, this volume), a hallmark of CSR is a commitment to methodological naturalism and on the whole CSR researchers do not (and should not) say anything about the ontological status of religion. Further, that religion is natural does not mean it is true, nor by extension does it mean that religion is good or bad for society. As I also discussed in Commitment 5, while it is almost inevitable that CSR research will be reinterpreted by others outside the field (at both ends of the debate), the vast majority of CSR researchers do not claim that their research supports or invalidates religion. Stoddard's characterization of the field is based on a 2003 book review. For religious studies scholars, this is akin to a critique of comparative religionists everywhere based on a book review of Frazer's *The Golden Bough*.

Consider the evidence provided by Wesley J. Wildman, publisher of *IBCSR Research Review*, a free monthly compendium of everything published in CSR and allied fields. Wildman reports an estimate from *IBCSR Research Review* editor Joel C. Daniels that the number of CSR articles whose aim is to invalidate or validate religion (as against discover its origins and functions) is at maximum 1 percent. Of course, there are articles that may not be explicit about this aim, and it is likely that an additional few percent would be added to this number. Overall, we can expect less than 5 percent of the total number of CSR articles published to abandon or imperfectly express proper scientific bracketing (W. Wildman, personal communication, March 22, 2016).

Stoddard extends this critique to "the Templeton Foundation's interest in funding CSR research, paying particular attention to the political, economic, and socio-cultural interests that motivate the research produced by Templeton Foundation-funded studies" (p. 116, this volume). Here, he places John Templeton Foundation in the second category, as promoting religion as a healthy aspect of human life to be encouraged and embraced. He claims that an answer to the questions he poses about the motivations of John Templeton Foundation funding CSR research would take up more allocated space than is supplied. Here evidence, not space, is the issue.

From 2006–2016, John Templeton Foundation have funded a total of 119 projects on religion. Eleven (9%) of these (12% of total funding to projects on religion) were in the area (broadly defined) of CSR.[1] John Templeton Foundation are certainly funding some CSR research, but the amount, as compared to the amount of John Templeton Foundation funding in other areas of religion, is modest. A more important question concerns the nature of this funded research. Specifically, does John Templeton Foundation funded research in CSR assume that some version of religion is good for human society?

Consider the aims of two projects cited by Stoddard. The aims of "Empirical Expansion in the Cognitive Science of Religion and Theology" are to "expose ... scholars to the cognitive science of religion, with an emphasis on quantitative research methodologies" and a grant competition "for quantitative hypothesis-testing or for theological and philosophical treatments of major, empirically supported claims in the field" (John Templeton Foundation 2007). Consider also the grant awarded to "Gods in Disorder: The Promise of Abnormal Religious Cognition for the Science of Religious Cognition", which aims to understand the etiology and cultural management of particular disorders in order to account for religious thought and practice (John Templeton Foundation 2015). Neither of these proposals appear to support the idea that (some version of) religion is good for society.

This tells us something about the nature of CSR research that gets funded, but what about the John Templeton Foundation funded research that gets published? A systematic review of peer-reviewed journals sponsored by John Templeton Foundation between 2006 and 2016 revealed 240 articles in over 10 journals (e.g., *Psychology of Religion and Spirituality, American Psychologist, Journal of Theoretical and Philosophical Psychology, Journal of Consulting and Clinical Psychology*).[2] A cursory glance at these articles suggests that there is no obvious link between John Templeton Foundation funded research in psychology and claims that religion is a positive component of human life. In fact, titles of some John Templeton Foundation sponsored research suggest the opposite. For example, consider "The Negative Association between Religiousness and Children's Altruism across the World" (Decety et al. 2015) or "My Brother's Keeper? Compassion Predicts Generosity More among Less Religious Individuals" (Saslow et al. 2013).

In sum, concerns about the motivations of funders should always be considered in light of additional processes, including the existence of a peer-review process that guarantees quality outside the reach of external control. Although certainly not exhaustive or conclusive, preliminary investigations into CSR research (funded and non-funded), suggests that CSR scholars are not concerned with the ontological status of religion and nor are they promoting a version of religion as either good or bad for society.

In the remainder of this response, I focus on Sheedy's commentary. Sheedy's appraisal of the exercise at hand is to provide an opportunity for CSR scholars to engage with others in the academic study of religion by clarifying, rather than assuming, that issues have been adequately addressed. For Sheedy, the "elephant in the room" is the definition of religion adopted in CSR research. Before turning to these questions in more detail, from the outset, I disagree that CSR should be guided by the aim of appeasing social constructionist critiques of religion. For example, Sheedy concludes that "If CSR is to meet the challenges of the social constructionist critique of the category 'religion,' it seems to me that it will need to move away from its operational desire to ground "religion" as a cognitive by-product of human minds, and pay much closer attention to historicizing the concepts that are used in each and every instance, in a phrase, the political uses that it is always and already caught up in" (p. 126, this volume). The aim of CSR is, and has always been, to provide an explanation of why particular kinds of phenomena (that we deem "religious") persist in remarkably stable forms within and across cultures. The aim has never been to provide a complete explanation of religion (whatever that enterprise may be envisaged to look like), including understanding every instance of when the term religion is used by scholars and laypersons. Whether or not CSR is a successful endeavor should be judged by scientific criteria for good research and against the aims it proposes. There are many relevant critiques of CSR research outlined in the target paper, but they do not include a historical lexicon of religion because it is simply not a relevant criterion.

Sheedy's response is based almost exclusively on Commitment 1 of the target paper, that for CSR scholars, "there is no single entity that constitutes religion but there are discernible patterns of thought and behavior that can be called religion"

(p. 98, this volume). Sheedy asks two questions about this commitment: What is religion in CSR? And: What are the implications of this definition? I wholeheartedly agree that opportunities to clarify what CSR is should not be missed, and I am grateful to clarify some points further. I am, however, also admittedly perplexed by the claim that CSR has not adequately addressed questions about the definition of religion adopted in the field. I would point Sheedy to the following references as a starting point: Atran 2002; Barrett 2007; Boyer 2013; Cohen 2011; Lawson and McCauley 1990; McCauley and Cohen 2010. What follows, then, is a summary of some basic points that have been addressed more eloquently, and in greater detail, elsewhere.

Sheedy asks how, from the perspective of CSR, religion would be differentiated from sport or music since they may also inspire similar responses in individuals? He points out why he thinks this question is important, namely, that by labeling certain ideas and behaviors religious CSR scholars are privileging them over other aspects of social life. Two points are noteworthy here. First, the comparators used in the paper (i.e., sport, music) direct attention to effervescent activities, thereby biasing the understanding of religion to that direction. This is indeed the case. There are other comparators that I could have drawn upon in the paper—for example, picnics, building maintenance and committees—that equally participate in similar cognitive-emotional-social defaults that underlie activities that we are willing to label as religious, but that are not based on effervescence. Second is the concern that labeling phenomena as "religious" in CSR equate to endowing it with a "specialness" or another privileged property over other similar forms of human life. On the contrary, the label religion designates phenomena as merely another property of human minds in their respective environments. This is one of the things we mean when we say that "religion is cognitively natural" (Commitment 5).

CSR scholars have an attachment to the scientific process not to the term "religion" (nor to any particular definition of that term). The term is a convenient tool that delimits a set of phenomena, but ultimately the goal of CSR is to explain how and why certain ideas and behaviors are culturally recurrent. It may be, for example, that the term only delineates superficial patterns that reveal little about the phenomena it designates and more about how we as humans tend to group things (see McCauley and Cohen 2010). As Barrett (2007: 768) put it, "if the explanations turn out to be part of a grander explanation of 'religion', so be it. If not, meaningful human phenomena have still been rigorously addressed." As I pointed out in the target paper, from the perspective of CSR, "religion is a convenient label that appears to characterize a cluster of recurring features" (p. 98, this volume). That is to say, it is a working term to designate a diverse array of phenomena, underpinned by diverse psychological predispositions that are not otherwise linked (see McCauley 2004). The ultimate challenge of course is to actually demonstrate how and when these aspects tend to cluster together to form "religious" systems. A challenge that a scientific study of religion is equipped to deal since it deals with identifying and systematically testing patterns. This is a challenge that I am confident will be met, but first, we must explain how and why the individual components (e.g., ideas about supernatural agents, religious rituals), arise and function (see Commitment 3: "to explain religion, we must fractionate it and reduce it into meaningfully constituent parts"; p. 103, this volume).

In contemporary practice, CSR is largely a bottom-up, piecemeal approach to the study of religion. First researchers fractionate aspects of what they take (or demonstrate) to be cross-culturally recurrent forms of ideas and practices, such as rituals, ideas about the continuity of persons after death and so on. The goal of CSR, then, is to explain how and why these phenomena persist in relatively stable forms by drawing on what is known about how humans tend to think (e.g., evolutionary, developmental and cross-cultural research) and how cultural input modifies these cognitive defaults (see Commitment 2: "religion can be explained scientifically"; p. 99, this volume). CSR is making steady progress, and some aspects (such as ideas about supernatural agents or religious rituals) have received greater attention because they are quite simply better candidates for scientific exploration (e.g., more obviously cross-culturally recurrent, logistically easier to study). This is how scientific knowledge progresses. In the future, CSR will continue to add to the repertoire of ideas and behaviors that may be construed as "religious", but that we have focused to date more on some aspects of religion than others does not mean, as Sheedy implies, that this is all that we conceive of religion as.

While CSR scholars have been clear in outlining how they conceptualize the phenomena they study, it is true that as a whole, we have not engaged in rigorous debates about the broader question of what constitutes religion in general. In fact, many see the value of a bottom-up approach like CSR precisely in the fact that it avoids the seemingly endless interpretative debates concerning what is religion and how do we define it. As I pointed out in the paper, such questions have characterized the study of religion from its inception and, to date, there is no general scholarly consensus. I am not saying that these debates are not important or that they should not take place, but the corridors of philosophical reflection can be much informed by the laboratories of scientific discovery (see McCauley 2004).

Rather than to only ponder questions of what religion is and what constitutes it, another complementary approach is to get the data. Much like the biologist observing the relationship between cells in the human body under the microscope as self-compartmentalized units and in interaction with each other, CSR scholars are examining some of the fundamental building blocks of human life in their respective environments. We are attempting to isolate common—perhaps even universal—aspects of human ideas and behaviors that we think designate "religion" to probe whether there are any patterns in the data. Through methods such as computer simulation modelling and controlled experiments, we are attempting to extract simpler representations from the data. Our aim is to predict and explain how and why humans tend to think and behave. We are optimistic about achieving this aim because we do not think that "religious" phenomena are so infinitely complex that we will not be able to make sense of them. This endeavor is not perfect; it will take time; perhaps it will progress with better technology.

To extend the analogy, by seeing the functions of cells in action, biologists are better equipped to answer the question of "what is life?" Likewise, through the scientific study of recurrent cultural phenomena such as ritualized behavior pertaining to ideas about supernatural agents or ideas about life after biological death we will be better equipped to answer the question "what is religion?" If we are wrong about what we thought of as the patterns designating religion, even better, because then knowledge has progressed on the basis of scientific discovery about how the world actually is rather than armchair reflection on how the world could be.

Claire White is Associate Professor in the Department of Religious Studies at California State University, Northridge. She is also Co-Chair of the Cognitive Science of Religion Group at the American Academy of Religion.

Notes

1. Total funding for 2006–2012 to projects on religion was $105,272,284, and that for CSR was $12,985,259. Data were derived from JTF records (www.templeton.org/what-we-fund/grant-search/results), along with the assistance of a research assistant, Jessica Levonian. Figures are based on performing a search for key words and then manually scanning the results for relevance to CSR.
2. The search was performed by my research assistant Jessica Levonian using PsychNet, a searchable database yielding psychological-based publications.

References

Atran, S. 2002. *In Gods We Trust: The Evolutionary Landscape of Religion.* Oxford: Oxford University Press.

Barrett, J. 2007. "Cognitive Science of Religion: What Is It and Why Is It?" *Religion Compass* 1(6): 768–786.

Boyer, P. 2013. "Explaining Religious Concepts: Lévi-Strauss the Brilliant and Problematic Ancestor." In Dimitris Xygalatas and William W. McCorkle (eds.), *Mental Culture, Classical Social Theory and the Cognitive Science of Religion,* 164–175. Durham: Acumen.

Cohen, E. 2011. "Out with 'Religion': A Novel Framing of the Religion Debate." In Wes Williams (ed.), *Religion and Rights: The Oxford Amnesty Lectures 2008,* §7.5. Manchester: Manchester University Press.

Decety, J., J. M. Cowell, K. Lee, R. Mahasneh, S. Malcolm-Smith, B. Selcuk, and X. Zhou. 2015. "The Negative Association between Religiousness and Children's Altruism across the World." *Current Biology* 25(22): 2951–2955.

John Templeton Foundation. 2007. "Empirical Expansion in the Cognitive Science of Religion and Theology." Available at www.templeton.org/what-we-fund/grants/empirical-expansion-in-the-cognitive-science-of-religion-and-theology (accessed July 10, 2016).

John Templeton Foundation. 2015. "Gods in Disorder: The Promise of Abnormal Religious Cognition for the Science of Religious Cognition." Available at www.templeton.org/what-we-fund/grants/gods-in-disorder-the-promise-of-abnormal-religious-cognition-for-the-science-of- (accessed July 10, 2016).

Lawson, E. T. and R. N. McCauley. 1990. *Rethinking Religion: Connecting Cognition and Culture*. Cambridge: Cambridge University Press.

McCauley, R. N. 2004. "Is Religion a Rube Goldberg Device? Or Oh, What a Difference a Theory Makes!" In Timothy Light, and Brian C. Wilson (eds.), *Religion as a Human Capacity: A Festschrift in Honor of E. Thomas Lawson*, 45–64. Leiden: Brill.

McCauley, R. N. 2012. "A Cognitive Science of Religion Will Be Difficult, Expensive, Complicated, Radically Counter-Intuitive, and Possible: A Response to Martin and Wiebe." *Journal of the American Academy of Religion* 80(3): 605–610.

McCauley, R. N. and E. Cohen. 2010. "Cognitive Science and the Naturalness of Religion." *Philosophy Compass* 5(9): 779–792.

Saslow, L. R., R. Willer, M. Feinberg, P. K. Piff, K. Clark, D. Keltner, and S. R. Saturn. 2013. "My Brother's Keeper? Compassion Predicts Generosity More Among Less Religious Individuals." *Social Psychological and Personality Science* 4(1): 31–38.

Slingerland, E. 2008. *What Science Offers the Humanities: Integrating Body and Culture*. New York: Cambridge University Press.

Slingerland, E. 2012. "Back to the Future: A Response to Martin and Wiebe." *Journal of the American Academy of Religion* 80(3): 611–617.

Part V

16

The Study of Religion, Bricolage, and Brandom

Matthew C. Bagger

In a by now well-known essay Bruce Lincoln laments the "(un)discipline of Religious Studies" (Lincoln 2012). His argument speaks to the dismay so many of us feel about the hegemony of the American Academy of Religion and provides indispensable historical context for understanding how the study of religion in America came "to straddle the interests of religion and the values of the academy ... while consistently tilting to defend the former against threats posed by the latter" (ibid.: 136). These divided loyalties, Lincoln suggests, prevent the study of religion from exhibiting the singleness of purpose, uniformity of approach, and critical intent definitive of an academic discipline. Asking us to "rethink the nature, goals, methods, and habituated dispositions of the discipline that claims religious phenomena as its own," Lincoln does not make clear how much unanimity in goals and methods he would prefer (ibid.: 135–136). It's probably revealing that he uses the terms "field [of study]" and "discipline" interchangeably, suggesting that he does not expect too much methodological or theoretical uniformity.

Regardless of what Lincoln would say, however, the dismal legacy he laments presents good reason to resist the impulse to conceive of the study of religion as a discipline, in a sense of that term (perhaps) stronger than his and that contrasts it to a field. Whereas a field is defined by the object of its study, a discipline is generally defined, at least in part, by the regimentation of its methods. The recent history of the study of religion suggests that the best antidote to uncritical, apologetic approaches to religion lies not in disciplinary regimentation, but rather in conceiving of the study of religion as a field that encourages theoretical diversity. If we share Lincoln's outlook, there's a sense in which we should celebrate the "(un)discipline" of the study of religion.

Initiatives that promote (or attempt to impose) a single theoretical approach in the study of religion have tended to end badly. Even when the theory yields insights, its exclusive employment erodes its critical edge. In the study of religion theoretical programs pursued in isolation from (or in opposition to) others generally find themselves rather quickly in the service of uncritical apologetic interests. The most egregious example, of course, is the history of religions approach championed by Eliade and others. At its high-water mark history of religions conceived of itself as a discrete discipline set apart from the others practiced in the university and equipped with its own distinctive theory. There's no reason to rehearse once more the ways in which history of religions amounted to little more than an uncritical crypto-theology resisting theory in the name of theory.

Few today would argue that the study of religion has its own distinctive theory, but the too exclusive reliance on one or another theoretical approach yields the same susceptibility to uncritical apologetics. Salutary post-colonial critique of Western scholarship, for example, when divorced from other approaches to the study of religion, predictably (and rather quickly) devolved in some quarters into the insistence that the "theory" found in non-Western religious texts is on a par with or preferable to Western academic theories (Radical Orthodoxy is a parallel phenomenon). As if it were an example lifted straight from Hegel's *Logic*, cutting edge critical theory here "dialectically overturns" into its uncritical, apologetic opposite. To take another instance, it was dizzying how quickly cognitive science of religion was put to apologetic purposes. One need only mention the appearance of "neurotheology" over fifteen years ago. More recently, Justin Barrett has argued on the basis of a purported cognitive predisposition to believe in God that belief in God is justified.

In the study of religion too exclusive an emphasis on any one theoretical paradigm seems to jeopardize the critical impetus. This tendency should lead us self-consciously to resist attempts to regiment theory in the study of religion. We should view ourselves as a field (not a discipline) and eagerly employ various methods developed in the various disciplines. A shared commitment to (in Lincoln's words) "rigorous, uninhibited, unintimidated, theoretically and empirically informed, wide-ranging, irreverent, and appropriately critical" study of religious phenomena is sufficient to provide the field with the requisite singleness of purpose, uniformity of approach, and critical intent (Lincoln 2012: 135). Not only as a field, moreover, should our work be theoretically eclectic, but also, ideally, as individuals. It should draw on diverse (but compatible) sources of theory. The theories we employ must all be naturalistic in orientation, stand up to reasonable criticism, and illuminate the objects of our studies, but beyond that need not bear some closer affinity.

Eclectic use of theory ensures that we always have independent critical perspectives available to us from which we can not only diagnose the kinds of lapses so prevalent in the study of religion, but also evaluate applications of theory more generally. The study of religion's contribution to theory comes not from the distinctiveness of our methods, but rather from the insight that our theoretical medley gives us about the limitations and potential uses of different theoretical perspectives when applied to the same material. Our eclectic use of theory puts our "foxy" field in a privileged position to assess the theory developed by the theoretical hedgehogs working in the disciplines.

This theoretical pluralism does not mean that our theoretical choices are arbitrary. What it does mean is that our research must be guided by questions. Genuine inquiry is generated by specific perplexities that emerge from a given epistemic context. In struggling to resolve a perplexity, we reach for whatever (defensible) theory relevant to that context best renders the perplexing phenomenon intelligible. The study of religion should be driven by questions about the material we study; it should not be the attempt to deploy systematically the latest theory. Rather than theory in search of questions, the study of religion should be questions in search of theory. The obvious fact that questions (like observations) are theory laden should not tempt us to divert our focus from first order inquiry in the study of religion. Neither should the fact that theory can lead us to critique our questions and abandon them in favor of others. The heart, soul and motivation of the study of religion is first order inquiry. At its best the study of religion avoids meta-theory. Sometimes, of course, meta-theory is inescapable (and even occasionally invaluable), but in general theoretical insight comes from the use (or the criticism of the misuse) of theory embedded in particular studies, answering specific first order questions about religious phenomena (think of Mary Douglas on the laws of *Leviticus* or Nancy Jay on blood sacrifice). Insight comes far less frequently from abstract theoretical discussions about theory, and almost never comes from books that assess the varieties of theory without seriously engaging the primary materials of some religious phenomenon. The burgeoning of this latter genre is not a hopeful development. The uses and abuses of theory manifest themselves in the work of scholars of religion, not scholars of theory.

To combat the impression that I'm simply offering my own set of meta-theoretical dicta, I will attempt to ground what I have said by addressing a specific question. I have chosen a longstanding perplexity about religion that dates to what is arguably the very charter for the critical study of religion, Hume's *The Natural History of Religion*. Hoping to demonstrate the virtues of theoretical open-mindedness, I avail myself of theory developed in analytic philosophy, a discipline much-ignored and frequently maligned in the study of religion.

Many of us in the study of religion define religion at least in part in terms of superhuman agents, but I suspect all of us define it either explicitly or implicitly, in part by its relation to human practice.[1] Lincoln, for instance, considers "*a set of practices*" (including both ethical and ritual practices) "*as defined by a religious discourse*" a "necessary" part "of anything that can properly be called a 'religion'" (Lincoln 2003: 6–7; italics original). Boyer (2001), tilling other theoretical soil, suggests that unlike mere myth and folklore religion involves actions and rules. Religious superhuman or supernatural concepts are distinguished as "serious" by their "aggregate relevance" to important social and moral processes (ibid.: 142, 298). For both Lincoln and Boyer religious discourse or concepts bear on practice and, although Boyer might not put it quite this way, it's clear that their bearing on practice consists in a kind of authority over practice.

It is (or, if not, ought to be) an axiom of our field that authority lies entirely in human dispositions to recognize or grant it. In the case of superhuman beings (or stories about them) the authority over practice that humans grant to them presupposes commitments to the superhuman beings' existence. Consider Santa Claus. He is a superhuman agent. More particularly he is (as Boyer would describe him) a "full-access strategic agent." He has full access to all the information strategically pertinent to social interactions ("He knows if you've been sleeping. He knows if you're awake."). He also prescribes certain ethical practices ("Be good for goodness' sake"; "Be nice to your little sister") as well as ritual practices (an annual audience and confession; offerings of cookies, milk, and carrots). Note that the discourse pertaining to the concept of Santa Claus bears an authority over practice for small children that it does not for adults. The difference in the discourse's authority obviously derives from the fact that children think the object of the discourse (i.e., Santa Claus) *exists.* That adults are committed to the non-existence of Santa Claus (except as a fictional character) and therefore do not recognize him as having any authority over their practices explains why we do not classify the cult of Santa Claus as religion, despite the analogies. This example shows that the authority over practice that religious discourse claims for itself depends on commitments about what exists.

In that ever-welling spring of insight into religion, *The Natural History of Religion*, Hume detects something anomalous and perplexing about the existential commitments informing religion. He writes:

> We may observe, that, notwithstanding the dogmatical, imperious style of all superstition, the conviction of the religionists, in all ages, is more affected than real, and scarcely ever approaches, in any degree, to that solid belief and persuasion, which governs us in the common affairs of life ... The usual course of men's conduct belies their words, and shows, that their assent in these matters is some unaccountable operation of the mind between disbelief and conviction, but approaching much nearer to the former than to the latter. (Hume 1956: 60)

In this passage Hume differs from the many cynical critics of religion before him, who charge the religious with imposture or insincerity. His interest is comparing the relative effects of different sorts of existential commitment on practice. Hume claims that the historical record reveals that the authority of religious discourse over human conduct does not appear as strong as the authority of common sense and experience over conduct. From this fact he infers a disparity between the existential commitments pertaining to religion and those pertaining to the mundane objects disclosed by the senses and past experience. Hume transforms a theological concern—how to conceive of the relationship between gods and humans—into a question for the study of religion: how to conceive of the relationship between two different sorts of existential commitment and their mutual bearing on human practice.

This question becomes acute for both theologians and theorists in the modern period with the development of historical consciousness and canons of historical inquiry that define commitments to historical existence more precisely. It is no surprise that Hume, best known as a historian in his lifetime, first posed the question. The question has perennially lurked in the background of our theoretical discussions. It's present in the age-old question whether the Greeks believed their myths. It also appears in debates about theological correctness and whether belief is an appropriate category in the study of religion. Modern Christian theology, moreover, essentially consists in recommendations about how to understand the claim that God exists. In what follows I will turn to Robert Brandom's social practice account of existential commitment to illuminate some varieties of modern religious apologetic.[2]

In *Making it Explicit* (1994) Brandom offers a philosophy of mind and language that is anti-representationalist and inferentialist. Anti-representationalists approach language as a sophisticated social practice and try to explain how and why semantic notions like truth and reference, as well as the notions of object and objectivity which the semantic notions presuppose, are useful or indispensable to the practice. For these philosophers pragmatics precedes semantics. They explain semantic (and allied) notions in virtue of the role they play in linguistic social practice, and view the "representationalist" strategy, which takes the notions of object and objectivity as primitive and tries to explain the semantic notions reductively in virtue of word/world relations, as misguided. Representationalism presupposes a certain word/world relationship as the point of departure for semantic theorizing: words refer to objects or states of affairs, which they represent, and those states of affairs make the representations of them true (or false). For representationalists truth and reference play a basic role in explaining the semantic content of mental states and linguistic performances. Understanding propositional content is explained in terms of grasping the conditions that are necessary and sufficient for its truth.

As a general strategy Brandom pursues an inferentialist as opposed to a representationalist account of semantic content. His version of inferentialism takes our practical attitudes regarding the propriety of material inferences as the point of departure for semantic theorizing.[3] His theory explains semantic content and intentionality in terms of a social practice that consists in the giving and asking for reasons. The fundamental move in this social practice is making a claim; that is, producing a performance (specifically, uttering or inscribing a sentence) that is propositionally contentful in that it can be offered as a reason and reasons can be demanded for it. Claims derive their contentfulness from their consequential relations to other claims. The content of a proposition is a function of its location in the inferentially articulated space of reasons. Brandom explains propositional content (i.e., content of the sort we express by the use of declarative sentences) in terms of the role that claimings play in the social practice of giving and asking for reasons.

Brandom explains the representational dimension of propositional content in terms of the perspectival features of communicating by claiming. He argues that to take a linguistic performance as a representing (i.e., treating it as purporting to represent objects and states of affairs correctly) consists in taking it to express attitudes concerning what there is and how things are. Such representational uptake means that the performance is liable to assessments of its correctness. Such uptake incorporates a distinction between representational attitude (how things are taken to be by the representation) and representational status (how things in fact are, which determines the success of the attitude). Objectivity (i.e., that things are the way they are regardless of what any or all of us assert about them), Brandom argues, is a structural feature of the practice of assessing the correctness of representations. Objectivity and the representational dimension of semantic content cannot be understood apart from the normative social practice of giving and asking for reasons.

Brandom believes the surface grammar of "true" and "refers" misleads us. It is a mistake, he suggests, to take "is true" as reporting the presence of some property of claims and beliefs and the sentences used to express them. The mistake is to think of truth as a property independent of our attitudes, to which they must answer. Likewise it is a mistake to take "refers to" as reporting some relation between linguistic and extralinguistic items. Avoiding the idea that reference is a relation between a word and something extralinguistic, and the related idea that truth is a property obtaining in virtue of a relation between words and extralinguistic states of affairs, Brandom's inferentialism offers an intralinguistic (word/word) account of truth and reference. Like pronouns "true" and "refers" anaphorically relate discursive tokens. Brandom explains these semantic terms by showing how their use enriches the expressive capacity of discursive practice. In Brandom's account these semantic terms serve a merely expressive function. They express explicitly the practical attitudes that make up the so-called representational stance that is implicit in discursive practice—the indispensable stance that takes our attitudes and claims as answering to facts concerning the objects the attitudes and claims are about. For Brandom this expressive function of semantic vocabulary precludes the explanatory function (i.e., explaining propositional content) attributed to it in representationalist theory because the expressive function presupposes propositional content.

As an anti-representationalist Brandom does not help himself to the idea of particular objects. Rather than beginning from particular objects in order to explain the singular terms (i.e., names or definite descriptions) that refer to them, Brandom begins by explaining singular term usage and then offers a transcendental argument for particular objects: particular objects are a condition of the possibility of propositional content. He offers a word/word account of singular terms. Brandom argues that to use an expression as a singular term is to take it "that its use is governed by symmetric simple material substitution-inferential commitments, that is, that there is some true non-trivial identity involving it" (Brandom 1994: 433). In other words to treat a term as a singular term, one must treat the term as intersubstitutable with some other expression in material inferences, intersubstitutable in the sense of preserving the goodness of the material inferences. "The substitutional commitments involving a singular term that" a participant in the language game "attributes [to others] and undertakes [himself] determine the pragmatic significance," for that participant, "of each use of that term" (ibid.: 423). For Brandom substitutional commitments of the sort that can be expressed as identities are crucial for explaining "why there are objects—not why there is something (to talk about) rather than nothing (at all), but rather why what we talk about comes structured ... as objects" (ibid.: 404).

Brandom's explanation of existence claims honors his anti-representationalist stance and relies on this notion of substitution-inferential commitments. According to Brandom to claim that something exists is to undertake a special sort of substitution commitment within the linguistic social practice. Existential commitment is a commitment that a referring expression is intersubstitutable with some member of a canonical class of substituends. It is a "disjunctive substitutional commitment" that the referring expression is identical with one member or another of the canonical class of substituends (ibid.: 442). Brandom calls these canonical substituends canonical designators. Entitlement to an existential commitment can be secured by entitlement to any identity between the referring expression and one member of the class of canonical designators. Canonical designators are referring expressions that are privileged in that we take their referential success as given or guaranteed. For a class of singular terms to have the status of canonical designators with respect to a kind of object is a matter of the attitudes of the participants in the relevant discursive practice.

Existential claims are given a sense by the relevant set of canonical designators. Brandom illustrates his account by elaborating on three distinct sets of canonical designators that give sense to claims about the existence of three different kinds of objects. He identifies the canonical designators that give sense to claims about numerical existence, physical existence, and fictional existence. In each case the canonical designators map out a structured space in which purportedly existing objects can be said to have an address. In the case of numerical existence, the canonical designators are the numerals. To claim that (to use his example) "the smallest natural number such that every larger one is the sum of distinct primes of the form $4n + 1$" *exists* (i.e., succeeds in referring) is to commit oneself to the identity of that referring expression with a numeral (e.g., 121). In the case of physical existence, the canonical designators are "spatiotemporal coordinates centered on the speaker" (ibid.: 444). To claim that some physical object exists is to commit oneself to the identity (i.e., intersubstitutability) of a name or definite description (e.g., "Jumbo") with an expression designating some spatiotemporal region traced out from the speaker.[4] In the case of fictional existence the canonical designators are the singular terms that appear in the fictional text. To claim that (again to use Brandom's example) Sherlock Holmes's housekeeper exists is to commit oneself to an identity between this referring expression and a singular term that appears in the text ("Mrs. Hudson"). Although Brandom illustrates his explanation of existence claims with just these three different kinds of objects and sets of canonical designators, in principle the number and variety of kinds of objects and kinds of existence are indefinite because kinds of objects and kinds of existence depend on the performances and attitudes of participants in discursive practice.

Brandom's theory of existential commitments clarifies Hume's observation about the relative effects of religious discourse and common sense on conduct. The disparity Hume notes is not best explained by postulating an "unaccountable" (i.e., inexplicable) propositional attitude distinctive to religion (neither "disbelief" nor "conviction"). Religion, rather, involves discursive commitments to a kind of entity with a distinctive kind of existence that nevertheless bears on other kinds of entities with their respective kinds of existence (which is not to say that all religious entities the student of religion will encounter are of the same kind or that they all share the same kind of existence). The disparity reflects efforts to integrate commitments to entities with different kinds of existence practically. To understand the bearing of religion on practice, one must:

1. identify the set of canonical designators specifying the particular sort of existence a religious object purportedly has when the religious discursively commit themselves to its existence, and

2. examine how the religious discursively relate the different sorts of existence to one another so as to grant the religious existent(s) authority over practice.

This analytic framework proves enormously useful in explaining some of the varieties of modern Christian apologetic.

When one claims that God the Father exists or that Jesus exists, one commits oneself to an identity between the referring expression, "God the Father," or "Jesus" and a canonical designator. To make sense of a claim that God the Father exists or that Jesus exists, one must determine the relevant set of canonical designators. What possible set of canonical designators might make sense of a claim that God exists or that Jesus exists? The Bible presents a likely source for the canonical designators that give Christian existential claims their sense. Because the religious narratives refer to people, places and things spatiotemporally arranged, it seems that one faces a choice between treating the narratives as ascribing to God fictional existence (in the same way that Conan Doyle's texts provide the canonical designators for existential claims pertinent to the Sherlock Holmes stories), or submitting the narratives to the sort of scrutiny we give other purportedly non-fictional texts and making them subject to the spatiotemporal canonical designators relevant to physical existence. In other words if the Biblical narrative supplies the canonical designators making sense of one's claim that God exists, one seems to saddle oneself either with a God who enjoys merely mythological existence (like Zeus) and whose existence wields no direct authority over practice, or with a God the record of whose activity is subjected to certain falsification by historical inquiry. When faced with this dilemma, one prominent Christian apologetic strategy has been to embrace the second horn and argue against all evidence for the historical veracity of the narratives.

Unwilling to bite that particular bullet, Hans Frei navigates the horns of the dilemma. In *The Eclipse of Biblical Narrative*, he emphasizes the realistic or history-like character of the biblical narratives, but distinguishes history-like narrative from historical narrative (Frei 1986). History gets its meaning, he argues, from its "ostensive-reference" to historical occurrences outside the text. By contrast, the biblical narratives, like fiction, get their meaning from the linguistic sense of the text. The history-like narratives of the Bible, moreover, invert the relationship of historical narrative to the world. Frei suggests that the world is to be read in light of biblical narrative and not vice versa. Brandom's account of existential commitments presents means of analyzing Frei's response to historical criticism and comparing it to other attempts to make sense of the existence and authority of superhuman beings. Like those who would treat the bible as fiction,

Frei locates the canonical designators that give religious entities (e.g., Jesus) their kind of existence in the narrative, but unlike fictional existence, biblical existents bear authority over spatiotemporal existence. "[T]he intratextual universe of this Christian symbol system is... the paradigm for the construal not only of what is inside that system but for all that is outside" (Frei 1986: 72). It provides "the interpretive pattern in terms of which all reality is experienced and read in the religion" (ibid.). As others have put Frei's point, the world of the text absorbs the world. Brandom argues that it is the attitudes of the participants in a discursive social practice that confer the status of canonical designators on a set of refer-ring expressions. The practical relationships between the kinds of existence also depend on the attitudes of the participants in a social practice. In his later work Frei insists that the authority of biblical narrative over spatiotemporal reality derives in precisely this way from the communal consensus institutionalized in the church.

Negative theology presents an alternative to Frei's narrative theology that is both medieval and modern. The contemporary negative theologian tries to disarm the critic of religion by happily denying all positive predication of God. Reflecting on the cosmological question—Why is there something, rather than nothing?—the negative theologian realizes that nothing can be predicated of God that attributes to him the qualities of a thing of any sort. If God is to be the expla-nation for why there is anything at all, God cannot be a thing. So, the negative theologian concludes, God is the necessary cause of the world, but any positive predication of him must be denied. As Denys Turner (2002: 32) explains, "I know that what requires me to say 'God exists' is true also denies me a grasp on what it means to say it." When Turner asserts that God exists, he asserts an identity between the referring expression, "God," and "cause of the world." In Brandom's terms "cause of the world" is the canonical designator that gives "God exists" its sense. That the set of canonical designators in this case consists of one member suggests, however, that Turner is correct to say that he has no grasp on what it means to say "God exists." It's also not clear that "cause of the world" qualifies as a canonical designator. The viability of the cosmological question has been impugned so thoroughly it's hard to see how the referential success of "cause of the world" could be guaranteed according to the norms of the relevant discursive practices.[5]

In Frei's view the church discursively relates the world of the text to the spatio-temporal world by endowing the paradigm that biblical narrative provides with authority over practice. Negative theology, by comparison, discursively inte-grates divine existence with spatiotemporal existence by deriving the one from the other. The cosmos results from the overflowing self-giving of the qualitatively infinite source of all being. As something created, human being participates in the divine self-giving, which authorizes an apophatic ethic of other-concerned self-giving and love.

Brandom's theory of existence claims even gives insight into the contemporary embrace of the language of "spirituality." Many have noted the vacuity of the term "spirituality." As it is commonly used, it seems to be defined by a series of negations. It's generally used contrastively with "religion." Spirituality is not to be understood in strictly moral terms either, and the language of the emotions or the aesthetic are taken to be inadequate to a characterization of it. It's not clear what it is when distinguished from those other more positively characterized domains of human life. The very vacuity of the term is what makes it so useful in democratic culture. Religious doctrines and institutions are what divides us. Despite our religious differences and even our moral disagreements, we can all agree that we are spiritual, as long as "spiritual" is semantically opaque. It's a useful placeholder term in democratic culture. Notice that the discourse of spirituality generally skirts the use of singular terms to describe the object of spiritual attitudes. Avoiding singular terms disengages spirituality from the substitution identities that confer meaning and that establish the sense an existential claim would have. Without "spiritual" objects the question of their authority over spatiotemporal existence cannot arise. This relatively inferentially disengaged discursive practice represents one response to a technological, democratic society.

Brandom's theory of existential commitments enables us to examine and compare the variety of kinds of existence attributed to religious entities, as well as the various ways religious entities are discursively given authority over practice, with analytic and terminological precision. Using Brandom as an example I hope I have sustained my claim that we should theorize eclectically, seeking to answer perplexities with whatever defensible resources we find helpful (even resources from such unlikely precincts as analytic philosophy). To foster theoretical innovation and prevent relapse into bad habits, the study of religion should construct itself as a field and encourage a diversity of theoretical approaches. Even from our failures we will learn much.

Matthew Bagger teaches in the Department of Religious Studies at the University of Alabama. He is the author of *Religious Experience, Justification, and History* (Cambridge University Press, 1999), *The Uses of Paradox: Religion, Self-Transformation, and the Absurd* (Columbia University Press, 2007), and editor of *Pragmatism, Naturalism, and Religion* (Columbia University Press, forthcoming).

Notes

1. Reflecting the influence of Hans Penner, Stan Stowers, and Bruce Lincoln, I define religion as belief in anthropomorphized superhuman entities—shading off into anthropomorphizing interpretations of the world—who confer a putative authority that transcends the merely human on at least some human preferences and practices.
2. In what follows I pursue a line of argument developed by Richard Rorty in his brilliant and underappreciated article, "Cultural Politics and the Question of the Existence of God" (2002).
3. Distinguished from formal inferences, material inferences are the kind of inference whose correctness essentially involves the conceptual contents of its premises and conclusions.
4. The canonical designators that give claims about physical existence their sense must include sortal information (e.g., The *elephant* located at x, y).

5. There's also the problem that singular terms must be associated with a sortal concept that specifies the *kind* of thing or object to which they purport to refer. Definite descriptions explicitly include a sortal ("the *chef* at the white house"). Names and demonstratives are implicitly associated with a sortal ("this" is always short for "this idea" or "this paper" or "this session," etc.). Incoherently, negative theology both requires that "God" not refer to an object because objects are sortally identified and individuated, and also requires that "God" be identical to a canonical designator guaranteeing reference to a kind of object.

References

Boyer, Pascal. 2001. *Religion Explained: The Evolutionary Origins of Religious Thought.* New York: Basic Books.

Brandom, Robert. 1994. *Making It Explicit: Reasoning, Representing, and Discursive Commitment.* Cambridge, MA: Harvard University Press.

Frei, Hans. 1986. "The 'Literal Reading' of Biblical Narrative in the Christian Tradition: Does It Stretch or Will It Break?" In Frank McConnell (ed.), *The Bible and the Narrative Tradition,* 36–77. New York: Oxford University Press.

Hume, David. 1956. *The Natural History of Religion.* Stanford, CA: Stanford University Press.

Lincoln, Bruce. 2003. *Holy Terrors: Thinking about Religion after September 11.* Chicago,IL: University of Chicago Press.

Lincoln, Bruce. 2012. "The (Un)discipline of Religious Studies." In Bruce Lincoln, *Gods and Demons, Priests and Scholars: Critical Explorations in the History of Religions,* 131–136. Chicago, IL: University of Chicago Press.

Rorty, Richard. 2002. "Cultural Politics and the Question of the Existence of God." In Nancy K Frankenberry (ed.), *Radical Interpretation in Religion,* 53–77. Cambridge: Cambridge University Press.

Turner, Denys. 2002. *How to be an Atheist.* Cambridge: Cambridge University Press.

17

Precision and Excess: Doing the Discipline of Religious Studies

Rebekka King

I want to begin by thanking Matthew Bagger for giving me the chance to return to the book that started it all for me. I first read Hume's *The History of Natural Religion* in college and was enchanted. We all had our conversion moments and mine was (at least in part) inspired by the eighteenth-century empiricist from Edinburgh. While I was inspired by Hume and while I now teach in a department of philosophy, I have tried in the interim to stay as far away from philosophy as humanly possible, dabbling first in biblical studies, religion and literature, sociology of religion, until ultimately I found my home in the anthropology of religion and the study of language ideologies. As someone with interests and training in linguistic anthropology I share a lot of the same forefathers (or ancestral kin) as the philosophy of language. Although my interests lie more in what language does than what language is. In some ways Bagger and I are almost what J. Z. Smith would call proximate others, reciprocally related as we seek out a theory of the self (Smith 2004). So I offer my comments as someone who has very little and everything in common with him. A point, which supports his introductory remarks, garnered from Bruce Lincoln, that we should conceptualize our work as a field, rather than a discipline.

Bagger's essay (Chapter 17, this volume) offers us three departure points: one which is practical, one which is methodological, or to a certain extent pedagogical, and one which is theoretical. In sum, he offers us the holy trinity of our academic vocation: service, teaching, and scholarship.

In this response, I work through each of these points to see if we can tease out more fully how they and the corresponding thinkers—Lincoln, Hume, and Brandom—are interrelated with a larger eye towards the theoretical component and Bagger's use of the philosophy of language. I think this is a helpful incursion with which to ask the question that animates this volume: what do we mean by excess? And what do we mean by saying that we are in a time of excess? Ultimately I want to argue that language occupies the sinewy space between excess and precision. What we think language is and what we think language does plays off our parallel desires to have both at once. And this is something that I think we can see in each of the components of Bagger's contribution to the volume.

Service—Field versus Discipline and Undiscipline

In the first section of his essay, Bagger asks us to consider what Lincoln sees as a conflict between the interests of religious agents over and against those of the academy. Lincoln belies this state of religious studies pointing out that the discipline at best results is an "ethos of inoffensiveness and a general intellectual timidity" and at worst comprises a unique discipline "consciously designed to shield its object of study against critical interrogation" (Lincoln 2012: 134). Lincoln uses the terms discipline and field interchangeably, but Bagger asks us to step back from this synonymous use and rather to think of religion as a field over and against as a discipline, so as to avoid homogenizing tactics from particular disciplinary orientations, such as the infamous history of religions approach which circulated around figures like Eliade et al., or more recently within certain apologetic adoptions of cognitive theory, and I would add to the list many working within my own methodological stratagem: ethnography.

While Bagger's refinement of Lincoln's terms may be a simple clarifying act for many religious studies scholars, I want to interrogate what might be lost in the shift from discipline to field. In doing so, I recognize that I am being selfish and speaking to my own situation and university setting. I have spent the last two years mired in bureaucratic paperwork, forms, learning objectives, etc., as I work with another colleague to develop a religious studies major at Middle Tennessee State University. We are fortunate to have the support of a Provost who in part sees the religious studies major as part of his legacy, but along the way we have hit opposition from a number of unlikely places, including, other departments in the College of Liberal Arts who feel that they adequately cover the study of religion in their course offerings; members of the administration who have helpfully suggested that we do not need to worry about expanding our faculty because the pastor at such-and-such a church has a Master's degree in church history so he can adjunct for us; administrators from the Tennessee Board of Regents who do not understand why we are not adopting a "world religions" model; or a certain dean who opposed our proposal to the University Curriculum Committee stating, "religious studies seems like a really nice hobby but I don't think it should be a major because it does not have a correlating career." In responding we have highlighted the differences between theology or religious devotion and the academic study of religion, explicitly explaining that ours is a discipline with distinct theories and methods that cannot be picked up by taking a smattering of courses in other departments but rather requires a sustained critical reflection on the development of the academic study of religion, a continued interrogation of the category and its systems of classification and descriptors, and an analysis of what it is religious people do and what the doing does in conversation with other scholars who share a commitment to these orienting frameworks.

Not to say that I think we should not draw from other disciplines or that there should be one overarching theoretical commitment that eclipses all others. As a cultural anthropologist, that field informs both the methods and theories that I employ in my research and also those which I incorporate into my teaching.

But religious studies remains my primary discipline: the questions I pose and the way I frame data are for scholars of religion and, more importantly, are in conversation with scholars of religion and presented with the assumption that they are part of a larger robust discussion generated through sustained conversations about the study of religion as a discipline. In other words, I wonder if the shift to field is at the expense of our academic enterprises and more practically speaking our livelihoods.

Pedagogical—The Methods We Employ

In his second section, Bagger turns to Hume, and notes that he is helpful for us to think about the origins of our scholarly endeavors because his approach is an early one in which we witness a shift from theological considerations of the data (either those that reject the content of religious claims as mere superstition or endorse it as truth). Instead Hume turns to a consideration of the social effects of religious claims. Particularly noteworthy is the quote that Bagger offers from Hume's *The Natural History of Religion* concerning the notion that "the usual course of men's conduct belies their words, and shows, that their assent in these matters is some unaccountable operation of the mind between disbelief and conviction, but approaching much nearer to the former than to the latter" (Hume quoted by Bagger, p. 142, this volume). Yes! This! Precisely! This is precisely what we do!

I see this as the pedagogical impulse because that is where we draw our students in. Particularly pertinent is Hume's notion that religious activity, which may or may not correspond to what adherents say religion is or does, lies somewhere along a trajectory between disbelief and conviction. Of course, this is old hat to many readers of this volume, but Bagger offers us the important reminder that what we see happening is a process by which "Hume transforms a theological concern—how to conceive of the relationship between gods and humans—into a question for the study of religion: how to conceive of the relationship between two different sorts of existential commitment and their mutual bearing on human practice" (p. 142, this volume).

Scholarship—The Theories We Choose

From this point of departure—first by attending to our roles within the academic study of religion and second by thinking through the methods we enact in selecting data—Bagger brings us to the meat of his paper which rests on the application of Robert Brandom's philosophy of language. As Bagger notes, analytic philosophy is somewhat maligned in the study of religion. Acknowledging that this material will be new to many of us (as it was for me), Bagger offers us a break down of Brandom's understanding of language which ultimately lies in its social dimensions and the 'attitudes' ascribed to communicative acts that center on claims. Particularly important is the concept of existence claims which makes use of a "special sort of substitutional commitment within the linguistic social practice" (p. 144, this volume). Bagger walks us through three of Bandom's examples:

numerical existence, physical existence, and fictional existence. These illustrations were a helpful preparation for his return to Hume and the type of existential claims made about God. According to Bagger, if God is linked to the Bible as its canonical designator then God's existence gets linked to the kind of object the biblical narrative is understood to be. He walks us through different options: it can be mythos or fiction (akin to myths about Zeus); it can be non-fiction (in which case it then gets scrutinized by historical designators that pose an obvious problem and generate an apologetics that is wrapped in a literalist model); or it can draw on Hans Frei's history-like model which has, of course, been adopted by many liberal Protestants as an allegorical or metaphorical theology. In this case the Bible's position as a canonical designator comes from the previous types of canonical status that it held in such a way that while the type of object existence has shifted the designator and the claims are retained: almost as if we are reorganizing the deck chairs on the Titanic.

The reason why this is a possibility is that these existential claims rest in the larger corpus of Western concepts of subjectivity and assumptions about the social roles of language. While there are certainly differences between the claims that the Bible is fiction, non-fiction history, or history-like, each of these designators occupy the same social location and are part and parcel of the same epistemological system. And so the question that I am curious about is: how would Bagger begin to work through these same questions within a different cultural context? I teach a course on global Christianities which looks at the processes of cultural translation when "non-Western" cultures convert to Christianity. Joel Robbins's work on Christian converts in Papua New Guinea who hold a non-referential understanding of language whereby it is not only impossible but also distasteful to know what others might be thinking comes to mind (Robbins 2008). Or Danilyn Rutherford's work on the Biak peoples in Indonesia whose cultural framework allows them to replace their protective idols with the Bible precisely because it is understood as foreign, alluring, and something that, like their former idols, "can be used up" (Rutherford 2006). In both cases we are dealing with assumptions about objects, representation, language, and the mind that come from very different worldviews but eventually arrive at a similar existential claim. Tying this point back to the question of excess and precision, what do we do in this case? Where does the theory go from here?

Bagger tells us that he's not interested in meta-theory, so perhaps his response would just be "chose a different theory." But if we are going to conceptualize the study of religion as a field, how and where do we connect? If we really have entered into a time of excess, what is it that we want theory to do? Do we see ourselves at a juncture where everyone claims to do method and theory, to be method and theory, which runs the risk of effacing our larger project? Avoiding this possibility is, in part, the vision put forward in the compilation of this volume. I wonder if there is something in Brandom's theory about how language works that might serve as a guide? Language, like theory, offers us an excess of representational possibilities with different existential claims that map on to the object and its designators. Perhaps the same could be said for theory? Like language, what theory does is as much about the assumptions we bring to its designators—theory does not happen in a vacuum—it too is derived from social practices that privilege certain ways of organizing data and ideas over against other ways. With this final point in mind, I want to move backwards through my own organization of Bagger's paper and suggest that perhaps the process of selection is not quite as eclectic as it appears at first glance. Certain theories make sense in the context of our research projects, our pedagogical aspirations, and our collective organization of our work vis-à-vis other scholars of religion precisely because of the social locations in which we find ourselves and our data. The methods through which we enact our theorizing and evaluate its effectiveness is somehow like Hume's trajectory between disbelief and conviction. It lies somewhere between precision and excess, and we author it as much in what we do as what we say.

Rebekka King is an Assistant Professor of Religion in the Department of Philosophy at Middle State Tennessee University. She is a cultural anthropologist and teaches courses on Christianity, ethnographic practices, and method and theory in the study of religion.

References

Lincoln, Bruce. 2012. *Gods and Demons, Priests and Scholars.* Chicago, IL: University of Chicago Press.

Robbins, Joel. 2008. "On Not Knowing Other Minds: Confession, Intention, and Linguistic Exchange in a Papua New Guinea Community." *Anthropological Quarterly* 81(2): 421–429.

Rutherford, Danilyn. 2006. "The Bible Meets the Idol: Writing and Conversion in Biak, Irian Jaya, Indonesia." In Fenella Cannell (ed.), *The Anthropology of Christianity*, 240–272. Durham, NC: Duke University Press.

Smith, Jonathan Z. 2004. "What a Difference a Difference Makes." In Jonathan Z. Smith, *Relating Religion: Essays in the Study of Religion*, 251–302. Chicago, IL: University of Chicago Press.

18

On Druids, the Dude, and Doing Excessive Theory

James Dennis LoRusso

In his influential essay "Map Is Not Territory," Jonathan Z. Smith paraphrases Paul Ricoeur, stating, "it is the perception of incongruity that gives rise to thought" (Smith 1993: 294). Smith is suggesting that "intellectual activity" springs from a suspicion that something does not fit or fails to conform to expectations. I find this maxim particularly appropriate for *thinking* through and responding to Matthew Baggar's "The Study of Religion, Bricolage, and Brandom" (Chapter 16, this volume) for two reasons. Not only does this echo Baggar's recommendation that good theory should arise from an observed problem, it also aptly captures my experience as a cultural historian of religion to engage an intellectual discipline, analytical philosophy, with which I am wholly unfamiliar. As Baggar rightly points out, the academic study of religion has only given scant attention to this field. I can sympathize with his sense of estrangement, as my own research on the intersection of business and religion frequently brings me into dialogue with scholars of management interested in spirituality. While occasionally one of these researchers may reference Williams James or Paul Tillich, their level of theoretical contact with religious studies never, in my experience, acknowledges scholarship more recent than the mid-twentieth century. Instead, I am often faced with business scholars employing uncritically ideas drawn from Joseph Campbell or Huston Smith. Yet they lack any awareness of the work of Bruce Lincoln and other who in more recent decades have revealed the shortcomings of phenomenology or the so-called "world religions" paradigm. In these situations, it is my responsibility to act as a translator across these arbitrary disciplinary lines that can hinder as much as they might enable fruitful research.

Bagger introduces scholars of religion, like myself, to Robert Brandom and asks us to wrestle with his ideas about language, practice, and meaning into the study of cognition and religious belief. While some of my colleagues have some exposure to this brand of philosophy, I am a historian and critical theorist by training, and even comprehending the basic dimensions of the intellectual space that Baggar occupies has proven quite challenging, but worth every effort. In this essay, I explore Baggar's argument through the lens of the history of religions and aspire, however unlikely, to do justice to the intricacies of Brandom's theories (I beg the reader's forgiveness if I fall short).

Before interrogating his specific application of Brandom, I would like to comment briefly on Baggar's guidelines for "doing good theory." He maintains that theorists of religion should obey certain rules. Scholars should embrace a certain theoretical eclecticism; questions should emerge from perplexities observed in the data, which in turn fosters theorizing. In short, as much as possible, *theory follows research*, not vice versa. Additionally, he states that theories should presuppose certain naturalism; a theory of religion built upon supernatural claims does not further social scientific knowledge of religion. Theories should be defensible, falsifiable but capable of standing up against rigorous critique. Finally, a theory of religion should illuminate the objects of our study—it needs to reveal something about the data that is otherwise obscured.

To illustrate these points, Baggar examines narrative theology through the lens of Brandom's taxonomy of existential commitments. He begins with Hume's observation that religious belief lies somewhere between certainty and disbelief. Religious belief therefore garners less authority over everyday human practices than "common sense." Baggar asserts that Brandom's schema demonstrates how narrative theology represents a strategy to overcome this liminal space occupied by religious belief. According to Brandom, objects can exist in three ways: numerically (represented as numbers), physically (represented in terms of a perceived spatiotemporal relationship to the speaker), or fictionally (as element in a story). Existential claims about supernatural entities, Baggar argues, imply neither the physical existence of god(s) nor their purely fictional existence in scripture. Echoing Hume, these lie somewhere in between, and narrative theology attempts to build a bridge between these exclusive cognitive domains.

Before assessing his analysis, I need to revisit Baggar's last point about doing good theory: that *it should illuminate the objects of study*. I would amend this with some advice from Tom Tweed. In *Crossing and Dwelling*, Tweed moves a step further. Not only should theories shed light on the data, they need to be comparative, providing "an illuminating angle of vision as you try to interpret religions in other eras and regions" (Tweed 2008: 27). In other words, theories should be applicable beyond the scope of the specific researched case. Baggar asserts his case is relevant for the cognitive science of religion, so I want to emphasize two aspects of comparison moving forward. As Tweed suggests, what can Brandom say about the study of religious cognition, and can other theories refine the work that Baggar has already finished here?

Historicizing Hume

In order to follow along with Baggar's argument, I must start with the assumption that Hume's observation actually reports something distinct about religious belief. However, as a historian, I am less inclined to take Hume at his word because I desire to know more about the context in which he is writing. Thus, in following Baggar's guidelines for good theory, I will ask the pertinent questions, as I understand them:

- What is at stake in Hume's claim about religious belief?

- What is Hume's implicit theory of religion and what does this reveal?

First, while he wants us to receive his argument as objective, grounded in empirical observation, I suggest that the ambiguity Hume ascribes to religious belief actually reflects his own struggles to make sense of belief rather than some inherent quality of it. Hume's writings about religion expose a deep uncertainty and inconsistency. He appears at once sympathetic and resistant. In *The Natural History of Religion* (first published in 1757), he states, "the whole frame of nature bespeaks an intelligent author; and no rational enquirer can, after serious reflexion, suspend his belief a moment with regard the primary principles of genuine Theism and Religion" (Hume 2010: 7). Even though Hume treats the notion of a Deistic creator as rational, he walks back this claim almost immediately, depicting religion as the product of baser human emotions, of "the terror of death, the thirst for revenge, the appetite for food and other necessities" (ibid.). Thus, one on hand, it is "reasonable" for one to commit to the existence of a deity, but conversely, religious belief arises not from rational thought but out of feelings. Philosopher David O'Conner asserts that Hume's "ambiguity suited his purposes," even as "this creates difficulty in definitively pinning down his final position on religion" (O'Conner 2013: 19). For Hume, although religious belief can be reasonable, it is never empirical, and more often in practice appears as a product of irrationality. In short, Hume's own position on religion wavers just as he characterizes the nature of religious belief itself wavering between certainty and disbelief.

Second, in setting religion apart from other forms of knowledge, Hume essentially downgrades its status; he situates it somewhere below empirical knowledge and just barely above disbelief. Despite his claims to objectivity, it is important to note how this move to downgrade religious belief reflects the larger sociopolitical order emerging in eighteenth-century Britain. The hierarchy of knowledge implicit here echoes the separation of the religious from other domains, particularly the political. The constitutional monarchy that arose in the wake of the so-called "Glorious Revolution" at the turn of that century upended historical political arrangements, disarmed monarchical authority, clipped the wings of Church authority, and elevated Parliament as the supreme political body of the nation. In essence, a nascent secular nation-state came into being, and Hume's ideas should be seen as a product of and a participant in these changes. Just as the Church lost ground to the secular nation-state, religious belief was losing epistemological status to an emergent modern rationalism. Hume's assertion—religious belief is closer to fiction than truth—merely takes part in establishing this modernist regime of knowledge; it actively reproduces a particular kind of social and political order taking shape at this time in the Euro-American world.

Yet, Baggar utilizes Hume's observation as if it lies outside the mechanisms of historical change, as a definitive statement about the quality of religious belief in all its manifestations and at all times. The argument proceeds as follows: Religious existential commitments always leave believers in a quandary, because they are asserting belief in something—a supernatural force—that is neither physical nor

fictitious. Believers therefore must find a method for working around this problem, typically in one or two ways. First, some parties, despite a total lack of empirical evidence, will stubbornly ascribe to god(s) a physical, historical existence.
Belief in the "inerrancy" of the Bible therefore, prevalent among Fundamentalist
Baptists today for example, can be explained as nothing more than a strategy to
deal with the plain fact that the epistemological status of religious belief begins
from a position of uncertainty. Others deal with this problem by accepting the
supernatural as utterly fictitious, as a symbolic concept that nonetheless reveals
truths about the world. Thus, when liberal theologians such as John Shelby Spong
(2003) declare the tradition of Jesus' resurrection as pedagogical rather than historical, Baggar understands this as a derivative move in which Spong is accounting for the clearly untenable position that a human being could possibly rise from
the dead after three days.

Yet, even though Brandom's schema allows Baggar to map these various strategies (that could, indeed, prove illustrative if framed differently), it seems to fall
short of augmenting our knowledge of religious belief generally. Rather, Baggar
sheds light on how individuals actively create theological assertions in order
to account for the precarious location that belief in supernatural entities holds
within a modernist regime of knowing. Under such conditions, Brandom's concept of existential commitments does allow us to see how those fundamentalist
Baptists might choose to reject historical evidence contrary to scripture: they
do so not because religious belief is inherently ambiguous, but because they are
developing their theological positions within a modern context where secular
reasoning rules over a privatized religiosity. For similar reasons, Spong conceives
of Jesus' resurrection in terms that reject a literal reading of the Gospels, instead
saying it only emerged gradually over some fifty years. The resurrection is important, Spong (2003) states, not because it accurately reflects historical events but
because it provokes a "conversation about the meaning of Easter" within the
Christian community. Spong, like the biblical literalists, makes these theological moves because of the ambiguous position that belief in God holds in relation to empirically based knowledge. However, this tell us less about religious
belief and more about how such beliefs have been downgraded in light of the
modern socio-political order in which secular reasoning represents the baseline
of authoritative knowledge.

By acknowledging the role of historical context in the production of beliefs, it
is easy to see how neither Hume's assertion nor Brandom's model of existential
commitments can account for religious belief in any universal sense. Conceivably,
contexts do and have existed where religious assertions could infer a kind of physical existence, or function like "common sense," connoting certainty. In the *Divine
Comedy*, for instance, Dante ascribes to "Purgatory" a spatiotemporal relationship to himself, locating it as a mountain on the far side of the world (Alighieri
1980: canto 34, lines 121–126). Of course, one could suggest that Dante's claim is
altogether different from stating, for example, that Manhattan is an island in the
northeastern United States because it cannot be verified. Again, however, this
requires the critic to impose a modernist epistemic order onto the pre-Columbian

world in which Dante is embedded. In a social order where religious truth is entangled with the political authority of the Church, as it was in Renaissance Italy, existential commitments about deities might conceivably begin from a place of certainty. European contact with the Americas facilitated more than empires, it shredded entrenched ways of experiencing the world and eventually made possible the anthropological and geological paradigms that would come to dominate in the nineteenth century.[1] Assertions of religious belief in different historical periods, therefore, might actually represent entirely distinct cognitive phenomena.

If it is possible that religious belief can reside in a place of certainty, then it might even originate and be sustained as wholly fictitious. I now briefly turn to two case studies, both newer religious movements, that can illustrate this point:

1. a neo-pagan group known as The Reformed Druids of North America, and

2. The Church of the Latter-day Dude, better known as "Dudeism."

While the doctrines of each have evolved in distinct ways, because their beliefs clearly began as fictions, it complicates how cognitive scientists might use Brandom's schema to locate religious belief.

Dudeism

The Church of the Latter-day Dude situates itself in the discursive world of the Coen brothers' cult-classic *The Big Lebowski* (1997), the tale of an aging ex-activist of the New Left whose relaxed, care-free disposition gets challenged when he is unwittingly caught up in solving an alleged kidnapping caper. While the film failed to achieve box-office success, it quietly acquired a devoted following of fans during subsequent years. Nearly a decade after the film debuted, as the legend goes, one of these fans, an American ex-patriot named Oliver Benjamin living in Thailand, formally organized the Church of the Latter-day Dude (LDD) in 2005 (Peskoe et al. 2007: 17).

Constituted primarily through its website, dudeism.com, the LDD offers adherents an amalgam of self-help resources, an online ordination service, and a network through which Dudiests may connect with each other, all framed within the satirical parlance of the film's protagonist, "the Dude" (Jeff Bridges). While claiming its origins extend back to "the original form of Chinese Taoism," these Dudeist Priests suggest that pure Dudeism became corrupted by belief in the supernatural, when it went, as they say, "all weird with magic tricks and body fluids" (Church of the Latter-day Dude undated). Being a Dudeist, instead, demands that one "take seriously" specific ethical teachings as inflected through the example of a fictional character, but does such seriousness imply that the Dudeist believer conceive of her beliefs as anything other than fictional? Are these theological fictions an attempt to deal with the presumably liminal space between fiction and literal existence that, according to Baggar, religious belief occupies?

Even though Dudeism relies heavily on humor for its appeal, it nonetheless articulates a theory of religion that contradicts Hume's statement about belief. According to the LDD website:

> *The Big Lebowski* is our founding myth; just as the Christian gospels, based on the Jesus of history, provide a portrait of the mythical Christ of faith who "died for all us sinners," the film, based on the Dude of history (Jeff Dowd), presents the mythical dude of film (Jeff Bridges) who "takes it easy for all us sinners." (Eutsey undated)

Identifying the structure of Dudeist belief with that of Christian orthodoxy gives Dudeism prestige, but it also transforms Jeff Dowd, a former political activist turned film producer that was the inspiration for the "Dude," into the postmodern hero, Jeff Lebowski, in the same way that the historical Jesus of Nazareth would become the Christ of a Triune deity. In short, belief, even when framed around historical figures, only becomes *religious* through acts of fictional narrations that authorize a certain brand of "take 'er easy" hedonism. Unlike Hume, who locates religious belief firmly between certainty and disbelief, Dudeists appear quite comfortable to reside in a world where belief or disbelief matter less than lifestyle choice. To use Brandom's schema, Dudeism begins and ends with only fictional existential commitments.

Neo-Druidism

The Reformed Druids of North America (RDNA) have a different story to tell. Founded on the campus of Carleton College in Minnesota in the early 1960s, the RDNA began not as a serious attempt to found a new religious group but as a student protest against the college administration. In 1963, the school attempted to enforce a new rule making some form of weekly participation in religious services compulsory for all students. Uncomfortable with this new policy, a small group of religiously diverse students, somewhat in jest, decided to form their own "religious" group in order to resist the requirement. "The sole motive was to protest the requirement," according to one of the founding members, "not to try for alternatives for worship" (Norman Nelson quoted in Clifton 2006: 153). The RDNA therefore parodied religion; its form and practice met the minimal criteria established at Carleton College to qualify as religion but only insofar as it could be used to undermine the legitimacy of these same criteria. Within a year, the protest proved successful and the administration removed compulsory religious worship. Despite achieving their initial goal, however, some members apparently found the community valuable and continued to meet. Apparently participants were drawn to its anti-institutional ecumenism where the specifics of belief proved less important than the benefits gained from understanding practices as "spiritual" (Reformed Druids of North America undated). Over time, however, as Reformed Druidism expanded and split into a network of loosely connected "groves" across North America, a certain orthodoxy has formed around devotion to the natural world. Sometimes referred to as "Earth Mother," "Goddess," or simply "Nature," the idea that "communing with Nature" can lead to an "awareness of religious truth" operates as a central tenet for the RDNA (ibid.).

Some of its splinter groups assert even more elaborated iterations of Nature worship. For instance, one such group, known as Ar nDaíocht Fein (ADF), describes Nature as explicitly "divine in Her own right," and that Druidic practice aims "to accept ourselves as part of Nature and not Her 'rulers'"(Ar nDaíocht Fein undated). Subscribing to what they refer to as the "Gaia hypothesis," that the "biosphere of our planet is a living being," the ADF turns environmentalist political action into "sacred duties:"

> We see talented and well trained Neopagan clergy leading thousands of people in effective magical and mundane actions to save endangered species, stop polluters, and preserve wilderness... We see Neopaganism as a mass religion, changing social, political, and environmental attitudes around the world stopping the death-mongers in their tracks. (Bonewits undated)

These bold declarations of the ADF depart drastically in tone and content from the parodic "religious" protests at Carleton College decades earlier. Yet, whatever the seriousness with which these neo-Druidic groups may approach their beliefs, it is important to note that the ADF's origins had little to do with serious beliefs about actually existing (super)natural forces. Sincerity arose out of historical change.

Perhaps even more than Dudeism, the example of North American Druidry complicates Baggar's usage of Brandom's model of existential commitments. Like the former, Reformed Druids begin not from a place of sincere belief in some concept of the supernatural but elsewhere. While Dudeists claim to reject frank religiosity altogether, Druids exhibit a varied attitude towards belief, with the RDNA leaving existential commitments largely to each individual, and its splinter groups like the ADF demanding a more robust devotion from adherents. However, both leverage humor founded on a fabrication to protest the status quo, be it a popular Hollywood film or a satirical "religion" invented by college students, respectively. In Brandom's schema, the existential commitments of these groups, at least in their inception, are demonstrably fictional. Moreover, the case of the Druids illustrates how existential commitments vary according to context. While the RDNA privileges practice over any sincere beliefs, its offshoots, like the ADF, espouse elaborate doctrines of social reform that demand ardent commitment to an actually existing "Gaia." Whatever we might call these "theologies" of Dudeists or Druids, it seems that we cannot exactly claim they emerged out of attempts to deal with some universal epistemological inadequacy of religious belief generally—that, as Hume suggests, religion rests on unstable ground because one can never be certain of its truth—because these groups crafted their beliefs with full knowledge of their invented status.

On the Very Idea of Supernatural Beliefs

If religious belief isn't naturally located between disbelief and conviction, then what can we say about other kinds of beliefs? Can non-religious beliefs operate in the same way that Hume suggests, in the Brandomian space that Baggar places supernatural existential commitments? I believe that a category such as "race," reveals this to be the case. In the postmodern context, many of us believe that "race" is a social construct, an empty signifier through which various human groups can be classified. Although it might signify certain observable attributes (skin tone, hair texture, ethnic heritage), race lacks empirical or scientific certitude. It doesn't "exist" as a naturally occurring, purely biological human trait. Rather, race functions at a socio-political register as a category that has been essential to the production of modernity. Theories of race, which typically placed "Caucasians" at the pinnacle of a hierarchy of global peoples, helped to legitimize an entire range of social arrangements in the post-Columbian world, including the trans-Atlantic African Slave trade, the subjugation, domination, and elimination of indigenous populations across the world, and global conflicts in the twentieth century.

If race lacks what Brandom calls physical existence, it nonetheless persists as more than pure fiction with bearing over some imaginary world. Instead, I suspect that most of us, at least in the US context, typically experience race *as if* it were empirically real because it continues to have real bearing on social relations. Acknowledging the constructed-ness of race fails to eliminate the continuing economic hardship or inordinate subjection to the policing power of the state facing African-Americans, as the BlackLivesMatter movement asserts. The residue of race theory is woven into the fabric of the society, shaping not only formal institutions and legal systems but the norms and habits governing individual subjectivities as well. When so-called "white nationalist" groups like the *Council of Conservative Citizens* declare that "the United States is a European Country and that Americans are part of the European people," or that "God is the One who divided mankind into different types," they are tacitly reproducing the naturalness of race.[2] Just as the fundamental Baptist will maintain the historical accuracy of Biblical narrative, some people continue to believe, despite evidence to the contrary that race is, in fact, a natural category that should hold great authority over life. Others, conversely, claim that because race is an invention, it can hold no legitimate power over life other than what we choose to give it. Consider, for example, the frequent charge that affirmative-action programs that benefit underserved minorities are themselves "racist" precisely because they perpetuate the salience of race as a category. Through the lens of Brandom's model, these two polar positions—the naturalistic and constructed notions of race—can be seen as strategies for overcoming the liminal status given to race in this postmodern epistemological order.

In sum, non-religious beliefs about race seem to exhibit the same lack of certainty as Hume's characterization of religious belief. Moreover, some of those beliefs deemed religious, such as pre-modern theological claims, appear to make spatiotemporal assertions, while others, like the Dudiests, comfortably recognize their doctrine as pure fiction. Therefore, what exactly can reasonably be stated about *religious* belief as a form of cognition, as Baggar argues? The most significant point to bear in mind for the cognitive science of religion is that religious belief differs little, if at all, from any other kind of belief. As Russell McCutcheon so aptly reminds his readers, "it is only when we start out with the presumption that religious behaviors are ordinary social behaviors—and not extraordinary private experiences—that we will come to understand them in all their subtle yet impressive complexity" (McCutcheon 2001: 14). Baggar, perhaps unintentionally, endorses a *sui generis* notion of religious belief. He argues from the proposition that existential commitments about supernatural forces are essentially distinguishable from other kinds of belief, and therefore a dataset that cognitive researchers can isolate, observe, and describe with scientific precision. Yet, I suggest that what Baggar calls "religious belief" or "existential commitments" does not represent an asocial unique domain of human cognition but rather a mode of believing unique only in relation to the socio-political and epistemological hierarchies of the modern period.

Thus, Baggar's application of Brandom is informative, but not in the manner he articulates. Brandom's model of existential commitments offers a useful vocabulary for discussing the rhetorical strategies of belief statements in specific contexts, from Dante to post-liberal theologians. Such taxonomies may be helpful for comparative work, but only insofar as they provide the scholar with a language to differentiate between discrete moments of believing. Brandom, however, cannot reveal the distinctive quality or qualities that render some beliefs or existential commitments "religious" and not others.

Furthermore, Brandom does remind the theorist of religion that an act of doing theory, like language, is a social practice, a part of a language game played by all. He highlights the pre-semantic quality of assertions, including the theoretical. In other words, doing theory is about more than explaining content; it is about, as Brandom might state, *making explicit* our inferred commitments about the order of things. This practice of theory does more than reflect one's assumptions; it simultaneously constitutes the theorist, her audience, and the wider scholarly community. Debates about theory, which I would argue can *never* be in excess, which occur in classrooms, in published scholarship, or at academic conferences, are ways of negotiating what it means to be a scholar of religion. To inflect on Smith's paraphrase of Ricoeur: *Theorizing is the unavoidable consequence of thought.*

James Dennis LoRusso is a research fellow in the Center for the Study of Religion at Princeton University. He completed his PhD in American religious cultures at Emory University. His research examines the intersection of religion, politics, and the marketplace in the United States.

Notes

1. See Bernard McGrane's monograph, *Beyond Anthropology* (1989), which unpacks how these changes overturned the dominant knowledge systems and established new grounds upon which moderns constructed notions of the "Other."
2. The Southern Poverty Law Center describes the Council for Conservative Citizens as "the modern reincarnation of the old White Citizens Councils, which were formed in the 1950s and 1960s to battle school desegregation in the South [USA]." See www. splcenter.org/fighting-hate/extremist-files/group/council-conservative-citizens for more information on CCC.

References

Alighieri, Dante. 1980. *Inferno* (trans. Allen Mandelbaum). Berkeley, CA: University of California Press.

Ar nDaiocht Fein. Undated. "What Do Neopagan Druids Believe?" Available at www.adf.org/about/basics/beliefs.html (accessed October 5, 2015).

Bonewits, Isaac. Undated. "The Vision of ADF." Available at www.adf.org/about/basics/vision.html (accessed October 5, 2015).

Church of the Latter-day Dude. Undated. "What is Dudeism?" Available at http://dudeism.com/whatisdudeism (accessed October 10, 2015).

Clifton, Chas S. 2006. *Her Hidden Children: The Rise of Wicca and Paganism in America*. Lanham, MD: AltaMira Press.

Eutsey, Dwayne. Undated. "The Take It Easy Manifesto." Available at http://dudeism.com/takeiteasymanifesto (accessed October 10, 2015).

Hume, David. 2010. *The Natural History of Religion*. Sioux Falls, SD: EZReads Publications.

McCutcheon, Russell. 2001. *Critics, Not Caretakers: Redescribing the Public Study of Religion*. Albany, NY: State University of New York Press.

McGrane, Bernard 1989. *Beyond Anthropology*. New York: Columbia University Press.

O'Conner, David. 2013. *Routledge Guidebook to Hume on Religion*. New York: Routledge.

Peskoe, Ben, Bill Green, Scott Shuffitt, and Will Russell. 2007. *I'm a Lebowski, You're a Lebowski*. New York: Bloomsbury.

Reformed Druids of North America. Undated. "A FAQ About Reformed Druidism." Available at www.rdna.info/faq.html (accessed October 12, 2015).

Smith, Jonathan Z. 1993. *Map Is Not Territory: Studies in the History of Religions*. Chicago, IL: University of Chicago Press.

Spong, John Shelby. 2003. "Easter: In Need of Reinterpretation!" April 23. Available at https://johnshelbyspong.com/2003/04/16/easter-in-need-of-reinterpretation (accessed October 30, 2015).

Tweed, Thomas. 2008. *Crossing and Dwelling: A Theory of Religion*. Cambridge, MA: Harvard University Press.

19

Reliabilism and the Limits of Pragmatism

Robyn Faith Walsh

Opening with a useful quote from Bruce Lincoln in his piece "The Study of Religion, Bricolage, and Brandom" (Chapter 16, this volume), Matthew Bagger identifies the "divided loyalties" or "theoretical ecelecticism" of the academy insofar as it concerns the "singleness of purpose, uniformity of approach, and critical intent" (p. 139, this volume) of our academic discipline. To rephrase this observation in slightly less erudite terms, one might say we have been guilty of a certain 'intellectual promiscuity' in the study of religion. Bagger goes on to delineate that Lincoln's "lament" signals an important distinction: while a "field" of study is defined in the main by its object of investigation and the question(s) at stake, a "discipline," by contrast, is tied to the implementation of method. In the case of the latter, Bagger explains that, in his view, when our investigations tether themselves too strongly to a single or orthodox method, our analyses tend to end somewhat like a Cubs baseball season (badly).

Bagger's assessment is well taken in that a narrow method for the study of religion does not make sense. That said, there remains utility in the notion of disciplinarity, albeit one that allows for dynamic interaction between disciplinarity and interdisciplinarity. In what follows, I will offer an example within my field, New Testament and Early Christian studies, where research divorced from discipline, and focused on the clustering of methods around a central question, has generated more mischief (including apologetics disguised as critical analysis) than perhaps concrete and useful outcomes—notably in the resurgence of the "oral tradition" or "oral transmission" turn for evaluating texts like the gospels. Building from this example, I will segue into a reconsideration of what lines of thought within philosophy can offer us in the study of religion. In the case of Brandom and pragmatism, I do not find that they get us very far—in fact, I argue that Brandom's brand of inferential semanticism leaves gaps too susceptible to interpolation from the same kinds of biases, interests, and concerns characteristic of uncritical or confessional approaches.

I see reliablism and a naturalized epistemology of the kind advocated by Hilary Kornblith as more promising—elevating our discourse from analysis on our *concepts of* or *intuitions about* knowledge, to analysis of the (scientific, biological) nature of knowledge itself; from investigations of *intuitions* or folk concepts of belief, to how belief actually *works* scientifically and cognitively. As Bagger quotes Lincoln elsewhere, we should endeavor to "employ ... methods" that are "rigorous, uninhibited, unintimidated ... *empirically informed* ... appropriately critical" (Lincoln quoted by Bagger, p. 140, this volume; emphasis added). I find in comparing these two philosophers—Brandom and Kornblith—we can begin to expose many of our blind spots in the field more broadly, and this will ultimately get us closer to answering another central question: can you justify religious belief in a philosophy of religion?

Beginning with Bagger's discussion of field and discipline, I do take some issue with his assessment that, "generally defined," a discipline is the sum of its methods. If a "field" is "defined by the object of its study," perhaps we can say that a discipline is a branch of knowledge within the academy devoted to the methods, questions, datasets of a particular object of study. I do not want to belabor this point, but I do want to caution against the notion of method determining discipline. The cognitive sciences, for example, are a diverse field of inquiry wherein there is not one approach. Pascal Boyer and Scott Atran certainly approach their understanding of the cognitive science of religion quite differently than, say, Justin Barrett (referenced in Bagger's chapter). Barrett is not shy about his brand of epistemology: he is a Christian within Calvinist circles whose later work attempts to locate evidence for God in our cognitive predisposition for belief in MCOs (minimally counterintuitive objects). But he is not a wolf in sheep's clothing. Moreover, his personal convictions do not render his research useless as long as we are able to distinguish his parochial interests from the utility of the results. "Uncritical apologetics" would be for someone with narrow aims shopping for a "cutting edge critical theory" that suits their predetermined purposes.

Now to be clear, Bagger is advocating for an approach to the study of religion "driven by questions about the material we study; it should not be the attempt to deploy systematically the latest theory" (p. 141, this volume). But I fear that an approach to the study of religion that focuses on diversity and eclecticism—for example, identifying questions and clustering theory around them—presents its own pitfalls. The eclectic use of theory can quickly shade into a kind of "theory shopping" for methods that are too aligned with our intuitions about a given object of study.

This brings me to the example from my field of New Testament, sometimes called Early Christian studies, sometimes called the study of Christian Origins (in any of these cases, a tortured descriptor that in itself reveals a variety of biases and apologetics)—that is, the oral transmission of "text." Usefully, Hans Frei helps contextualize the issue.

In the eighteenth and nineteenth centuries, the texts of the New Testament were increasingly viewed through a "critical" lens within the academy. The field of what would come to be known as early Christian or New Testament studies imagined itself as departing from what Frei termed a "pre-critical" reading of these ancient writings. As these vanguards of the field began formulating their questions for critical inquiry, however, their beliefs and intuitions about the social world of the first-century rendered their efforts futile from the start. Moreover, their assumptions about their own "field" directed them to eclectic methods and theories from the fields of literature, folk studies, archaeology, classics and so on, broadly conceived.

First, the field continued to advance the view that the literature and social history of the first-century Jesus movement are best understood within the context of "early Christian communities." Upon reflection, the concept of "community" employed by these early critical scholars, in many respects, mirrored coeval, German Romantic ideas on folk speech, oral traditions and communal authorship. This uncritical adaptation of certain Romantic concepts by the field represented a fundamental flaw in the historical-critical efforts of the thinkers Frei describes as "explaining the thoughts of the biblical authors... on the basis of the most likely, natural, and specific conditions of history, culture, and individual life" (Frei 1974: 18).

Rather than offering an historical analysis of the writing culture of the first-century, studies that referred to communities of early Christians reified the mythic origins of Christianity as established by texts like the Acts of the Apostles.[1] In so doing, these so-called "critical" treatments of the New Testament participated in maintaining a theological narrative about the miraculous development and cohesion of early or "primitive" Christianity, ignoring the reality that writing texts in the first-century was largely the purview of the educated who possessed associated means for the production and dissemination of writings. This more plausible historical and social context for the gospel writers—that is, that they were elite cultural producers, writing a creative biography about a Judean teacher—was *and continues to be* overlooked as scholars persist with investigations into the, frankly, presumed "oral traditions" behind these texts. While certain oral precursors may certainly have existed, this possibility must be discussed and (re)described with a great deal more nuance and with greater attention to the specific details of the social practices being postulated.

And this isn't a problem exclusive to New Testament studies. More broadly, (what we might call) Biblical scholarship has believed too forcefully in the alleged superior ability of the ancients to transmit their traditions orally. For example, Romantic-era thinkers interpreted the prevalence of perceptual metaphors in the Hebrew Bible as evidence that the ancient Israelites were cognitively primitive but nearer to nature and God than themselves. There was no concrete cognitive evidence cited for this claim. Scholars associated with this school of thought posited that the poetry of the Hebrew Bible was somehow more "pure" than other literatures and also representative of an underlying oral tradition.

Again, shades of this kind of thinking persist to this day. The work of folklorists Milman Parry and Albert Lord in the early twentieth century, for instance, greatly influenced Homeric and New Testament scholarship with their suggestion that recurrent "themes" in literature, such as repetitions or certain grammatical formulae (e.g., "wine-dark sea," "swift-footed Achilles") indicated the presence of lost verbal cues for oral poets (see, for instance, Lord 1991). By the mid-twentieth century, scholars began to associate nearly any literary device, variations in syntax, repetition or even lacunae within a text as evidence for an oral precedent.

Moreover, oral poetry became increasingly synonymous with illiteracy and the concept of "oral societies," which were imagined to possess unique and superior techniques of memorization, memory retention, and transmission of "oral texts." Approaching the end of the last century, trajectories in Early Christian studies began to speak of the fixed nature of oral poetry and prose and to take for granted the reliability of the ancient Hebrew poet and early Christian author to preserve the speech and sayings of notable figures like Jesus.[2]

In reference to more recent scholarship in the field along these lines, comparatively few studies have consulted emerging research in the cognitive and neurosciences on the structures and reliability of memory. Research on constructive memory frameworks, for instance, reveals that memory is highly transient and affected by a variety of forms of bias (e.g., encoding memory with elements from previous experience), or suggestibility or misattribution of ancillary events to a given subject. Increasingly, memory is viewed not as a reliable recording of the past, but as a complex and dynamic construction of aspects of memory coupled with a variety of neuropsychological, heuristic, and other associations. But if one is committed to the question: "How did illiterate early Christian communities transmit their oral traditions from the foot of the cross to the ear of a gospel writer two generations later," one is likely to gravitate to an eclectic bundle of theory that confirms this particular intuited myth of origins.

In my view, this is where Brandom raises some red flags. I have already outlined that Brandom's pragmatic and social semantic approach emphasizes the idea that meaning comes from making inferences and giving reasons. Thus, when it comes to something like belief, a Brandomian approach would be not to study *belief* but *ideas* about belief. One would not study *knowledge* as, to borrow a phrase frequented by Kornblith, "a natural kind" but to study *concepts* of knowledge. Brandom also tends to prefer somewhat "contrived situations" in his analyses (take his hypothetical scenario of concentric circles of barn façades, for example) rather than concrete evaluation of a human being's natural environment (Brandom 1994: 209–210). Thus a Brandomian approach also presupposes the following (most of which can be found in his *Making it Explicit*):[3]

1. Adult human beings—not non-human animals and not human children—are the only beings or agents with the ability to form second order beliefs based on reflective mental states.[4]

2. Adult human beings are the only beings able to acquire new information about their environment and adjust or modify their beliefs, whereas non-human animals and human children have fixed belief.

3. Adult human beings are the only beings with concepts of belief, reason and truth (see Brandom 1994: 195ff.; Kornblith 2014: 207ff.).

4. Only adult human beings are "epistemologically responsible" and not "passive information processors."

5. Only the belief of adult human beings is "apt for normative assessment" and only adult human beings are "responsive to reason." Thus, adult human beings are the only beings "capable of genuine knowledge."

6. While the mental processes of non-human animals can be evaluated by the sciences, adult human cognition is immune to such scrutiny and, therefore, is not a natural phenomenon (see Brandom 1994: 199–271; Kornblith 2014: 208).

7. Thus, adult human beings have a "special epistemic access" to what is in our minds because our account of knowledge amounts to understanding our "humanly created concept." Kornblith describes this elsewhere as an "a priori knowledge of the content of our concepts" (Kornblith 2014: 139).

Brandom's pragmatist "meditations" rely upon the same nineteenth-century speculative frameworks that have long assumed: (first) the mind is a blank slate; (second) language and mind are holistic; (third) language (as we understand it) is all encompassing; and (fourth) that humans are (really) the only subjects that matter. Current research in the sciences does not support Brandom's operating assumptions. Neural signatures for human infants as young as eighteen months of age indicate that they can both acquire information about their environment in order to form beliefs and attribute beliefs to others (see, for example, Kampis et al. 2015). Cognitive research on the neural basis of the category of belief ("certainty in the truth or falsity of a non-testable proposition") indicates that adult human beings process the truth value of propositions with the medial prefrontal cortex, caudate, posterior cingulate, and the middle temporal gyrus, as evidenced on fMRI (functional magnetic resonance imaging); in other words, it is a *natural* process, observable and testable (Howlett and Paulus 2015: cit. 1). Contemporary research on animal behavior demonstrates that non-human animals possess more dynamic cognitive processes than pragmatism might otherwise allow. One might even argue that pragmatist assumptions about animals and the natural world harken back to an age that claimed that any beings understood in social dis course and practice to be "soulless" (e.g., human slaves and non-human animals) felt no pain and were little more than machines (e.g., Descartes 1897–1913, 1957, cited in Harrison 1989: 79). Further research examples are legion.

By contrast, philosophers like Kornblith who adopt a naturalism approach suggest that we are paying a huge price for accepting premises like those of the pragmatists above. For instance, certain assumptions about the nature of our data can foster category mistakes. When philosophers *assume* and then assert that animals do not have knowledge or belief, they commit the unforced error of naming (and, thus, defining) an adult human's ability to adapt to environmental change as "reflection," whereas with other beings this activity is described as Pavlovian. A truly naturalistic account of knowledge calls for a different approach to our subject matter. First, it would not rely on a humanly created concept of knowledge.

While Brandom's emphasis on the *social* is, indeed, an important corrective to approaches like that of Frei, we also know that human society is rife with false beliefs and folk intuitions. Science almost always has been able to *empirically* undermine such missteps. Kornblith explains:

> If we regard the category of knowledge as a human creation, we might think that it is thereby more easily accessible to us than if it is located out in the world. Thus, if giving a philosophical account of knowledge amounts to understanding our humanly created concept, then on some views, we will thereby have a kind of special epistemic access to it that we do not have to the outside world in our minds ... If knowledge is a natural kind, rather than a humanly created concept, it being a natural kind need make it no more epistemically remote or inaccessible than water and gold ... (Kornblith 2014: 139–140)

Elsewhere, Kornblith clarifies that human interests and definitions cannot define an organism's environment or what we in the humanities might call "context" or "milieu." Observations about the nature of knowledge and how it is obtained must be grounded in the observation of an organism's adaptation to change "where the notion of environment is not given in any way by human interests or practices" (ibid.: 65).

With this brief overview and comparison of Brandom and Kornblith, I hope the utility of a naturalistic epistemology for the study of religion comes into sharper relief. Under Brandom, something like "canonical designators" certainly provides us with one entré into reconsidering the frameworks of "participants in a discursive social practice." But Kornblith takes us a step further by emphasizing the need to treat our understanding of the sociology of knowledge as a demystified category for scrutiny. To illustrate what I mean by this, allow me to return to my example from New Testament/Early Christian studies. If I were to take for granted that the categories of "religious community" for the early Christian writers, a social analysis of the kind Brandom provides might help me talk more fruitfully about the imagined social dynamics of that exchange in the first-century. But my premise would be fundamentally based on false intuition. Kornblith, on the other hand, would encourage a reexamination of the concept of oral transmission and cognitive difference that might help reveal that my intuitions about oral traditions and communities are misguided. It is a more empirical methodology. In this respect even Barrett with his apologetic stance engages the empirical to a degree even greater than Brandom.

Robyn Faith Walsh is Assistant Professor of New Testament and Early Christianity at the University of Miami (Florida). Her research interests include the letters of Paul, the history of the interpretation of the Synoptic problem, Greco-Roman archaeology, and cognitive science. She is currently working on the influence of Romanticism on the field of early Christian studies and authorship practices in antiquity.

Acknowledgements

I would like to thank Matthew Bagger and the NAASR group for the opportunity to respond to such an interesting paper. I would also like to thank Stanley Stowers for our many conversations about this topic and my student at University of Miami, Quinn McKinnon, for assisting me in researching relevant studies in the cognitive sciences.

Notes

1. On the subject of Romanticism's influence on early Christian studies, see Stowers (2011: 238–256).
2. I am thinking here about scholars like Richard Horsley using the work of folklorists and ethnomusicologists like James Foley, translating the means and methods of beat poets to first-century, Palestinian scribes and so on (see, for example, Horsley and Draper 1999; Foley 2002).
3. For a thoroughgoing critique of Brandom and his cohort, see Kornblith (2014). I heavily rely on Kornblith's account of reliablism in my own critique and he raises many of these same objections, albeit without this precise enumeration.
4. Brandom distinguishes between adult humans, human children, and animals on the basis that human children and animals are unable to ask and give reasons. Thus, given that knowledge depends on judgment for Brandom and, in his estimation, animals do not judge, animals do not "think" (see Brandom 1994: 199–271; see also Kornblith 2014: 207ff.).

References

Brandom, Robert. 1994. *Making it Explicit: Reasoning, Representing, and Discursive Commitment.* Cambridge, MA: Harvard University Press.

Descartes, René. 1897–1913. "Letter CXCII (to Mersenne)." In Charles Adam and Paul Tannery (eds.), *Oeuvres de Descartes*, vol. III, 85. Paris: L. Cerf.

Descartes, René. 1957. *A Discourse on Method* (trans. John Veitch). London: Dent.

Foley, James Miles. 2002. *How to Read an Oral Poem*. Urbana, IL: University of Illinois Press.

Frei, Hans W. 1974. *The Eclipse of Biblical Narrative: A Study in Eighteenth and Nineteenth Century Hermeneutics.* New Haven, CT: Yale University Press.

Harrison, Peter. 1989. "Theodicy and Animal Pain." *Philosophy* 64(247): 79–92.

Horsley, Richard and Jonathan Draper. 1999. *Whoever Hears You Hears Me: Prophets, Performance, and Tradition in Q.* Harrisburg, PA: Trinity Press International,

Howlett, Jonathan R. and Martin P. Paulus. 2015. "The Neural Basis of Testable and Non-Testable Beliefs." *PLoS ONE* 10(5): e0124596.

Kampis, Dora, Eugenio Parise, Gergely Csibra, and Ágnes Melinda Kovács. 2015. "Neural Signatures for Sustaining Object Representations Attributed to Other in Preverbal Human Infants." *Proceedings of the Royal Society B* 282: 20151683.

Kornblith, Hilary. 2014. *A Naturalistic Epistemology: Selected Papers.* Oxford: Oxford University Press.

Lord, Albert Bates. 1991. *Epic Singers and Oral Tradition.* Ithaca, NY: Cornell University Press.

Stowers, Stanley K. 2011. "The Concept of 'Community' and the History of Early Christianity." *Method and Theory in the Study of Religion* 23: 238–256.

20

A Reply

Matthew C. Bagger

Let me begin by extending my thanks to Rebekka King (Chapter 17, this volume), James LoRusso (Chapter 18, this volume), and Robyn Walsh (Chapter 19, this volume) for giving my essay (Chapter 16, this volume) such attention. What a rare delight to have one's work subjected to extended analysis and searching criticism from sharp readers who home in on the crucial issues! Although I might wish to engage these readers on a variety of lesser topics (e.g., Hume interpretation), I will reply to the concerns they raise about the two central components of my essay. In the essay I argue that students of religion should view themselves as working in a field (rather than participating in a discipline), and then I try to exemplify the usefulness of this theoretical pluralism by putting Robert Brandom's philosophy to work in the study of religion. The responses to my essay express reservations about both the general point and the specific application.

King cites all-too-familiar practical worries when she queries the wisdom of configuring the study of religion as a field. We work in a time of crisis for the humanities. Short-sighted, anti-intellectual administrators seek ways of saving money, and what tidier way than disbanding the Department of Religion and distributing its interdisciplinary faculty among the disciplines? If we frame ourselves as a discipline, she implies, we might fend off ravening administrators. I have no simple rejoinder to this argument or answer to the practical worry generating it. I spent several years as the sole student of religion housed in a philosophy department. Despite the congeniality of my colleagues, I would not wish that such an arrangement become the norm! Presenting ourselves as "a discipline with distinct theories and methods" addressed to shared questions might well help us to preserve ourselves institutionally, but I wish King had elaborated on just what "distinct theories and methods" she has in mind. If we list the thinkers most responsible for the theories and methods we tend to employ, how many belong to a theoretical matrix distinct to the study of religion? Durkheim? No. Weber? No. Marx? No. Nietzsche? No. Evans-Pritchard? No. Lévi-Strauss? No. Douglas? No. Festinger? No. Goffman? No. Geertz? No. Horton? No. Turner? No. Foucault? No. Said? No. Bourdieu? No. Butler? No. Bloch? No. Nancy Jay did truly innovative theoretical work from a position within the study of religion, but that's hardly reason enough to think her theory is distinct to a discipline called the study of religion. Those, by contrast, whom we can easily identify as belonging to a theoretical matrix distinct to the study of religion, or who have tried to impose one, have become cautionary tales told to our undergraduate students (e.g., Eliade).

In my chapter I characterized a discipline as generally defined, at least in part, by the regimentation of its methods. Walsh takes issue with this characterization and recommends a substitute. "A discipline," she tentatively suggests, is "a branch of knowledge within the academy devoted to the methods, questions, [and] data sets of a particular object of study" (p. 166, this volume). This alternative formulation effaces the distinction I attempted to draw between a field "defined by the object of its study" and a discipline defined in part by its methods. Walsh makes her intention to blur my distinction clear in subsequent sentences, in which she warns that one should not consider "a discipline the sum of its methods" and cites the example of the cognitive sciences. The cognitive sciences, while presumably a discipline, "are a diverse *field* of inquiry wherein there is not one approach," she writes (ibid.; italics added). I have nothing invested in my definitions and do not necessarily resist Walsh's effort to muddy the terminological waters. Nothing of importance rests on the terminology. The crucial question remains, regardless of how one defines "discipline": precisely how "diverse" (to use Walsh's word) or "eclectic" (to use mine) should the approaches employed in the study of religion be?

Walsh impugns my position by adducing an example from her field, New Testament and early Christian studies. Early historical criticism, which adopted methods originating in the "fields of literature, folk studies, archeology, classics and so on" (p. 167, this volume) failed to interrogate certain theological assumptions about Christian origins. The legacy of this scholarly tradition continues to distort scholarship on the Bible. Recent psychological studies of memory have, however, helped to identify and rectify the unrecognized apologetic influence on work in the field. Walsh takes this example to demonstrate the dangers that a commitment to theoretical eclecticism presents. I draw the opposite conclusion from the example. As I see it, the willingness to consult work in psychology provided the critical distance necessary to critique central assumptions. What she takes to be a counterexample, in fact, resoundingly supports my central claim: theoretical diversity presents "the best antidote to uncritical, apologetic approaches to religion" (p. 139, this volume). Again, however, the question arises: how much diversity? Walsh points out that the cognitive sciences themselves exhibit a diversity of approaches. I find it hard to believe that she would limit the study of religion to the approaches found in the cognitive sciences. Granting that psychology disclosed a blind spot in New Testament Studies, would she entirely abandon the methods found in the "fields of literature, folk studies, archeology, classics," and, of course, history? I do not believe she would. She's too good of a scholar. When pursued without sufficient attention to archeology, classics, history, and, yes, even philosophy, the cognitive science of religion has produced embarrassing blunders. Walsh's training in archeology, history, classics, etc. puts her in an ideal position to diagnose those blunders (as well as to discern the truly significant work in the cognitive science of religion). Theoretical eclecticism of the sort I advocate provides reciprocal critical leverage.

In my use of Brandom, LoRusso accuses me of treating religion as *sui generis*, whereas Walsh takes me to task for not treating knowledge as a natural kind. To put the criticisms in less arcane language, I am too essentialist ... or not essentialist enough. I am not sensitive enough to "human interests and definitions"... or too sensitive to "human interests and definitions." As for my intellectual sympathies, Walsh is closer to the truth. I am as thoroughgoing an anti-essentialist as the pragmatists (who are generally credited as being the first anti-essentialists) would have me be. In her criticism of Brandom (and, by implication, me), however, I think she is unfair. Nothing Brandom says suggests (or even "harkens back" to claims) that slaves felt no pain. The distinction between sentience and sapience that he employs rules out the suggestion that animals feel no pain. When, moreover, Brandom rejects Kornblith's variety of "naturalism," that does not mean that Brandom denies that language processing is natural or that it occurs by means of the brain! He points out that concepts involve norms of application and to apply a concept is to make a move that is subject to norms (e.g., If I say that cats require periodic tune-ups, oil changes, and tire rotations, I am violating the norms for the application of the term "cat"). Norms obtain, furthermore, in virtue of a social practice. Insofar as propositional belief requires the application of concepts, social practices, therefore, rather than the brain, are the appropriate locus of inquiry. In an interview Brandom explains:

> One of the central tasks of philosophy is to understand the normativity of human belief and agency, the dimension of responsibility it involves, the way we bind ourselves and make ourselves subject to assessments of the correctness or appropriateness of our attitudes. I don't think there is a natural scientific story to be told about this sort of conceptual normativity. But that is not to say that it is *supernatural*. I think it is an essentially social phenomenon: we brought commitments and entitlements into the world when we started to take or treat each other in practice not only as doing things, but as *committed* or *entitled* to do them. One can no more understand this normative dimension of our activity by looking into our brains than one can understand what it is to join a political party or to mortgage one's house by studying carefully the marks on paper that constitute the signature by which (in the right social setting) one did those things. (Penco 1999: 144–145.)

The role of social practice in generating norms means the lab may not be the place to investigate concepts. We can, however, learn much about cognition in the lab, including, for instance, the processes of memory. Brandom's anti-essentialism in no way imperils science, even much cognitive science (remember that pragmatism was first and foremost a philosophy of science). Discursive social practice is embodied practice that includes interaction with the environing world. Despite Walsh's assertion to the contrary, there's no reason to think that on Brandom's view inquiry could not prove our intuitions (even about ourselves) false.

Brandom's insistence that social practices generate norms, and therefore concepts, builds conceptual diversity into his model *ab initio*. Concepts will be as various as the norms instituted by the participants of different discursive practices interacting with their environments. Kinds of existence will likewise be as various as the practical attitudes of the participants in different discursive practices because practical attitudes determine which class(es) of singular terms serve as canonical designators. How discursive practices relate various kinds of existence to one another will also depend on the practical attitudes of the participants. All this room for diversity should cast doubt on LoRusso's claim that my analysis "holds [only] within a modernist regime of knowing" (p. 158, this volume), and begin to answer King's questions about the applicability of Brandom's analysis apart from "Western concepts of subjectivity and assumptions about the social roles of language" (p. 153, this volume).

In my chapter I make reference to Hume because he articulates an issue that has perennially recurred in the study of religion. To add to the examples I mention in the paper, Robin Horton's classic essays on African religion compare belief in the existence of religious entities to belief in the existence of non-religious entities. Geertz subtly asks about how religious worldviews are rendered (variously) realistic. I turn to Brandom because he provides us with a way to analyze and reframe the issue (so as to avoid the shortcomings of Hume's discussion) that enables us to attend to the indefinitely diverse ways that religions as "we" define them conceive of the existence of their superhuman authorities and how they relate that kind of existence to the other kinds of existence their discursive practices generate. Hume marks a point of departure for my inquiry, but he does not fix the terms of my inquiry. With Brandom's theoretical vocabulary we can consider cases at odds with Hume's summary claim about religious belief. I discuss Frei in particular because his explicit discussions of history and fiction make the dynamics I'm trying to illuminate easier to see because of the way they echo the *examples* of kinds of existence Brandom provides. Frei's narrative theology functions for me as an especially convenient illustration of an attempt to revise the norms of a discursive practice that give sense to claims about God's existence and his authority over other types of existence.

LoRusso argues that Neo-Druidism "illustrates how existential commitments vary according to context" (p. 161, this volume). Exactly. Brandom gives us both a way of understanding how this diversity could be the case (whereas much cognitive science would seem to stymie such an understanding) and a useful theoretical vocabulary for comparison. As LoRusso rightly notes, Brandom "cannot reveal the distinctive quality or qualities that render some beliefs or existential commitments 'religious' and not others" (p. 163, this volume). As I read J. Z. Smith, to whom LoRusso refers at the beginning of his paper, we scholars of religion must take responsibility for the definition of religion we employ in our research, keeping in mind the implicit comparisons and taxonomies our definition inscribes. Smith's anti-essentialism serves the cause of definition and theory building. It allows us to have self-conscious control of our definitions, the theories they imply, and the data domains they circumscribe. In my chapter, I try to be explicit about my definition and the commitments it entails. Neither LoRusso nor I would include race in the category of religion, but I think he astutely recognizes the usefulness of Brandom's account of existential commitments for analyzing discourse about race. When someone says that races exist, we must locate the relevant canonical designators that give existence its sense in this case. Stephen Jay Gould wrote somewhere about the irony that the same biologists who insist that races don't exist are called upon by the police to identify the race of badly decomposed cadavers. The biologists are clearly denying the intersubstitutability of race with one set of referring expressions (those treated as canonical designators by the Council of Conservative Citizens, perhaps?) and implicitly affirming the intersubstitutability of race with another set.

I appreciate the opportunity King, LoRusso, and Walsh have afforded me to rethink and rearticulate the position I take in my original paper. I hope someday to return the favor.

Matthew Bagger teaches in the Department of Religious Studies at the University of Alabama. He is the author of *Religious Experience, Justification, and History* (Cambridge University Press, 1999), *The Uses of Paradox: Religion, Self-Transformation, and the Absurd* (Columbia University Press, 2007), and editor of *Pragmatism, Naturalism, and Religion* (Columbia University Press, forthcoming).

Reference

Penco, Carlo. 1999. "Interview with Robert Brandom." *Epistemologia* 22: 143–150.

Part VI

21

Theory Is the Best Accessory: Branding and the Power of Scholarly Compartmentalization

Leslie Dorrough Smith

In a chapter from her book *No Logo*, social activist Naomi Klein describes a situation that may have some purchase for those of us interested in the study of religion. Klein recalls how, as a member of the "progressive youth" of the late 1980s and early 1990s, she and others were fighting for visibility in media and marketing that would provide the queer community equal identity representation at the same time that it would overturn old stereotypes (Klein 2009: 107).

While Klein goes on to discuss the naivety of thinking that all things can be solved through equal airtime, her interest lies more in considering what must be bought and sold to make such publicity possible. While at one point in time the LGBTQ movement was despised by mainstream culture, she notes, the tables turned very quickly as various corporations caught wind of the marketability of diversity talk and subsequently flew their rainbow flags (ibid.: 112–113).

What Klein is interested in analyzing is not just the evolution of a category, but how such categories become brands. As with all brands, the diversity campaigns she describes were (and still today, are) designed to do two specific things: first, and perhaps most obviously, they are designed to generate capital. In this sense, things that are marketed under a brand cannot stray too far from the boundaries and constraints of what the brand's designers need it to be—that is, edgy enough to entice, but conservative enough for buy-in.

Second, the brand is designed to obscure. The critical function of diversity branding, Klein notes, is to fend off what she calls the corporate "nightmare moment," which is that point when the public realizes that what we are being sold by corporations of all stripes is nothing other than the products we have always been sold, but simply with different packaging (ibid.: 117). Questions about what diversity is, or whether it has been achieved, may end up mattering very little when it comes to the success of the campaign.

In light of Luther Martin and Don Wiebe's reflections from more than a decade ago (reprinted as Chapter 1 of the present volume) on what was then NAASR's twenty-year history, we have reached an interesting point, and, some might claim, a paradoxical one: perhaps now more than ever, it seems like many scholars in our field feel the need to describe to others the nature of their relationship with method and theory. As we are aware, though, recognizing the existence of method and theory is different from actually engaging them, even if we are tempted to take this recognition as some sort of progress. The fact that it is now fashionable to say that one "does" method and theory without any serious interface with either one feels more to me like a sign of just the opposite, however, for reasons that recall Klein's analysis: while it is encouraging to have positive attention for something important, that attention may backfire if the thing itself is somehow completely misunderstood or lost in the process.

I want to consider the notion that method and theory are, together, the hot new item being sold under the brand of religious studies, and like all branded things, their joint appeal is maintained only to the degree that they are construed in specific ways that offer the aforementioned edgy conservatism. This conservatism can take many forms, but I am particularly interested in thinking about how methodological and theoretical engagement are trinkets given lip service in our field, at the same time that they are systematically undermined in the name of preserving the field's longstanding reverence for certain types of *sui generis* discourse.

This undermining happens by treating method and theory more like accessories to scholarship rather than scholarship's very foundation. It is important to note that most religious studies scholars would probably argue that method and theory are vital to good scholarship. After all, if we cannot rigorously examine how and why we study something, and then go on to formulate large scale analyses about how the social dynamics that drive religion operate, then much of our work has no integrity, they might suggest.

But as I will shortly discuss, methodological and theoretical concerns are often not applied with such care. Many scholars now function with intentionally incomplete models of method and theory and/or confuse any sort of analysis with theory, leaving the category itself with little meaning. In addition, the branding of method and theory talk has permitted others to compartmentalize theoretical work as a matter of preference, allowing many to discuss theory as something one simply "doesn't do," in much the same way that some of us "don't do" Renaissance Christianity or Islam in Indonesia.

But if we are to earnestly consider what circumstances have caused method and theory to emerge as the latest and greatest disciplinary widget, then I suspect we will need to turn our attention to the very ways that we are first taught to professionally conceive of them when we are graduate students. The rite of graduate training (and what, for many, is the immediately pursuant job search) seems an important place to start, as many recent graduates are using the category "method and theory" as a noteworthy line on their CVs. The fact that it is often listed as a specialty alongside their teaching certificates and other sorts of supplementary training should give us some pause, for many now presume that their required graduate coursework on the topic makes them qualified to teach it in much the same way that a couple of weekend seminars provides the know-how for an IT or service-learning credential. This is but one piece of evidence to demonstrate the growing treatment of method and theory as a marketable fad or trend, one that, I will suggest, is only fashionable because it has become something that can be so easily discarded.

Thus the task of this essay is to consider the role that graduate training in our field may play in generating some of the present attention given to method and theory, attention that may nevertheless render the category as little more than a flash in the pan. My observations may sound, at times, rather simple (not to mention anecdotal), but I want to suggest that they describe formative moments in graduate training, the importance of which we may otherwise overlook. Many of the dynamics that I am about to discuss were relatively invisible to me until I began graduate work in a field outside of religious studies (women's and gender studies) that tends to approach theoretical issues in a different way. To be clear, such tendencies are not isolated to a particular university, school, or program. Rather, I think they are the result of a disciplinary blindness to political realities within religious studies that enable an intolerance for specific facets of critique. I think we will see that certain elements of method and theory have been and continue to be excluded, re-appropriated, or otherwise truncated for the sake of maintaining our branded discipline, a move directly reflective of the field's current political landscape.

Ambivalence and Invisibility

We are all probably aware that having students take method and theory coursework does not ensure that they have a clear sense of the significance or centrality of that work, despite the fact that it is now standard to have a course or series of courses that cover method and theory in virtually every graduate program. But rather than chalk that up to student naivety, it is important to recognize that even scholars have wildly different expectations about the "proper" uses of method and theory.

While there are a number of approaches to teaching about them, perhaps one of the most common models has method and theory coursework operating separately and co-terminously from the topical courses that presumably address the "real" reason why most students perceive they are there, not unlike our undergraduates who see their core/general education courses as possibly interesting but ultimately inconsequential stops on the road to a major.

This is not a "separate but equal" approach, however, for there is often an unspoken ambivalence that surrounds the merits of theory coursework, a disease that does not exist in more topical courses. I sense that this is not because religious studies graduate students misapprehend the importance of those courses. Rather, I think they rightly perceive that the field is in a state of denial, for scholars of religion are highly reticent to discuss our discipline as a thoroughly political exercise. At the same time, they teach graduate students that method and theory—the resources we use to describe and explain the nature of power relationships—are important. Since both method and theory involve a certain degree of self-reflexive work, taking them seriously often involves taking disciplinary power seriously. This means that, in many realms of religious studies,

one can reconcile this dissonance only if method and theory are accessorized—
that is, if they become some sort of attractive, but removable, bauble.

From a personal standpoint, I discovered this through an interesting comparative experience. I pursued graduate training in religious studies and women's
and gender studies simultaneously, and was surprised by the differences in how
method and theory were described by the scholars defining both fields at that
time. While my religious studies theory exposure was quite comprehensive in
terms of the content I received, I was nevertheless aware that:

1. it was presumed that I knew what to do with my method and
   theory coursework, despite the fact that that nugget of information
   remained unspoken;

2. "method and theory" really meant "theory," which I will address
   shortly; and

3. I could intellectually bypass the content of those courses and still
   produce acceptable scholarship in our field, for I was seeing both my
   peers and established scholars do it all the time.

On the other hand, the very first readings that I encountered in my women's
and gender studies coursework introduced the term "theory," described its necessity to the entirety of our intellectual enterprise, and presupposed that rigorous
self-examination was an important part of research production. We discussed
how it was impossible to engage in solid critical analysis without theory, for the
very sorts of meta-analytical perspectives that theory engages are what drive
group interests, and that was what made the world go round. This attitudinal
difference (if we might call it that) between these disciplines might also explain
why, in graduate school, I was usually most concerned in my religious studies
courses about overlooking some bit of local analysis or whether I could choose
some incredibly unique and sparkling topic to explore, but in my women's and
gender studies courses, my biggest fear was that I had inadequately assessed my
own political positionality.

It is possible that the very presuppositions that fuel these fields are responsible
for how method and theory are treated—and the differences between them are
politically telling. Because women's and gender studies scholars tend to embrace
an openly activist identity at the same time that they do not presume their own
cultural popularity, I would wager that many do not assume that any aspect of
their argument will be taken for granted. In my women's and gender studies
training, I was constantly pushed to defend my positions in ways that directly
interfaced with critical inquiry and which demonstrated applicability outside of
specific contexts. The very fact that many scholars of religion have the luxury of
denying or ignoring their politics is revealing of the epistemological basis upon
which a large portion of our field rests.

As anecdotal as this might be, I hope it nevertheless communicates the point
that, at least in my training and later entry into the job market, I picked up on

the difference between a field that is ambivalent about method and theory and one that, in many respects, values them as the basis of its credibility, even if it sometimes applies them in questionable ways. I came to see self-critique and meta-analysis as built-in, disciplinary components of women's and gender studies, and thus I had a tangible scholarly model for what such political awareness looked like. Even if I produced scholarship that was critical of that field, within the parameters of my women's and gender studies training I was still doing something recognizable *as* scholarship. I never got the idea, in other words, that I was picking at a sore spot, or even worse, that I had gone rogue.

Discomfort and Alliances

I mentioned earlier that the existing ambivalence over method and theory in religious studies might be one reason for its compartmentalization in graduate coursework, keeping it relatively separate from content courses. The practical reasons given for this arrangement are many, but the most common is that it is an efficient delivery system for a diverse group of students with wide-ranging interests.

But if we are being perfectly honest, we should acknowledge that pedagogical models can be endlessly reworked, and yet method and theory cannot be divorced from content and still remain anything with substance or significance. Put differently, there is no need for method and theory unless we have something to which to apply them. The fact that we do not see *that* as a practical consideration in course structuring is revealing, for what such an arrangement tacitly permits is the exploration of a data source outside of methodological or theoretical concerns.

If students are taught to be ambivalent about method and theory more broadly, then it becomes quite easy for these very same scholars-in-training to abandon such concerns when a theoretically and/or methodologically robust analysis leads to uncomfortable places. While this can happen in many ways, there are two specific situations that come to mind that I believe briefly deserve our attention if only because they are so common. My sense is that because a fair number of our students come to the field with liberal political commitments and/or some sort of Eliadian interpretation of religion (even if they don't label it as such), these are the areas where they are least likely to be pushed to engage in critical analysis.

Specialization as Anti-Theory

Selective theorizing—that is, engaging theoretical insights only when convenient—may be something that happens as a byproduct of the way we train students to think about the scope of their data. For many graduate students, the sign that they are embarking on "serious" scholarship is the continued narrowing of their research focus so that what began as a student interested in "American religion" becomes someone examining "New England Unitarianism between 1890 and 1894." Of course, these constraints are often necessary in order to create manageable research projects, but at the same time it may be possible that the focus on narrowness as a scholarly virtue enables us to choke off method and theory's possibilities in the name of eliminating unnecessary fluff.

For instance, I can think of several junior scholars, who, as religious studies graduate students, were discouraged from engaging with theory because an advisor argued that a particular theorist was irrelevant if that theorist did not directly address the student's data in their theory-making. Still others have been discouraged from pursuing theoretical engagement because their work was historical; the presumption was that theoretical and historical angles are somehow mutually exclusive, or, at the very least, that the theoretical would detract from the "real" historical work at play.

These are fairly logical conclusions to draw if one views method and theory as accessories rather than foundations. What is enabled in this narrowing or even omission of method and theory is a model for scholarship that has been popular, if not predominant, in our field for decades. This model favors a more encyclopedic approach to scholarship, where focus is placed on lists of characteristics that describe various groups (including beliefs, myths, rituals, ethics, etc.), and featuring few, if any, questions about the nature of those lists.

(Even More) Selective Theorizing

Another way in which this selective theorizing happens is in the countless examples of scholarship that engage reductionism only when it aids in the deconstruction (and thus perceived discrediting) of unpopular groups. Since the brand of religious studies is often marketed as something expressive of a progressive theological voice, or concerns over "justice" (or any number of other ideological positions that are taken to be neutral or ethically self-evident), these preconditions make it such that a scholar can excuse him/herself from applying theories consistently across a variety of social groups when doing so may prove counterintuitive to that scholar's own political vision or projects.

It is already intriguing to consider the dynamics behind the assumption that reductionism is an anti-religious stance. But for those of us who study these unpopular groups (which, in my case, is evangelical Christians) the lopsided reductionist critiques become hard to miss. As a very straightforward example, consider the fact that while the false-consciousness model is still a prominent explanatory framework used to explain Christian fundamentalism (whose adherents, this model contends, are misled by conservative patriarchal structures to embrace a rigid, dichotomous reality that does not exist), that theoretical position seems to be employed much less frequently in the study of what is called the "spirituality" of more progressive religious groups whose claims and behaviors, although just as possibly the product of the same dynamics, are far more popular and thus escape that analysis.

Consider also that when I was thinking through how to turn my dissertation about the political activism of the Christian Right into a book manuscript, virtually every example of a theoretically engaged book on that topic that I referenced ended with a statement on the dangers that conservative evangelicalism creates for American democracy. A warning such as this would rarely be found in a book on a more popular group, and in fact, would probably be seen as a violation of scholarly objectivity in that context.

Whether one can logically defend the false-consciousness or democracy-killing power of evangelicals is actually not the point; rather, the more pressing issue is that such perspectives have often been portrayed as self-evident, ahistorical, depoliticized fact. As a newly minted Ph.D., I had virtually no other models to look to within my subfield for how to do scholarship differently. As a side note, I had nothing like that in women's and gender studies, either, an interesting commonality that demonstrates the critical weaknesses that might occur when scholars deny that they have activist positions—in other words, that they pursue interests.

Omission and Separation

Finally, I wonder if we have construed to our graduates that "method and theory" is a phrase that links two things that otherwise need not be connected—in other words, that method and theory can be separated from one another and still each retain their integrity. I want to entertain this idea because I think it is the most expedient way to disempower the category while at the same time giving it ample praise; put differently, it is a highly effective way to support the brand.

I suspect that one of the most common manifestations of this splitting of theory from method occurs in the selective theorizing just mentioned; that is, theory is turned "on" to the degree that it is used by a scholar to aid in the development of some sort of explanatory schema, but then is turned "off" when its larger conclusions about the nature of the phenomenon in question departs from the standard religious studies script that has focused, as of late, on "lived religion," "authenticity," and other *sui generis* references.

While I was just situating this as a problem in the sense that it allows one to simply stop being critical in ways dictated by the political winds, I want to also suggest that such selective theorizing permits us to use bits and pieces of theories as we wish, and in this way, to entirely discard what might be their larger methodological implications. For instance, I suspect we are all familiar with the many scholars who have used Jonathan Z. Smith's work in astonishingly creative ways; his famous remarks regarding "no data for religion" and the need for rigorous self-consciousness have been invoked to justify any number of competing claims (Smith 1988: xi). Domesticating Smith's larger point by decontextualizing it offers a rather efficient way to produce what is considered "respectable" research that ends up ruffling few feathers. Because graduate students have much to lose if they do not please a number of parties simultaneously, treating method and theory as things that might be selectively engaged when convenient allows students to perfectly mirror the ambivalence that they may encounter in their own training, nicely replicate the status quo with analyses that fall short of any serious critical or meta-analytical engagement, and politically protect themselves at the same time.

Moreover, there is some reason to believe that this may also happen through method and theory pedagogy. It would be an interesting exercise to be able to look panoramically at how professors who teach method and theory courses define those terms, split the content time between them, and how, if at all, they discuss their interrelationship in the classroom. If one peruses the available syllabi on the web, it appears that approaches to this sort of course are all over the board. However, what stands out as a general trend is the relatively *small* amount of time spent discussing the nature of the field today and the methodological issues that underscore its present state, and a much *larger* emphasis on what is treated as the history of theory (as approached through the works of Eliade, Durkheim, Freud, Marx, etc.).

This is not to imply that such theorists are irrelevant, but it is a call to carefully consider how they are portrayed and situated as contributors to our discipline. If their theories are depicted as still-relevant analytical tools (even if we no longer find them as helpful as other models today), then we might possibly read their longevity as a sign of the enduring importance of method and theory. But if they are viewed as little more than historical artifacts the fading relevance of which is mentioned only to tip the hat to our discipline's own brand of origin story, then this may indicate, again, the compartmentalization of method and theory.

Of Brands and Buzzwords

While my observations suggest that things have not changed much since Martin and Wiebe's retrospective on NAASR's history, perhaps we can say that they now stand more exposed for us to critique. The problem, then, is not that we have a paucity of theory; the issue is that we are working within a system the integrity of which hinges on praising the use of method and theory while simultaneously rendering it ineffectual. My suggestion is that if we are interested in Martin and Wiebe's effort to establish a "beachhead" that might secure the status and use of method and theory as fundamental scholarly components in religious studies, then we must re-imagine how their importance takes hold *before* new waves of scholars receive substantial professional, economic, and social rewards for bartering with this particular branded model that threatens to undercut method and theory's significance.

If graduate training is a time where one's notions about the worth of method and theory are forming, this means that we should be thinking about changing the educational experiences of our future colleagues just as much as we should consider their participation in the organizations that later foster their entrance into the profession. In particular, we should carefully contemplate how we may inadvertently add to the confusion surrounding our field's politics and how we may deny our own role as political agents, as well.

This may happen, in part, by failing to describe this branding process as a system of privilege. The idea that one can avoid, undercut, or otherwise accessorize method and theory is a sign of this privilege because, simply stated, it means that those who downplay their importance have opted out of having to formally explain themselves in the sorts of critical ways usually demanded in other fields of study. Lincoln puts it more directly when he remarks that "Reverence is a religious, not a scholarly, virtue" (Lincoln 1996: 225–227). This particular system of privilege depends on tokenism in the sense that the copious but relatively empty attention now being given to method and theory, or the vitality of organizations like NAASR, could be read by some as a sign that there is no issue. In religious studies, method and theory's own proverbial glass ceiling has been shattered, or so the rumor goes.

But the other reason why I think there might be some merit in this description is that "privilege" remains a powerful buzzword within many liberal theological circles at the same time that understanding the very concept demands a certain degree of methodological and theoretical engagement. The study of privilege is, after all, the examination of large-scale social advantages that often go unspoken, and understanding how privilege shapes identities and perspectives is a first and yet vital step in the self-critique that is part of a rigorous methodological process. By using the word "privilege" to describe the manner in which method and theory are accessorized in our field, we will, ironically, be using a sort of privileged language (about privilege!) while simultaneously finding common ground with young scholars who may be familiar with the concept even if they are unskilled with applying it to the politics of their scholarship.

And if we have gone that far, might we publicly consider what we mean by the terms "method and theory," and more specifically, how we present these concepts to our students? I tend to think of method and theory as the parameters one places around an object of study in order to render an analysis that has critical integrity. Specifically, I think of "method" as a process that involves considering the philosophical foundations that one uses to analyze the subject in question. The hope, of course, is that rigorous self-examination will result in a tweaking of one's presumptions if the foundations and later analysis they inspire are based on, or can only result in, conclusions that fail to effectively interface with critical analysis. "Theory," to me, is the process of creating a meta-analytic web capable of explanatory power that is built upon the local analyses first generated by those very methodological considerations.

While those are my rudimentary definitions, I acknowledge that others' may differ, particularly as we together situate related words like "critical," "analysis," "logic," and even "study." This is not a new conversation, nor am I suggesting that there must be one final answer, but I sense that the discussions about these things have happened in places and formats generally out of earshot from those graduate students just forming their own philosophical commitments, and may be particularly silent in schools and programs where the current branding project of the field is at its most robust.

I began this essay examining Naomi Klein's discussion of corporate branding and want to end it there as well, for among her other observations, Klein notes that in many cases, corporate brands matter far more to corporations than the actual products they sell. One reason for this is that the brand allows corporations the power to nimbly navigate any number of capital-generating events to tap those that are, at that moment, the most fruitful, while more imperceptibly cutting away those that are not (Klein 2009: 3).

I think that we may be able to strike yet another parallel between corporate branding and the current state of our field, for I suspect that method and theory may end up a discarded fad relegated to the back of the drawer just as soon as our field's power dynamics shift. In fact, it strikes me that the very reason why method and theory are accessorized—that is, compartmentalized—is that it will be that much easier to discard them when they are no longer in fashion. This highlights the importance of directing our attention to our future colleagues, that group most philosophically and economically at the whims of those trends. Those of us interested in a rigorous approach to method and theory must also continue to remember that the reason why this branded conservatism is currently so edgy is that the privilege that drives it can be so blinding.

Yet in my appeal to call this system "privilege" as a way of using privilege for our own purposes, there arises the issue of the impossibility of speaking outside of our *own* political position, as if what we are promising our students through a method and theory approach is a sort of special, objective legitimacy. This sentiment is discussed in Jane Flax's classic feminist essay "The End of Innocence," wherein Flax chastises certain feminist theorists for claiming that it is possible to manufacture a scholarly position that is neutral, free of self-interest, or that is otherwise, as she puts it, "innocent" (Flax [1992] 2015: 32).

Flax's project here is to push feminist theorists to boldly state what they want from the exercise of theory-making, and to recognize that arguments over what we call "truth" and "critical analysis" might be completely incompatible with meeting particular goals. In her case, she notes, she theorizes not to "speak the truth," but to dismantle patriarchy (ibid.: 34). Indeed, her push to her fellow theorists is to say out loud what they want and to stop wrestling with truth claims (or whatever else one wishes to call them), for those turn into a confusing sideshow, she notes, becoming the euphemisms we use to justify "the game" of academics (ibid.: 33).

While Flax provides us a lot to unpack, what I think is immediately pertinent is that it is fair that graduate students may ask us what we want from our field and our efforts, and what role our conceptualizations of method and theory play in that vision. We should not only be prepared to answer that question, but also to admit that we, ourselves, are political agents with privilege in a rigged game. If we claim to be something other than representatives of the aforementioned edgy conservatism that currently characterizes our discipline, then they—our students—deserve to hear how we have developed and wrestled with our own set of answers.

Leslie Dorrough Smith is Associate Professor of Religious Studies and Director of the Women's and Gender Studies Program at Avila University. Her research is primarily focused on how sex, gender, and reproduction issues are used by American conservative Protestants to change public opinion and policy.

References

Flax, Jane. [1992] 2015. "The End of Innocence." In Susan Archer Mann and Ashly Suzanne Patterson (eds.), *Reading Feminist Theory: From Modernity to Postmodernity*, 32–35. New York: Oxford University Press.

Klein, Naomi. 2009. *No Logo*. New York: Picador.

Lincoln, Bruce. 1996. "Theses on Method." *Method and Theory in the Study of Religion*. 8: 225–227.

Smith, Jonathan Z. 1988. *Imagining Religion: From Babylon to Jonestown*. Chicago, IL: University of Chicago Press.

Afterword

Feast and Famine in the Study of Religion

Russell T. McCutcheon

I'm pleased to offer a few concluding words to this collection of essays—a volume that not only resulted from a program that marked NAASR's thirtieth anniversary, but which appropriately opens with Luther H. Martin and Donald Wiebe's co-written history of the association. That I was working toward earning my M.Div. degree in 1985 and still a couple years away from becoming a graduate student in religious studies at the University of Toronto (where I studied under Wiebe)—back when they, along with Tom Lawson, first came up with the idea to establish NAASR—and that I was still several years away from my involvement in *Method and Theory in the Study of Religion* (*MTSR*) (which later became NAASR's official journal), makes this opportunity, three decades later, to reflect on the state of the field, and NAASR's place in it, rather significant to me. For despite whatever disagreements some of us within NAASR may have had over the years concerning what we might profitably mean by method and theory (on this see McCutcheon 2014: ch. 1), it's fair to say that the institutional space created by the efforts of NAASR's founders, not to mention the now worldwide discourse that *MTSR* has helped to establish, has provided me with much of the operating conditions of my own career. For, long before helping to set the theme for the 2015 meeting (along with Aaron Hughes, Willi Braun, and Craig Martin), I attended a NAASR session at my very first American Academy of Religion/Society of Biblical Literature conference back in 1992 (held in San Francisco that year) and the second conference paper listed on my CV was one presented at a NAASR session in 1995. (My first was an IAHR paper presented, as part of a panel on Benson Saler's work, in Mexico City earlier that same year.) And it was because of NAASR's initiative that *MTSR*'s editors (Willi Braun, Darlene Juschka, Arthur McCalla, and myself) met, at that same 1992 conference, with a representative of Mouton de Gruyter, which had been persuaded (presumably by Don and Luther) to be interested in acquiring the journal, thereby beginning the transition from a periodical completely edited and produced by graduate students just twice a year to what it has become today: one of the premier international peer review quarterlies in our field. And when *MTSR* was unceremoniously let go by Mouton de Gruyter, just five years later, NAASR once again rose to the occasion and ensured that Brill's editors understood the opportunity that had just been presented to them. That *MTSR* has since those days been successively and successfully led by several different editors, all unrelated to the journal's University of Toronto days (Jeff Ruff, Matt Day, and now Aaron Hughes), that it recently celebrated its twenty-fifth anniversary with a "best of" volume in its newly inaugurated supplements book series with Brill (Hughes 2013), and that NAASR itself has now passed the thirty year mark tells us, I think, much about the viability of the alternative that these two sites still offer the field—and I say "still" because it seems to me that, despite some in the study of religion claiming that we are now somehow post-theory, i.e., that we have come through the fires of methodological controversy and are now the better for it (on that topic see Hughes's introduction to this volume), the issues that have long animated both the journal and NAASR are still as relevant now as ever.

And this was the very topic that prompted the theme to NAASR's 2015 meeting, the result of which you have in this very volume. For what is the enduring relevance of an organization devoted to promoting explicit and sophisticated reflection on our tools and both the motives that animate our work, as well as the ends it serves, if everyone in the field today seems to claim that they too are a theorist (something made plain, as Hughes's opening noted, from most early career CVs, which—presumably as a result of method and theory courses being established, as required in many of their programs, over the past decade or two—now list "method and theory" as being among most people's specialties)? Given that, as I write these very lines, NAASR has just announced the participants for its 2016 program ("Method Today" is its title, with major papers on description, interpretation, comparison, and explanation, along with responses as per the papers in this very collection), it should be evident that the consensus within the organization is not to close-up shop, in response to that question of relevance, and hang up a "Mission Accomplished" sign. There are those in the field who might think this would be a reasonable response, however; for given that few in our field talked openly or approvingly about theory thirty years ago yet nearly everyone today seems to see him or herself as a theorist, suggests that the issues that NAASR and its members (or at least its sympathizers—a group more than likely far larger than actual dues-paying members) have been promoting have had an effect, inasmuch as a veritable feast of theoretical alternatives now seem to present themselves in the academic study of religion (i.e., from cognitive science to empathically studying religion on the ground). But the question remains just what this effect has been—for it would not be difficult for some to hear that the span of theoretical choices that I just named fails to identify comparable approaches and thus to conclude that there is instead only a light sprinkling of theory, one that hardly quenches an appetite. What's more, this minimal role for theories of either religion or "religion" could be understood as an inoculation against the threat of there being more; that is, upon closer examination of the work of many of those who claim to work in theory it becomes evident that longstanding assumptions about religion being an obviously important, deeply felt human universal remain and, at least for many, the role of theory is some sort of secondary add-on that, much like cooking with seasonings, one uses sparingly and only as needed. Should one instead think that theory provides the enabling conditions of any intellectual pursuit—that theories orient us, as scholars, and enable us to distinguish and demarcate items in the world as worth paying attention to or not (thereby the old line about definitions being theories in miniature)—then the problem in the field today is that more people need to be aware *that they've been theorists all along*, even when they're simply describing the world around them. For even the religion on the ground and lived religion people, who aim to study religion in its authentically local and personal instances—who strike me as simply rebranding an old phenomenological approach (inasmuch as their work examines meaning being embodied, as opposed to essences being manifested)—operate with a set of assumptions about what religion is and does; for somehow they know what to describe and what to ignore. This tells me that they have a theory—though, sadly, it is one that is largely unrecognized and thus unacknowledged, as if their viewpoint was instead in lockstep with reality on the ground.

Contrary to this fantasy of immediacy and presence, I would argue that without an *a priori* way *explicitly* and *self-consciously* (both key points if we're to call ourselves scholars) to narrow our gaze, focus our attention, and thereby delimit the spectrum of possible points of interest one will quickly find that there is far too much in the world in need of description. In a move not unrelated to how Wiebe, my teacher, would try to get me just to identify how many books were on the shelves of his office, in Trinity College, presumably designed to establish that, contrary to my newly acquired postmodernist tendencies, there were such things in the world as disinterested facts. But instead, I now simply ask students (who have dropped by to discuss such topics) if there's any data in my office. It houses plenty of books, of course, much as you'd expect from a university professor, but it is also filled with plants, an old typewriter, disorderly piles of stuffed file folders not to mention filing cabinets, a variety of framed pictures and documents, and quite a variety of trinkets from either my travels (e.g., a mug from this or that university or name badges from a variety of conference) or tokens left by former students. (Our department secretary has a master key, after all, and periodically lets students sneak into my office to leave little surprises for me, such as the romance novels scattered throughout the shelves, the wild-eyed Nicolas Cage cut-out heads that appear all over the room, or the *papier-mâché* dinosaurs that adorn my shelves.) Sooner or later, and after looking over the whole room, the student will play my game and name something—say, my desktop computer or maybe one of the fridge magnets from around the US that adorn my filing cabinets. (Yes, they're from a student who periodically mails them from her travels around the continent.) My next move in this chess game is to ask *why* that particular item *stood out for them*, in hopes of doing two things: (i) getting them to become self-conscious on the criteria and interests they used in order to single that one item out from the background noise of my hectic office; and (ii) moving them to a position that can entertain that, contrary to what I just wrote, nothing in the room "stood out" of its own accord (i.e., the mugs and magnets do not have agency—they do not *stand* out—but, instead, they became an item of discourse because of the student's own interests). So contrary to how this pedagogical parlor trick might have been used on me when I was a student (and it was always the occasion for a lively exchange with Don, to be sure—something we talk about to this day), I've repurposed it to make evident how implicated we each are in animating the world around us with the appearance of curious and thus significant things—curious and significant *to us*, that is, for this specific reason and at that particular moment. For surely the University of Alabama's heating and cooling maintenance crew entering room 211 in Manly Hall will pay attention to rather different things than will the interior design major or business student stopping by during office hours—and none will likely care (or even "see") that there's a box of Shreddies on my shelf, from a student who, several years ago, mailed it to me from Vancouver. But enter a fellow Canadian ex-pat who grew up eating that "crisp and crunchy cereal, that's good to eat (good to eat) ...") and, well, that old jingle will likely come to their mind and we'll end up growing nostalgic and lamenting that Coffee Crisp bars are not available here. What's more, that the building bears the name of our university's second president, a man known in the years prior to the U.S. civil war as one who advocated for the institution of slavery, will surely attract the attention of some prior to even stepping into my office.

But a further point remains to be made: although I think that this is how signification *always* works (i.e., that the world does not come pre-packaged for our passive enjoyment), if we happen to be the type of people known as scholars then among our jobs is to identify those interests and assumptions as best we can and then to make them as explicit as possible (as noted above), organizing it all into what we'll just call a theory, that (i) directs our gaze, (ii) makes it possible to see something as more or less interesting to us (i.e., as an object of inquiry or datum), and (iii), inasmuch as it is explicit, empowers our peers to call us to task when inquiring as to the warrant for, or implications of, what it is that we do.

This was a point, at least as I read him, nicely made by the philosopher of science Karl Popper, in a passage I've quoted before, when he reports having asked his students, without elaboration or further instruction, simply to observe (i.e., to use a method of analysis). Concerning that episode, Popper writes as follows:

> The belief that science proceeds from observation to theory is still so widely and so firmly held that my denial of it is often met with incredulity. I have even been suspected of being insincere—of denying what nobody in his senses would doubt.
>
> But in fact the belief that we can start with pure observation alone, without anything in the nature of a theory is absurd; as may be illustrated by the story of the man who dedicated his life to natural science, wrote down everything he could observe, and bequeathed his priceless collection of observations to the Royal Society to be used as evidence. This story should show us that though beetles may profitably be collected, observations may not.
>
> Twenty-five years ago I tried to bring home the same point to a group of physics students in Vienna by beginning a lecture with the following instructions : "Take pencil and paper; carefully observe, and write down what you have observed!" They asked, of course, what I wanted them to observe. Clearly the instruction, "Observe!" is absurd. (It is not even idiomatic, unless the object of the transitive verb can be taken as understood.) Observation is always selective. It needs a chosen object, a definite task, an interest, a point of view, a problem. And its description

presupposes a descriptive language, with property words; it presupposes similarity and classification, which in their turn presuppose interests, points of view, and
problems. (Popper 1962: 46)

Updating Popper, I think of the difference between, say, Narrative Clip—a small,
wearable camera that automatically takes a picture every thirty seconds—on the
one hand, and an Instagram photo on the other. Whereas the former, attached to
the lapel of your coat, for example, documents unfailingly, recording every single
raw and uncomposed setting that happens to be in front of it, with no editorial
input ("Capture authentic video and photos effortlessly," their website says),
the latter produces highly crafted, filtered images based on preferences that are
applied to the selected photo—making evident that choice (i.e., selection) and
interest play a fundamental role in the latter (though it may not be as apparent,
we must recognize that, in the case of the former, human agency plays no less a
role, of course, since the camera didn't put itself on your coat, let alone the front).
So, from one we get breathtakingly dazzling images of vibrant sunsets while the
other produces hundreds, even thousands of supposedly authentic (but more
than likely uninteresting) photos of undecipherable things, such as whatever it
was that the camera happened to snap as you took your coat off and threw it over
a chair. That this little camera is called Narrative is a bit ironic, if you stop to think
about it, for only by means of a subsequently spun, developmental tale would the
disparate photographed moments of a life become part of a story; for, at the level
of unending thirty-second photographs, there is no narrative arc to the day but,
instead, just the monotony of disconnected, raw happenings.[1]

Looking through library shelves or doing fieldwork are much the same, I'd
argue: without a clearly-stated reason for going there and thus a way to pay
attention to just some of the things you find, it is an endless series of disconnected happenings of no consequence.

That too few in our field seem to recognize that, as Jonathan Smith once
quipped, "one wears eyeglasses when one gazes at these naked facts" (Smith 2007:
76), is the enduring problem of the field—I take it that this explains the resistance
I often encounter to historicizing the category religion itself, inasmuch as we all
just seem to know that some things are religious. I therefore often find scholars whose descriptive language is used as if it comes with no preconditions or
implications (i.e., as if it is assumed to be a natural fit with whatever it is used to
name). For example, I rarely find an explicit theory of myth but, instead, simply
see things in the literature called myths that the observer somehow just knows
to be tales in distinction from all of the other stories about the past that some
group of people tells on occasion—a distinction usually presumed to be rooted
in some necessary quality or inherent feature of the object rather than in the
contingent eye of the beholder. And so the distance between recognizing that
our work is possible.because of scholarly interests (that exist at a distance from
the so-called lived reality of the people whom we study) as well as the technical
terminology that we develop in pursuit of those interests, on the one hand, and,
on the other, those who carry out their work as if their claims passively document

self-evident realities outside themselves constitutes the landscape of our field's enduring debates.

Come to think of it, it's a distinction nicely captured in Bruce Lincoln's straight-forward definition of religion, which he proposes in the second of his (I would hope) now well-known theses on method:

> Religion, I submit, is that discourse whose defining characteristic is its desire to speak of things eternal and transcendent with an authority equally transcendent and eternal. (Lincoln 1996: 225)[2]

As we've often seen in the history of our field, when studying people who them-selves aim to speak with a legitimacy attributed to such an authorized domain, there is a temptation for scholars also to claim that authority for themselves and their own scholarly claims—as if this or that action or item just ought to attract our attention; in such cases, the if/then conditional of scholarly discourse—one I'd say Lincoln goes on to characterize as "that discourse which speaks of things temporal and terrestrial in a human and fallible voice, while staking its claim to authority on rigorous critical practice"—is dropped; for here there is presumed to be no theory, no lenses, and thus no posited (dare I say necessary?) gap between scholarly interest and matters of fact or actual state of affairs (thus, speculations on the motives and intentions of actors are repeatedly made in our field, as if hardly speculative, let alone the many totalized claims made by colleagues about this thing called the universal human condition). And so, rather than making clear the posited starting point and set of assumptions that provide the ground upon which a claim can be made, followed then by the implicit "If you grant to me all this, then here's what I make of this or that ..." (which, I'd further main-tain, carries with it an invitation to test those assumption utility, i.e., what do you think about what it allows me to say about the world?), scholarship takes on the form of assertion or proclamation, since its first principles need no argumenta-tion because there's nothing conditional or contingent about them; rather, such speakers act as if their claims are in lockstep with reality itself—as if whatever a student happens to see as interesting in my office necessarily must also attract the attention of anyone else who walks in the door.

So those who mean by theory some sort of secondary step after an obviously significant thing "catches their eye" (of its own agency, perhaps?)—even those who claim an interest in rigorous explanatory theorizing sometimes presume the self-evidency of their datum and understand theory only as what they use to explain its existence or function—seem to fail to acknowledge Popper's point: that a prior set of interests was needed to make something in the world "stand out" as worth talking about, making it worthwhile to dig through the archives or travel to the other side of the world in order to examine it in greater detail. So the challenge of theory, then, as I would describe it, is to make plain one's starting point. But that not just every set of prior interests counts as part of the discourse of the academy is important to consider—I recall again the definition of History, as opposed to Religion, offered by Lincoln (the uppercases are his). In my reading it's a distinction informed by Roland Barthes's 1957 preface to *Mythologies*, where we read about what he characterizes as his motivation for writing the pieces collected in that volume:

> In short, in the account given of our contemporary circumstances, I resented seeing Nature and History confused at every turn, and I wanted to track down, in the decorative display of *what-goes-without-saying*, the ideological abuse which, in my view, is hidden there. (Barthes 1972: 11)

Staking itself instead on, as Lincoln puts it, "rigorous critical practice," what we might as well just call an historical discourse, one that contributes to the academic pursuit that I understand the study of religion to be, always keeps the fallibility of the if/then conditional in view, mindful that nothing goes without saying (for then we wouldn't say it, now would we?); for the critically minded scholar whom I have in mind presumes that there is no outside of history and thus no final resting place where our work will be done—"it's turtles all the way down" is the shorthand some have come to use for this position—and thus that there is also no absolute origin or ultimate end. For with each new set of eyes or ears that appear on some scene there also come new interests. What we therefore have to take into account is situation and interested observer, arriving with questions that are more than likely alien to the interview subject or which have been previously unasked of an artifact—what we might otherwise name as a generic object that those very interests have already plucked from the obscurity of Trotsky's "dustbin of history" to make it into an item worth our time.

But, as I said, I find too few in the field interested in defining theory in this way and thus, despite the so-called reflexive turn, few seem open to scrutinizing their own position as a scholar and the contributions they offer to making the world seem interesting. Instead, as already noted, theory is assumed only to be a subsequent step, only sometimes used to explain religion itself.

In looking for a contemporary and easily described example of this problem, I came across a recent post at the Wabash Center for Teaching and Learning in Theology and Religion's blog, entitled "Integrating Theory and Research in the Undergraduate Islamic Studies Classroom"; it reflects on the challenge of using theory in courses where students expect an emphasis on a descriptive approach. As Caleb Elfenbein writes in his opening line: "More often than not, it seems, students register for courses on Islam [not to mention any number of the other world religions, I would add] wanting to learn 'stuff'" (Elfenbein 2016). But, as he then goes on to elaborate, "if we don't spend time really developing theoretical frameworks for understanding that stuff, then are we ultimately doing much more than presenting curiosities, intellectual knick-knacks?" This is a crucial point, of course, but given how I usually find this notion of theory being used in our field, I admit to a suspicion when reading comments such as these, for I'm inclined to wait for the other shoe to drop by learning that everything but religion needs theorizing. And, sure enough, despite soon after rightly warning his readers that "[w]ithout explicit and sustained theorization, we create the mistaken impression that information stands on its own," it turns out that not religion or the idea of tradition are theorized but, instead, the idea of "the public" requires theoretical treatment. Therefore, an undergraduate course entitled "Being Muslim in America," in which the aim is for "students ... to consider the conditions in which Muslim communities have been or sought to be included or excluded from broader American public life," invites students "to spend some time figuring out what exactly 'public life' means, which requires us to ... theorize" (ibid.).

Now, as one who has spent some time thinking through the way our own society employs the rhetorically effective private/public distinction, I am hardly unsupportive of those wishing to have students examine what it is that differing senses of "public life" can accomplish for social actors, but it was the following line that confirmed the suspicion mentioned above, for it made plain that while the environment in which religious things take place need theories, religion is itself somehow exempt; he writes:

> There is a rich body of literature analyzing the place of religion in public life ... (Elfenbein 2016)

We see here what I would characterize as an untheorized, folk notion of religion as being something originally apart from the public domain and which then interacts with it in some secondary manner; it is a well-known, philosophically idealist conception of religion, akin to some sort of private emotion or experience, that, in my assessment, informs much of the literature on "religion in public life"; for if, instead, we theorized the very category religion as a socio-rhetorical term that some actors use to name and thereby manage elements of their social world then the phrase "religion in public life" would be heard as redundant and unhelpful, for the fact that this or that claim, action, or organization *is called* religious (either to be privileged or critiqued) would itself be seen as the trace of a prior social situation.

One may counter that my critical reading here is overly ambitious; in support of it, I note that, a little further into the blog post, we find a no less philosophically idealist social theory:

> By the time we got to the end of the session we had come to the conclusion that what [Michael] Warner means by a "text" [in the reading for that day's class] is really *an expression of an idea*—in any medium—that grounds a common experience of some kind for people. *This common experience is then what generates a public.* (Elfenbein 2016; emphasis added)

Perhaps best exemplified in the much earlier work of William James, scholars simply reproducing the presumption that private inner states (called such things as ideas or experiences) are the primary ground of public domains (such as texts or groups) leaves unexamined the way in which certain social circumstances are legitimized as if they originated from a pre-political personal realm. The problem, then, is that binary pairs (i.e., private/public) are often not treated by scholars *as a binary* and, instead, one pole (in this case privacy, such as a folk conception of the self as *expressing* private meanings into the secondary, public realm) is naturalized while the other (the so-called public) is historicized. The effect of this, of course, is that traditional understanding of religion as an experience or interior disposition that is only subsequently projected outwardly (where it is prone to misinterpretation and pollution, to recall James's classic approach) is employed as if it was necessarily accurate, and thereby reinforced. For, contrary to this idealist approach, there are others (some of whom are represented in Martin and McCutcheon 2012, for example) who would see not common experiences as generating a public but quite the other way around. Case in point: as I've noted on previous occasions, without the vocabulary and grammar taught to each of us by others, who were themselves parts of even more prior institutions not of their own making, none of us would not be *experiencing* the *meaning* of this very thing that we call a text.

So despite the fact that he concludes by noting that his "students did a great job locating varied 'texts' that sought to include or exclude American Muslims from public life," the trouble is that this understanding of theory leaves unexamined not just the thing that we call religion, but, more specifically, how the identity "American Muslim" is itself constituted; instead, we look only at how it is expressed in this or that setting. According to this model of what it means to theorize, then, both are presumed to be prior, coherently existing things that only interact, in some secondary manner, with the world; that is, are Muslims included or excluded from public life? The more interesting theoretical question, I'd argue, is to examine how (along with asking *by whom* and *in what occasions*) certain groups of people are constituted *as* Muslim in this or that setting. For my presumption is that this particular identity is not a naturally occurring fact but, instead, is operationalized by various people in different manners and at different times.

I think here of the then candidate for the Republican Party's nomination, Donald Trump; in response to a December 6, 2015, speech from the Oval Office by President Obama—in which Obama had said:

> Muslim Americans are our friends and our neighbors, our co-workers, our sports heroes—and, yes, they are our men and women in uniform who are willing to die in defense of our country ...

—Trump tweeted as follows:

> Obama said in his speech that Muslims are our sports heroes. What sport is he talking about and who? Is Obama profiling? (December 6, 2015)

In response to this tweet, a number of news outlets began listing all of the Muslim sports stars in American history, going so far as to note that Trump himself had won the Muhammad Ali Entrepreneur award in 2007 and even met the famed boxer at the event. But my guess is that such retorts entirely miss the point, for at the time of composing the tweet, African Americans or members of the Nation of Islam were probably not what Trump (or whoever manages his Twitter account) had in mind as constituting "a Muslim." My point was nicely evidenced in the parodies that followed the controversy, at least for some, of Beyoncé's 2016 Super Bowl halftime appearance (in which her dancers' costumes referenced the Blank Panthers), as well what was then her new single, "Formation" (released just the day before). The parodies of reactions to both lampooned many white Americans' apparent shock to realize that the singer was African American (inasmuch as they heard her music to explicitly engage what they saw to be racially charged topics, such as featuring the Black Lives Matter movement);[3] this nicely illustrates that the idea of the Other is not an inherent quality as much as it is a subject-position ascribed to oneself by others (with a nod here, of course, to Louis Althusser's notion of interpellation). To return to my point: the interesting question may not be which conditions allow Muslims to be included in public life, as if their Muslim identity was a constant and uniform possession, but, rather, which conditions do or do not constitute various people *as* Muslims.

The problem, then, with how many in the field use theory is that it naturalizes the very thing that we might instead be scrutinizing. For as Elfenbein (2016) concludes, "applying a theory heightened their [i.e., his students'] capacity to learn about and reflect on the conditions of public life for American Muslims," but, judging by the blog post on this class exercise, at no time did it examine the constitution of that very identity itself—instead, it seems to have been taken as a given—let alone tackle the implications of conceiving of it as a specifically *religious* identity about which we, as scholars of religion, ought to have something to say. And so, when this way of understanding theory is used, an exercise in *applying* theory ends up also being an exercise in *limiting* theory by ensuring that students understand that only certain things need to be theorized or, better put, not all things are the discursive products of prior curiosities, assumptions, interests. After all, something that pre-dates theory is the thing to which we subsequently apply it, no?

Because this is the way in which I see many of our peers to be theorizing it strikes me that NAASR's role is now as relevant as its founders thought it was thirty years ago—if by theory we mean to develop analyses of religion as a mundane element of the human, rather than just offering accounts of some interior dimension's interactions outside the so-called believers' hearts and mind. Most recently, I think of Amy Paris Langenberg's use of Mary Douglas's work on purity systems as a positive counterexample for the field, inasmuch as Langenberg draws upon the anthropologist's theory to make sense of (i.e., to see as comparable to examples from other groups[4]) diverse pollution taboos and rituals, on the one hand, and the production of social and gendered identity in classical Indian texts, on the other—specifically those regulations involving blood taboos, as she terms them, associated with menstruation (Langenberg 2016). The result of her use of Douglas is a conclusion separate from how elite insiders might have understood their own texts and injunctions for, following Douglas's understanding of the need to study total systems of purity (i.e., think here of how Douglas explained the role of the Levitical dietary codes), Langenberg makes novel claims about these practices—exemplifying that theory allows us to produce new knowledge about the world that is not constrained by the way the people we happen to study see the world. For, *if* you grant to her Douglas's theory on the social function of pollution taboos, *then* this is what we can now say about disparate texts not previously understood as related. That much of the issue of the *Journal of the American Academy of Religion* in which Langenberg's article appears is devoted to rather different, normative topics in the field makes her essay stand out as exemplary of a marginal but nonetheless important position in the field.[5]

And it is just such a position that, in my reading, NAASR aimed to represent and encourage back in 1985; it's an old position, to be sure, that (though we now differ from them in many regards) dates to our intellectual predecessors in the late nineteenth century (if not even earlier—at least according to the late Sam Preus): that those things some people privilege as religions can be productively studied by non-participants, doing so cross-culturally and comparatively, and then analyzed as accomplishing mundane (but not unimportant) things; and it is a position that I maintain is no less in need of representation and encouragement now—especially when we still find such scholars as Wilfred Cantwell Smith being appreciatively cited in the field and such figures as Rudolf Otto called a "theorist of the holy."[6] So consider the preceding essays, responses, and rejoinders, all focused either on ways of theorizing religion today or ways of understanding this notion of theory in the study of religion, as a still relevant dispatch from one edge of the field, sampling issues and conversations that ought to have an impact far wider than the panels where they initially took place. And in doing so, readers should note that many of the participants in that conference, and thus the contributors to this volume, were rather early in their academic careers when they first wrote and presented these papers (several were doctoral students at the time, in fact), which suggests to me that this is an edge to which we should pay attention, in hopes of seeing even more intellectually provocative developments in the near future. For the scarcity of theory in our field, at least as I believe many of these contributors understand the term, will hopefully not continue to characterize the field for too much longer.

Russell T. McCutcheon (Chair of the Department of Religious Studies, at the University of Alabama) is the President of the North American Association for the Study of Religion (2015-18) and a longtime contributor to debates on theory in the academic study of religion.

Notes

1. Gordon Bell's (b. 1934) noted experiments in so-called life-logging (i.e., Microsoft's "My Life Bits" project)—documenting every one moment and sound from a life via wearable devices—also comes to mind as one example.
2. It may or may not be surprising to learn that a number of the undergraduate and even graduate students who routinely find me on social media, to start up a conversation about their frustrations with the field, are not aware of Lincoln's "Theses on Method."
3. I have in mind Saturday Night Live's skit, from February 13, 2016, entitled "The Day Beyoncé Turned Black," which can be seen at www.nbc.com/saturday-night-live/video/the-day-beyonce-turned-black/2985361 (accessed March 18, 2016).

4. "[H]ere I take the view that, at least for now, more is to be gained from viewing Buddhist impurity as a total system normative for social reality and comparable to ritual impurity systems in other religions than in focusing on how it is unique and specific" (Langenberg 2016: 164).
5. For instance, a set of papers, originally from a roundtable at the 2013 meeting of the American Academy of Religion, published in this same issue of *JAAR* and devoted to defending various senses of normativity in Islamic studies scholarship, was the focus of a recent critical essay of my own (see McCutcheon forthcoming).
6. On my former claim, see the previous *JAAR* editor's inaugural editorial (79(1) [2011]: 4–5) or some of the above-mentioned papers on normativity in Islamic studies (*JAAR* 84(1) [2016]). On the latter, this is a claim made by Robert Orsi in his own chapter, "The Problem of the Holy," in his edited volume, *The Cambridge Companion to Religious Studies* (2011: 86); see also his podcast discussion on this same topic, in which he characterizes Otto—the German Lutheran theologian—as a "theorist of religion" within the opening moments of the interview: www.religiousstudiesproject.com/podcast/robert-orsi-on-rudolf-otto (accessed March 17, 2016).

References

Barthes, Roland. 1972. *Mythologies* (trans. Annette Lavers). New York: Hill & Wang.

Elfenbein, Caleb. 2016. "Integrating Theory and Research in the Undergraduate Islamic Studies Classroom." Available at http://wabashcenter.typepad.com/teaching_islam/2016/03/integrating-theory-and-research-in-the-undergraduate-islamic-studies-classroom.html (accessed March 18, 2016).

Hughes, Aaron W. (ed.). 2013. *Theory and Method in the Study of Religion: Twenty Five Years On.* Supplement to *MTSR* vol. 1. Leiden: Brill.

Langenberg, Amy Paris. 2016. "Buddhist Blood Taboo: Mary Douglas, Female Impurity, and Classical Indian Buddhism." *Journal of the American Academy of Religion* 84(1): 157–191.

Lincoln, Bruce. 1996. "Theses on Method." *Method and Theory in the Study of Religion* 8: 225–227.

Martin, Craig and Russell T. McCutcheon. 2012. *Religious Experience: A Reader.* Sheffield: Equinox.

McCutcheon, Russell T. 2014. *A Modest Proposal on Method: Essaying the Study of Religion.* Leiden: Brill.

McCutcheon, Russell T. Forthcoming. "Identifying the Meaning and End of Scholarship: What's at Stake in Muslim Identities?" *Journal of Comparative Islamic Studies.*

Orsi, Robert (ed.). 2011. *The Cambridge Companion to Religious Studies.* Cambridge: Cambridge University Press.

Popper, Karl. 1962. *Conjectures and Refutations: The Growth of Scientific Knowledge.* New York: Basic Books.

Preus, J. Samuel. 1987. *Explaining Religion: Criticism and Theory from Bodin to Freud.* New Haven, CT: Yale University Press.

Smith, Jonathan Z. 2007. "The Necessary Lie: Duplicity in the Disciplines." In Russell T. McCutcheon, *Studying Religion: An Introduction*, 74–80. Sheffield: Equinox.

Index

CPSIA information can be obtained
at www.ICGtesting.com
Printed in the USA
BVOW09s2359121216
470392BV00007B/9/P